T0132818

Electronic Tribes

Electronic Tribes

The Virtual Worlds of Geeks, Gamers, Shamans, and Scammers

EDITED BY TYRONE L. ADAMS AND STEPHEN A. SMITH

University of Texas Press ♆ *Austin*

The editors of and contributors to *Electronic Tribes* dedicate this work to Dr. Leonie Naughton (1955–2007).

We will all miss you.

Copyright © 2008 by the University of Texas Press
All rights reserved
Printed in the United States of America

First edition, 2008

Requests for permission to reproduce material from this work should be sent to:
  Permissions
  University of Texas Press
  P.O. Box 7819
  Austin, TX 78713-7819
  www.utexas.edu/utpress/about/bpermission.html

♾ The paper used in this book meets the minimum requirements of ANSI/NISO z39.48-1992 (R1997) (Permanence of Paper).

Library of Congress Cataloging-in-Publication Data

Electronic tribes : the virtual worlds of geeks, gamers, shamans, and scammers / edited by Tyrone L. Adams and Stephen A. Smith. — 1st ed.
     p.   cm.
  Includes index.
   ISBN 978-0-292-71773-2 (hbk. : alk. paper) — ISBN 978-0-292-71774-9 (pbk. : alk. paper)
   1. Online social networks.   2. Internet—Social aspects.   3. Tribes.   4. Communication and technology.   I. Adams, Tyrone.   II. Smith, Stephen A., 1949–
   TK5105.88817.E53   2008
   306.4'6—dc22

                                                                    2008001906

Contents

Foreword

RONALD E. RICE

Introduction

The authors of this edited book—Adams and Smith; Davidov and Andersen; Olaniran; Standerfer; Dewberry; Russ; Brignall; Skinner; Vance; Rosenthal; Zalot; Naughton; Abrams and Grün; Roy; O'Neil; and Kperogi and Duhé—have written a very interesting and diverse collection of essays and studies on "e-tribes." One indication of this intriguing diversity is some of the words appearing in these chapters. Consider, for example: anarcho-primitivists, craftsters, craftsterbate, cybercrews, cyberhate, cybertime, digital dreamtime, eco-brutalism, electronic tribal warfare, e-tribes, fetish, fictive kinship, flist, gift economy, hierarchies versus heterarchies, Horde versus Alliance, kerfuffle, massively multiplayer online role-playing game environment, mayhem, online shunning, palimpsest, resurrection, retribalism, slash, talisman, technoshamanism, transparency. It is entirely possible that no prior book (possibly not even a dictionary) includes all of these words.

Rather than make some vague and general statements about the importance, irrelevance, contributions, or threats of e-tribes, I am going to highlight some of the main themes from these chapters: what are e-tribes, sites of analysis, methods, theories, and social implications. In that sense, everything that follows comes directly from the chapters, so in essence I am citing all the authors.

What Are E-Tribes?

The chapters take different positions on the concept of "tribe" and "e-tribes." Some are more traditional, historical, anthropological, even technological. Some are more positive, others more negative. Here are some of those positions.

Tribes are more organized than bands, but less than chiefdoms or communities. Tribes coalesce around conflicts with outsiders over scarce resources. Civilization weakens tribes, increases resources, and promotes individualism. Tribes are associated with war, civilization with peace. This rejection of mainstream civilization may also mean racism, stereotyping, eco-brutalism. Tribes self-identify as unique, with shared affinities, and are often narrow, exclusionary, undemocratic, and antagonistic to open debate. Tribes are homogenous and autonomous with common speech, culture, and territory. Tribes involve extensive hierarchies of status, power, gender, age, fears, taboos. Tribalism may involve fragmentation, struggles, competition, and hostility.

Alternatively, tribes may encourage individual identity; there may be only a little formal structuring, and that based primarily on frequency of interaction. Tribe members are empowered within the tribe, through collective responses and through projecting identities into the tribal network. Tribalism may reduce hierarchy and inequality. Tribes have fluid boundaries externally, and heterarchies (webs, networks) instead of hierarchies (strict vertical subsets) internally. Tribes are not amenable to centralized control and persuasion. Tribes may not have historical reality beyond being a conceptual and political artifact of colonial relations with indigenous political elements.

E-tribes may be similar to or different from online discussion groups, forums, and communities. They may represent, in the modern world, a retribalization and return to affiliation groups; they may be quite similar to "lifestyles" or both represent and foster "fictive kinship" ties. E-tribes may consist primarily of those with strong shared interest, and either few ties or strong ties. But people may move from one online tribe to another, or even become members of multiple e-tribes (nearly impossible in their real-life counterparts).

Sites of Analysis

There are Internet sites on more phenomena than people could imagine, and indeed even on many that some would be unable to imagine. The topics analyzed here cover a wide range, including: the creation and maintenance of online culture or tribe; e-tribes versus communities; fostering different versions of traditional identities, such as people

engaged in making crafts; maintaining community online after the dev-
astation of the physical community; how online tribal groups can foster
as well as inhibit civil discourse; how physical and virtual relationships,
and offline and online companies, are parallel and reinforcing; how to
inhabit and make habitable online territory; human life as fundamentally a network of communication; increasing organizational transparency whether intended or not; massively multiplayer online role-playing
and tribal behavior; online Aryan tribalism and hate groups; online role
games as fairy tales or Aboriginal myths; online tribalism as a form of
fictive kinship; organizational relations with e-tribes or stakeholders;
similarities of music downloading with the Aborigine Dreamtime; slash
fans; and the validity of online ethnography.

Methods

The approaches to studying these sites are also varied, including: conceptual essay; content analysis of forum postings and replies; ethnography; grounded theory; historical recounting of foundations of types of
online tribes; informal interviews; reflexive note-taking; online surveys;
participant-observation (including a major sacrifice toward academic
goals—extensive multiplayer video gaming over fourteen weeks!); rhetorical analysis of language and argument strategies within and across
online tribes; semistructured interviews; and review of theory and
implications.

Theories

While some of the chapters are primarily analytical essays, many ground
their approaches in specific theories, including: adaptive structuration;
civil society; communication rules; communitarian theory; complex
adaptive systems; complexity science; crisis and disaster communication;
critical mass; field theory; group cohesion; hyperpersonal computer-
mediated communication; identity formation; interpersonal and intercultural theory; prescriptive and descriptive dialogue; public discourse
and positive public dialogue; rules of dialogue; social constructionism;
social fields; social individuation and deindividuation theory; social influence; and uncertainty reduction.

Social Implications

A central question, of course, is what kinds of social implications are associated with e-tribes. Among the primary issues I've identified in these chapters are inclusions/exclusions, norms, paradoxes, and structure.

Inclusions/Exclusions

E-tribes may foster both utopian and dystopian aspects of tribalism. E-tribes may well foster various kinds of inclusions. People can find others with similar identities; online groups can provide networking and pointers to other authors or sources; organizations may improve their relations with e-tribes and stakeholders; and e-tribes allow participants to overcome the isolation of rural areas. Indeed, in e-tribes comments, interactions, and hyperlinks represent cliques of friends and other relationships. Social networking software can be said to invoke and re-create an idealized historical society, or "fictive" kinship relations.

However, e-tribes can also foster exclusion. Consider just the range of terms for members and nonmembers, such as "slashers" versus "mundanes." Members can set filters (friends groups, friends lists), conceal and protect themselves from the traditional/outside world, and easily avoid nonmembers and social critique or discrimination by nonmembers. Some online groups reject outside groups, at the same time emphasizing divisions within their groups (examples of e-tribes exhibiting both include primitivists and Aryan hate groups); a minority group in a tribe can found its own online tribe, using its own terms and accepted discourse. Digital music players, playlists, and stored songs can be forms of inclusion and exclusion, both of people or groups, as well as of times and places.

Norms

A crucial aspect of e-tribes is the extent and nature of their norms. Online groups may perpetuate social norms; online guilds often replicate real-life ethnicities and orientations. E-tribes may foster ritualized ingroup/outgroup relations, and online game actions are ritualized. Shared music tastes and knowledge can be the basis of cultural tribes, manifested through aural signals. Online group rituals may be central to maintaining an e-tribe identity, such as frequency of mail checking, fake/humorous as well as real/serious titles, shared stories, acceptable formats, and responding or not responding to posts. Strong tribal norms can suppress disagreement. An online cultural identity can be fostered through enforcement of norms and in-group beliefs, and expel intruders and doubters.

Alternatively, some virtual tribes are very egalitarian, supportive, and dialogic, allowing for discussion of opposing positions. Individuals are free to start over with a new pseudonym and new norms. Hard-core players may prefer online to offline socializing, and some video game players or forum members reject central norms. Participation in certain kinds of postings can maintain users' membership in a group, and reinforce the ideology and values of an otherwise dispersed tribe.

Paradoxes

While in no way a central theme of these chapters, some intriguing paradoxes are noted. Using modern Internet technology to participate in neotribalism, primitivism, pantheism, and antitechnology resistance seems pretty clearly paradoxical. For example, Dreamtime ritual and myth, from a timeless, atechnological spiritual perception, are being obtained through commercial, corporate, technological digital music. There is also the paradox of participating in fashion tribes to experiment with alternate, noncommercial identities, but most of these opportunities are generated through commercial and manufactured experiences (such as online video games). Underlying some broad-based concerns about the negative social or individual effects of Internet technology are deep-seated anxieties about loss of or threats to kinship.

Structure

Finally, an ongoing theme has to do with both the structure and structuring of e-tribes and related technology.

Internet technology allows people to participate in multiple groups, and maintain weak and heterogeneous ties. The anonymity of participants and accessibility to posted materials decrease some tribes' control over peripheral members (such as skinhead cybercrews). New communities may form, but they may be ephemeral or temporary; however, that may be appropriate, such as in the case of contact, grief, support, and relational links after Hurricane Katrina. The ability to search, obtain, store, retrieve, mix, and update digital music allows and represents transient personal and group identities. The organizational use of online connections to stakeholder tribes allows proactive development of dialogic and more reciprocal relationships with those stakeholders. Thus, computer-mediated communication may inhibit the emergence of a dominant or centralizing user. However, analyses of e-tribes founded by a proactive leader (whether an Aryan supremacist group, an academic discussion list, or a support group of baby-boomer women) provide counterexamples.

The rules and rewards of a video game may foster tribalism, in the form of guilds and quest parties, competing to kill rivals; limited or pre-assigned icons and avatars may reinforce stereotypes. Role-playing and video games invoke the magic and myth of folklore, and allow manipulation of time and sequencing, crossovers into other worlds, and resurrections from in-game deaths. The digital media experience is a way to cross temporal, physical, and spiritual boundaries; and downloaded music and associated material talismans (personal digital music players, as well as shared playlists) are social resources. The Internet allows the words/texts of actors to be used, manipulated, recorded, and precisely critiqued by tribal rivals, generating an ongoing discourse of appropriated and critiqued arguments.

Conclusion

Clearly, there is not only a wide range of interesting and intriguing topics here, but also diverse and contrasting perspectives on those topics across the chapters. To what kind of e-tribes do you wish to belong?

Acknowledgments

It has been our previous experience that anthologies are rather difficult to assemble. And, while we did have our fair share of difficult decisions to make concerning which pieces were selected for inclusion in *Electronic Tribes* and which were not, this collection of essays seemed to come together rather easily. For that very reason, we would first like to acknowledge our contributors for being so patient with us while we painstakingly read, analyzed, and assessed their work. There were *many* excellent essays submitted for our review, and we had many difficult decisions to make. We hope that we did justice by our decision-making process, and selected those essays that reflected the best perspectives on electronic tribalism possible.

Second, we would like to acknowledge our own tribes (families) for being a support structure for us while we amassed this volume. Too often, projects of this nature consume an unfair amount of time away from family, friends, and loved ones. In both of our cases, as editors for *Electronic Tribes*, we found that our families not only helped us through the late nights of reading, essay selection, and ultimately editing—but were collaborators, as well. At times, it seemed that our families were more interested in our final product than we were, as evidenced by their inquisitive conversations and consistent timetable checking. Accordingly, we both love the fact that our families are supportive. And, we both love each and every one of them, dearly.

Also, we would like to acknowledge our sponsoring editor at the University of Texas Press, Allison Faust (and her support staff), who, from our initial inception of this idea, was intrigued by our notion of tribalism in the new Information Age. She pushed us very hard to make this volume what it is today, and we are grateful for her unrelenting precision and attention to detail. Additionally, her support of this body of work throughout the process has been remarkably passionate. And, at times, when our energy and stamina seemed to be running low, a well-timed supportive e-mail could always be found in both of our inboxes. A toast to you, Allison, and the Longhorns! Cheers!

Finally, to our "silent partner" in this publication endeavor: Mr. Farooq A. Kperogi of Georgia State University in downtown Atlanta. Many of you do not know Farooq, yet. But, certainly, you soon will. As a Ph.D. student of communication studies at Georgia State University, he takes historical-critical research to new heights, and does so with an exacting meticulousness. Farooq is originally from Nigeria, which, many of you will come to learn, is the birthplace of the dreaded 419 e-mail scam. In fact, he and Professor Sandy Duhé have a wonderful chapter on this very issue in this book. Farooq was kind enough to serve as an unofficial editorial reader of this work before final copy went to UT Press Editor Allison Faust. As an editor from the *Daily Trust* in Nigeria, his command of the English language is brilliant. We owe Farooq an immeasurable debt of gratitude and thanks. The communication field is much better, now, for having you in it as a scholar, teacher, and future disciplinary leader. Another toast! Huzzahs to Farooq!

A special thanks to Emma Jean Guillory for her sharp reading eyes.

Electronic Tribes

Where Is the Shaman?

JIM PARKER

T he Internet has undergone tremendous transformations since the introduction of the Mosaic browser in 1993 by the National Center for Supercomputing Applications (NCSA). Mosaic, the precursor to Netscape, Internet Explorer, Firefox, and other graphical browsers, opened up the Internet in ways that were never imagined by most of us. Use of the Internet has exploded over the past decade, with penetration in the United States estimated as high as 70 percent. One of the auxiliary consequences of the explosion of the Internet has been the radical transmutation of our conceptions of sociability. The Internet has become the site not only for the composition and recomposition of new, intriguing, Internet-specific identities; it has also given vent to the recrudescence of hitherto premodern social formations such as the tribe and all the consequences that come with this.

Electronic tribes have existed since well before the present Internet explosion. Personally, I was involved in an e-tribe, or virtual community, in 1986, nearly a decade before the introduction of Mosaic, which started the present revolution in communication. The e-tribe I was part of at that time was a group of computer and media enthusiasts who connected to each other via a primitive bulletin board system, which ran on a repurposed computer that lived in the dresser drawer of one of the members of the group. I am not sure anyone knows the exact date that online tribes began, but we do know that the WELL (Whole Earth 'Lectronic Link) began in 1985 and continues to this day. The beginnings of the WELL, the development and the problems encountered in its evolution, are well documented in Howard Rheingold's *The Virtual Community*.

Even these early efforts at building community on the Internet are well over ten years after the first introduction of e-mail on ARAPA-NET and other precursors to the Internet. One of the interesting questions addressed by this volume is, what is an electronic tribe? What is the difference between a tribe and community? And what is "virtual" about these concepts? Webster's online dictionary has a definition of "virtual" that includes existing on a computer network.

In the chapters that follow, you will be exposed to all sorts of electronic tribes, those that exist in e-mail lists with very few members, those that follow the more traditional format of a message board that can be found at the WELL, and even tribes that are less formal than the e-mail lists but use the Internet to accomplish the goals of the group. At the upper end of participation, the reader will encounter MMORPGs (massively multiplayer online role-playing games), where literally millions of people can interact with each other online.

When I think of tribes, I think of the tribes I encountered in the media of my childhood. These tribes could be either Native Americans or the tribes of Africa. Certainly, to me, a component of this type of tribe was the interdependence among members of these groups. They were often isolated by factors such as geography, language (though, of course, on TV and in the movies everyone spoke English), and dress, and differed from other tribes or larger groups in terms of religion, housing, and worldview. The reader will come away from this book with a better understanding of what a tribe is. How does a tribe differ from a community or a culture? The authors in this book present a variety of approaches to the concept of tribe and explore the ramifications of these approaches.

As the title suggests, the work explores the implications of Internet communication. Just what are we moving toward in terms of human interaction? Is the Internet bringing us closer together or leading us to lives of isolation where our only connection to other human beings is through the pixels on a computer screen? In many ways the Internet seems to be taking us closer to Marshall McLuhan's Global Village, but just what will that Global Village look like? Will the humans come to a greater understanding of each other, developing relationships that span the globe, overcoming the barriers created by cultures, languages, and distance, or will we retreat to tribes of like-minded individuals who, given the marvels of technology, will find it easier to contact each other? Do we reach out and explore new worlds or retreat into imaginary worlds of our own creation? Certainly, we live in an age when it is easier than ever before to be in contact with others, to find friends with whom we have lost touch. But what sort of world does this create? Have we lost privacy because it is now easier than ever before for people to find out where we are and what we do? With even a limited amount of effort, most anyone searching for others can find them. Even those who are not great Web searchers can employ any number of services to this very end. People obviously want to find each other. The popularity of such services as Classmates.com and alumni.net supports this assertion. What of the people who do not want to be found? What many see as a wonderful new world, they may see as a nightmare. To see the dark side of this newfound ability to find out about others, we only need to look to identity theft. Though people have been stealing others' personal information long before the Internet, we now live in a world where we must constantly be aware of the dangers of others trying to use the Internet for nefarious purposes. Chapter 16 of this work takes a look at how an age-old scam has migrated to the Internet. Not a day goes by that most of us don't receive some suspicious e-mail trying to get us to invest in some bogus scheme or phishing for personal information to be used to access our records or bank accounts.

Are we creating an online utopia that will bring us closer together, as suggested by McLuhan? Many of the chapters in this book demonstrate how people are working together, sharing information, and leading happier, more productive lives because of new ways of interacting that the Internet engenders. The opposite side of the coin is that we are just beginning an age of dystopia, as envisioned in movies like the *Matrix* series or books such a William Gibson's *Neuromancer*. Again, some of the articles show us a darker side of the uses of Internet communication. Is the Internet more of a threat to our families and our children than comic books, radio, or television? Every medium has both positives and negatives associated with it. What this work does is help us to better understand both sides of the equation.

One of the important concepts that I noted while reading the articles in the book is that the Internet cannot be considered a single medium. The term Internet covers a wide range of communication tools. The Internet provides us with tools that range from purely text-based artifacts such as plain e-mail to multimedia tools that employ audio, video, text, and interactivity in nearly any combination you can dream of. If you have not thought of it, someone will tomorrow. Each of these different media has a unique impact upon how we interact with others. The Internet provides us with a cornucopia of environments for study as well as for personal use. The Internet also provides scholars with a unique opportunity for study because many of the ongoing interactions are archived—whether they were created in discussion boards, e-mail groups, instant messages, wikis, or chat rooms. Never before have scholars had access to so much data created without the intrusion of cameras or observers. While certainly Internet communication is not the same as face-to-face communication, we have been presented with an opportunity to examine the interactions between people in ways never before available. The media are new and different and most certainly influence the interactions. However, because the interactions are often stored, we can examine these new types of interactions in ways we have never been able to examine interactions in the past. Several of the authors make excellent use of the stored interactions, allowing them insight into the lives of people that in the past has been rare at best.

A question raised about Internet communication and Internet relationships is: are they real? Do they have the same value or depth as real-world relationships? Are they just ways to hide from real interaction? The philosophical implications of this question are not easily answered, but I see the Internet as providing more capacity for communication and, as with other media, how it is used is up to the individual. For years, we have been talking about long-distance relationships. As long as there has been mail, people have had pen pals. Are these relationships real? Often, pen pals end up meeting in real life. Some couples survive long-distance relationships, while others do not. Just because we call Internet relationships electronic tribes, virtual communities, online friends, IM buddies, etc., doesn't negate the relationships. The way that we interact with others certainly affects the relationship. Just as many relationships cannot survive a physical separation, I assume that some online relationships could not survive a face-to-face encounter. People who meet online often meet face-to-face. Sometimes, this face-to-face meeting makes the relationship grow stronger; at other times, the face-to-face meeting is a disappointment. Internet communication is just a different way of getting to know people. We are still learning how it works. Certainly many of the people we encounter online will never become part of our physical reality, but that does not mean they don't affect us nor us them.

Even within electronic tribes where people interact with each other in fantasy realms, taking on characters that may transport individuals to places they could never visit in reality, as examined in Chapter 7, on guild life in World of Warcraft, people develop relationships. Are we who we are? The online world gives people the opportunity to try out new selves. Is this dishonest? Certainly it can be. We are shown on an almost daily basis the specter of sexual predators pretending to be someone they are not to lure underage victims into situations where they may prey upon them. On the other hand, who can find harm in a woman, an African American, a young person, or practically anyone else not revealing everything about herself during a discussion in order not to have her words filtered by sexism, racism, ageism or other forms of prejudice? Hiding can be used both for nefarious purposes and for protection.

While we can use Internet communication as a place to hide, it also offers us great freedom to think and express ideas and feelings without being bound by the constraints placed upon us by our physical appearance. Just as mail and shortwave radio in the past gave those physically confined a broader world, the Internet has opened up an even broader world. Anyone can find a place to express ideas, whether popular or unpopular. Electronic tribes exist that have a place for anyone, whether it is for innocent pastimes such as crafting, as in Chapter 6, or the more menacing activities of skinheads, as shown in Chapter 14.

So who is the shaman of the e-tribe? Who is the chief? Who are the warriors? Electronic tribes develop norms, and people take on various roles just as those in real life do in face-to-face interaction. Some electronic tribes have a formal structure with elected leadership and assigned roles just as in formal organizations. Some electronic tribes are merely extensions of existing organizations where the online structure is a carryover from an existing organizational structure. Some electronic tribes are informal communication structures within organizations. Electronic tribes give people a chance to be chiefs or shamans when in real life they are much lower on the organizational chart. The article by Ann Rosenthal addresses how Gerald Phillips became an e-tribal chief without even expecting it to happen. Many people think of Howard Rheingold, the author of *The Virtual Community* and *Smart Mobs*, as the guru of electronic tribes. He was most certainly one of the early adopters and chroniclers of the phenomenon. Many people take on roles and head up electronic tribes simply because they have slightly more technical expertise than others. For anyone willing to put out the effort and invest the time, a place exists in the online world. All of us who use the Internet to connect with others and develop relationships owe a debt of gratitude to many people who will probably forever remain unnamed who began this journey and keep pushing it forward.

Allow me to take you on a quick tour of the book. The first section seeks to conceptualize electronic tribes. The chapters in this section investigate just what is a tribe and how electronic tribes differ from other types of online groups, and they begin to look at the potential impact of online tribalism.

The second section deals with the social consequences of electronic tribalism. This section looks at existing electronic tribes on MySpace. com, discussion groups, online games, and mailing lists. This very intriguing section examines how people justify electronic tribes as a means of holding groups of people together despite being separated physically, how people join together based upon interest rather than proximity, and even how some people prefer virtual friendships to real-world friendships.

The third section is concerned with the development of online culture. How do electronic tribes develop norms and rules? How is deviant behavior managed? How do leaders develop online? What is the culture that relates to downloading music?

The final section takes the reader to a darker side of electronic tribes, crime and counterculture. As stated earlier, a place exists for everyone on the Internet. This section looks at the places where some of those people live. How do we manage threats? I think most of you will find very interesting the origins of the Nigerian scam that most of us have found in our e-mail inboxes at one time or another.

This volume doesn't pretend to investigate every aspect of electronic tribalism, but does offer many different points of view and points the way to a very interesting future for both the online communicator and those investigating that communication. We are no longer tied to just our computers and either a dial-up or an Ethernet connection for participation in electronic tribes. The Internet is now available on many wireless devices—whether a person is sitting at Starbucks with a laptop computer, accessing his or her Blackberry while sitting in the park, or using a cell phone almost anywhere in the world.

We are finding more and more ways of connecting. Groups can be called together at a moment's notice via members' cell phones or through such services as Dodgeball; or you can tag locations to let your friends know about a good restaurant or hotel nearby using Socialight.

Most of us belong to some type of electronic tribe. A tribe may be a simple mailing list of the people with whom we work. This may be no more than a supplement to our face-to-face communication. A tribe may be a group we belong to that plays games. Friends on Facebook constitute overlapping tribes. Friendster even provides charts of how these tribes overlap, giving us instant sociograms of our online world. We may go online to discuss politics or to learn how to arrange flowers. We share bookmarks and create tribes based on similar interests using del.icio.us. The range seems limitless. The variety of modes for communicating is just as varied. We can work online to create content with others through wikis. We can discuss any subject via bulletin boards. We can find love at Match.com. We can use our cell phones to find friends who may be close by. We have entered a world very different from that of just ten years ago. Let's move forward on the journey and explore what the electronic world has to offer.

PART I

CONCEPTUALIZING ELECTRONIC TRIBES

CHAPTER 1

"A Tribe by Any Other Name . . ."

TYRONE L. ADAMS AND STEPHEN A. SMITH

W hen we initially imagined what this collection of essays might become, we must admit that we were awestruck by the term "tribe." Before engaging in a discussion of electronic tribes, we will note our intrigue with the term tribe, and how it relates or does not relate to other terms similarly used to describe groups. Tribe is a core construct in sociological, anthropological, and political thought, with hotly contested significations. Its use evokes different imageries, even passions, in different scholarly traditions. We hope that the essays in this book will do the same.

While it is customary to conceive of the term "tribe" as denoting an aggregation of people who are bonded together by ties of consanguinity, territorial contiguity, and cultural singularities, postcolonial theorists have called attention to what they perceive as the invidious Eurocentric bias inherent in the reservation of the term to exclusively describe non-Western people. David Wiley, professor of African Studies at Michigan State University, made the case that Western scholars and journalists have been enamored of the category "tribe" for over a century primarily because it helps them oversimplify for readers the complexity of the sociohistorical experiences of non-Western societies in Africa, Asia, Latin America, and the American plains. It is no accident, he said, that the contemporary uses of the term were developed during the nineteenth century, when the rise of evolutionary and racist theories denigrated nonwhite peoples as inferior or less civilized, and not yet evolved from an atavistic, acephalous, and primeval state.[1]

An additional epistemological burden imposed on us in the use of the term "tribe" is the negativity, misleading stereotypes, and intense disapproval with which "tribalism," a derivative of tribe, has been associated in the popular imagination. The term conjures images of internecine wars, primitive savagery, irrationality, superstition, and even occultism. The combination leads to portrayal of violence and conflict in non-Western societies as primordial, irrational, congenital, and immutable among "tribes." This image resonates with habitual Western racialist imaginings and can suggest that irrational violence, coarseness, depravity, baseness, and malevolence are in-built in the conception of "tribe."[2] The president of the University of Oregon, Dave Frohnmayer, gave expression to this sentiment when he defined what he called "the New Tribalism" as

> the growth of a politics based upon narrow concerns, rooted in the exploitation of divisions of class, cash, gender, region, religion, ethnicity, morality and ideology—a give-no-quarter and take-no-prisoners activism that demands satisfaction and accepts no compromise. It is a raw permissiveness that escalates rhetorical excess sometimes even to physical violence.[3]

This attrition of culture and good breeding in public discourse, he continued, is only an outward expression of the New Tribalism. Beneath it, he said, "are the tribes themselves, small groups of like-minded people who zealously support narrowly focused political issues."[4] Thus, according to this view, the multiplicity of self-interested, fragmentary enclaves that populate cyberspace, which we have termed "electronic tribes," represents a descent to barbarism, primitivism, and other unsavory premodern practices. Technology, especially Internet technology, is often implicated in this putative descent from the heights of culture and civilization. This stance complicates any attempt to conceptualize the term "tribe" outside the confines of this widespread imputation of vulgarity that unfortunately enjoys pseudointellectual endorsement in the form of pious, self-righteous, but barren statements such as that above.

The epistemological and even taxonomical utility of the term "tribe" in the sociological and anthropological literature is as robustly variegated as it is self-contradictory. Some authors deploy the term to denote linguistic affinity, others common culture, some ancestral provenance, and yet others government by common rulers. Consequent upon the semantic fluidity and conceptual inexactitude of the term, some scholars have suggested that it should be thrown into the intellectual trashcan by social scientists.⁵ Instructively, the eminent Kenyan professor of African politics and TV director, Dr. Ali Mazrui, doesn't even mention the term "tribe" in the entirety of his seminal and hugely influential book and TV series, *The Africans: A Triple Heritage*.⁶ While the objection by post-colonial scholars to the use of the term "tribe" is perfectly valid and legitimate from a political standpoint, our object in using it to approximate the social and relational intercourse that takes place in cyberspace by social aggregates is predicated on its classical anthropological conception. Tribe is originally a community of people united by common blood descent. In later historical periods, tribes consisted of people who domiciliated and whose ancestors had domiciliated in a common territory, regardless of blood relationship. In anthropology, it is usual to construct a gradational hierarchy of the human family and place "tribe" at the top, outrivaled only by the "nation." The taxonomy usually places gens at the bottom, followed by a phratry, a tribe, and a nation. A gens (plural gentes) was composed of the progenies descended from a common ancestor. Marx and Engels, influenced by Lewis H. Morgan, the nineteenth-century American anthropologist, believed that the gentes were originally based on common female descent, but as father-right dislodged mother-right, the gentes shifted to the basis of common male descent. The importance of the gens is that it was the most basic, irreducible unit of organization of primitive society. The monogamous family as a unit of organization emerged only later. Thus, under gentile conditions, the husband and wife belonged to different gentes while the children belonged either to the gens of the father or the mother, depending on which system of common descent was in effect. Lewis Morgan concluded that the gens was the unit of analysis for the Iroquois, Greeks, Romans, Scots, Irish, Germans, and others.⁷ The head of the gens was predominant over the head of the family. Clan is sometimes used as a synonym for gens. A phratry was composed of several gentes, while, originally, a tribe was composed of several phratries. To quote Engels directly, "Just as several gentes constitute a phratry, so, in the classical form, several phratries constitute a tribe."⁸ The term tribe was later used to designate those living in the same territory; hence, common territory displaced common descent as the basis for the term. Finally, a nation, in one of its many conceptualizations, represents the coming together of two or more tribes.

We draw inspirational strength from the above to construe the term "tribe" as a unit of sociopolitical organization consisting of a number of families, clans, or other groups who share a common ancestry, spatiotemporal particularity, and cultural artifact, and who are united by a consensual imagination of social and biological affinity. This definition is commonly reflected in the work of many sociologists, anthropologists, political scientists, and liberal arts scholars as a basic understanding of "tribal" human organization. But, in our opinion, this understanding merely scratches the surface of what a *tribe* really is. You see, to us, tribes are much more than sociopolitical, ethnic, or ancestral divisions of states or cultures. They go beyond the classical historical divisions of the ancient Romans—the Latin, Sabine, and Etruscan. They are much more than the twelve tribes of ancient Israel, or even a polis in ancient Greece. They extend well beyond the known historic and extant tribes of Asia, Africa, or Latin America.

Our opinion (and also guiding argument) is that "tribes" are an active confederacy of humans interested in sharing something—an occupation, an interest, or even a habit. Tribes are collections of people who share similarities in beliefs or behaviors. Tribes are modalities of thought. They are the vehicles of the socio-interactional and ideational intercourse among human beings. But then, what distinguishes a tribe from a small group or a larger organizational collection? We believe that there exists a void between the small group (three to eight people) and organizational groups, which denote a more structured, complex, and hierarchical classification. We believe that tribes exist between and within formal organizations in varying numbers and sizes. They are throngs of people dedicated to an idea, purpose, function, or even a way of being. Their number can be small or large enough to encompass an entire community.

The insightful reader may be tempted to ask a fundamental and critical question: *What distinguishes a community from a tribe?* There are two widely accepted definitions for a community used among the general public, which are somewhat helpful here: "a group of people living in the same locality and under the same government" and "the district or locality in which such a group lives." These definitions of community are bound more by geocentric raison d'être than are tribal designations. Yet, sometimes the word community can hold a highly charged logocentric structure as well, such as when it is conceived as: "a group of people having common interests" (e.g., the academic community or the international business community). And sometimes, the word community can be explicatory of a discrete segment of a given society, where the "gay community" or the "African American community," for instance, demonstrates a sociocultural human tangent. All in all, it is our opinion that: (1) communities are much larger human aggregates than tribes; (2) communities are bound to geographies, generally speaking; and (3) communities foment utopian idealism, where tribes incorporate both utopian and dystopian formations.

Carrying the tribal lens over into the digital environs of the Internet, without a doubt, is a relatively easy task. The case can be made that the cartography of cyberspace encapsulates such an enormous assortment of neotribal formations that migrating the concept from offline reality will not be difficult. However, we do not discount the reality that the notion of what constitutes "tribe" in cyberspace is still a contested terrain. This is precisely because the scholarship that should foreground the epistemology of electronic tribes is still at the formative stages. Unfortunately, it promises to be no less susceptible to theoretical dissensions and acrimony than the conventional, preexisting conception of the term. Because the emergence of cyberspace in many significant ways heralded the "death of distance,"[9] time, and space, tribal formations on the Internet dislocate our habitual notions of tribal bonding. Tribes on the Internet at once transcend and encompass biology, spatial distribution, and all the singularities of the traditional conception of tribe, without losing the associational specificity and other socio-interactional quiddities of conventional tribal formations. As the succeeding chapters demonstrate very clearly, tribes have been formed on the Internet on the basis of geography, common descent, intellectual interests, recreational passions, political ideologies, social concerns, age, unity in adversity, and so on. Sometimes the tribes conflate. At other times they are very noticeably divergent. And they can be antagonistic and/or mutually congenial. In sum, cyberspace is inhabited by congeries of tribes that are at once benevolent and malevolent, similar and dissimilar.

Although in principle the Internet is intrinsically democratic, producing consensual, equalizing, and "horizontalizing" effects—assuaging, not multiplying or exacerbating, social stratifications—it spawns specialized groups of "hundreds or several thousand people . . . and no traditional medium offers a personally available means to do this"; "it can shatter institutional control over knowledge that relies on geographical proximity of members and boundaries on knowledge distribution." Specialists in several provinces of knowledge deploy the Internet to construct exclusive loci of knowledge, resulting in "cliques of experts . . . electronic tribes linking people in associations not possible in any other way."[10] Further, organizational "tribes" emerge as the Internet reproduces itself in terms of "microgroups" within organizations, that is, closed corporate intranets and private extranets to "broadcast" to and secure high-quality links with branches, partners, suppliers, and customers.[11]

What, then, is an electronic tribe? As is evident from the foregoing discussion, four indispensable constituents can be isolated in the conception of electronic tribes: people, purposes, protocols, and technology.[12] The members of electronic tribes are bound by collective purposes, and they interrelate socially by adhering to both notional and clearly defined protocols, rituals, and roles using Internet technologies that support online sociability.[13] The technology needed to create an electronic tribe is not complicated. A simple e-mail–based electronic tribe can be formed by setting up a listserv for a group of users. Others are created using a mishmash of Web pages, chats, bulletin boards, e-mail, instant messengers, Internet relay chats, and databases. The key characteristics of these technologies are their ability to: (1) facilitate synchronous and asynchronous interaction; (2) enhance the convergence of different genres of information-sharing through multimedia; (3) provide an incredibly robust assortment of information for a variety of information-processing needs; and (3) be easily accessible, as well as immune to spatiotemporal constraints. Further, their ease of use, centralized symbol capacity, mass-market appeal, affordability, simultaneity in message dissemination process, vast outreach, and uniform operating standards have heightened their network effects.

Humans aggregate in social organizations for relational development and mutually beneficial expression and exchange of views and opinions. The paramount purpose of aggregating is often information sharing and exchange of life experiences tied to their common concerns, problems, and anxieties. Continuous flow of information is, therefore, the pith and marrow of electronic tribes; it is what defines their essence. Researchers have tagged this tribal behavioral attribute "storytelling."[14] Storytelling here is used to denote the practice of participants asking questions, posing problems, and providing answers and solutions in online social interactions. Through this, online tribal participation satisfies many multidimensional needs of participants.

This ritualistic storytelling actuates profound emotional soldering and guarantees the continuity of the tribe; community participation is strengthened by the affinity offered by the tribe, what Joseph Gusfield characterized as "consciousness of kind."[15] Consciousness of kind is the proclivity for members of a close-knit unit to construct a consciousness of emotional attachment toward one another, and a corresponding sense of group difference from others who are notionally located outside the orbit of the tribe. Consciousness of kind is collective consciousness, the outward manifestation of a "we-versus-they" mentality. It is a shared knowing of mutual solidarity. It encapsulates a sense of collective distinctiveness or the amity that members feel toward one another. We therefore define an electronic tribe as *an exclusive, narrowly focused, network-supported aggregate of human beings in cyberspace who are bound together by a common purpose and employ a common protocol and procedure for the consensual exchange of information and opinions.*

In constructing this definition, we are not unaware of the intense terminological bickering between competing conceptions of "tribes" and "neotribes." Albert Muniz and Thomas O'Guinn, for instance, stated that "Tribes are networks of persons gathering for social interaction. Neo-tribes are unique in that they are fluid, ephemeral, and nebulous; they form, gather occasionally, disperse, and form again."[16] We think that this distinction is at best tenuous and at worst forced in a computer-mediated context. All identities in cyberspace invariably are, or have the potential to be, transitory, provisional, tentative, situational, and sometimes narcissistic. We are, therefore, persuaded to regard electronic tribes and neotribes as synonymous.

Eminent French sociologist Michel Maffesoli is often credited with being the earliest scholar to deploy and locate the term "neotribalism" in an intellectual framework.[17] Maffesoli predicted that with the relentless waning of the cultural and institutional props of modernism, industrial societies would eventually roll back the wheel of their historical progress and re-create the organizational principles and shibboleths of the prehistoric tribal past for direction. He concluded, therefore, that the recrudescence of neotribalism and the rebirth of tribes—or neotribes— would be a hallmark of the postmodern era. These neotribes, he said, are "characterized by fluidity, occasional gatherings and dispersal."[18] Building on Maffesoli and extending more into consumption realms, Bernard Cova characterizes members of these neotribes as uninhibited by spatiotemporal limitation, but displaying "a local sense of identification, religiosity, syncretism, group narcissism."[19] That explains why Robert Kozinets, for instance, conceives of e-tribes in terms of associational bonding of groups for purposes of consumerism.[20]

The reality of cyberspace seems to be lending credence to Maffesoli's predictions. Electronic tribes of different hues are luxuriantly proliferating in cyberspace in ways that closely approximate traditional tribes, except for their impermanence, flexibility, and imperviousness to the limitations of traditional tribal formations. The emergence of electronic tribes challenges the time-honored contention that postmodern individuals are solipsistic isolationists who take delight in being ensconced in their lonesome worlds. Electronic tribes make obvious the truism that humans have ingrained desires for communication and the construction of a sense of community. These desires especially become apparent in times of disasters such as hurricanes, wildfires, and so on, or when people find themselves marginalized by mainstream society. In the fragmentary milieu of postmodernism, they appeared to shrink, but in reality they flourish and burgeon in many innovative ways.

It would seem safe to contend that we are actually experiencing a relentless onslaught on individualism, a powerful reversal of the social atomism that the Industrial Age spawned. We are now experiencing the deconstruction and reconstruction of our ultra-atomistic society to what Rob Shields called "heterogeneous fragments, the remainders of mass consumption society."[21] These heterogeneous fragments come in the shape of electronic tribes. Even though they are not tribes in the traditional anthropological signification of primitive arcadian congeries, they are nonetheless social aggregations that closely approximate the sense of community of the tribe. In the Electronic Age, these tribes are imprecise, illimitable concatenations of individuals and groups for the purpose of social interaction and information sharing. They form, disband, and re-form as something else—reflecting the perpetually transforming and kaleidoscopic character of postmodern identities.

Though the thesis of postmodern society of today posits pervasive social dissolution and extreme individualism,[22] we may very well be witnessing the emergence of an antithesis in the attempts by postmoderns to reconstruct the social fabric on their own terms, with "links of their own" making and choice, which Michel Maffesoli has labeled "neo-tribalism,"[23] but which we have chosen to call electronic tribes. This is important in itself, and it demands the attention of communication scholars. It will be interesting to watch how the synthesis between this postmodern thesis and antithesis plays out over time. The electronic agora will undoubtedly be the site for this postmodern dialectical push and pull.

Notes

1. For an excellent discussion on the use of the "tribal" lens by Western scholars and journalists to gaze at African societies, see David Wiley, "Using 'Tribe' and 'Tribalism' Categories to Misunderstand African Societies" (African Studies Center, Michigan State University, mimeo, 1981).

2. Robust academic debates on the appropriateness of the use of the term "tribe" abound. See, for instance, *The Oxford Companion to Politics of the World*, ed. Joel Krieger (New York: Oxford University Press, 1993). A. B. M. Mafeje's article "Tribalism" and Okwudiba Nnoli's article "Ethnicity" are particularly insightful and instructive. Similarly, a succinct, overarching essay from a standard textbook in African Studies, "On the Concept of Tribe," can be found in John N. Paden and Edward W. Soja, *The African Experience* (Evanston, Ill.: Northwestern University Press, 1970), 2:20–22.

3. See Dave Frohnmayer, "The New Tribalism," http://president.uoregon.edu/tribalism.html.

4. Ibid.

5. An oft-quoted early statement by a prominent anthropologist disapproving of the term in academic discourse is Aidan Southall, "The Illusion of Tribe," in *The Passing of Tribal Man in Africa*, ed. Peter Gutkind, pp. 28–51 (Leiden, the Netherlands: Brill, 1970). Carolyn Fluehr-Lobban, Richard Lobban, and Linda Zangari, writing in UCLA's *Ufahamu* ("'Tribe': A Socio-Political Analysis," vol. 7, no. 1 [1976]: 143–165), also pooh-poohed the use of the term and argued for the discontinuation of its use in scholarly discourse.

6. See Ali A. Mazrui, *The Africans* (London: BBC, 1986).

7. This discussion is distilled from Frederick Engels, *The Origin of the Family, Private Property, and the State* (orig. 1884; Moscow: Progress, 1948).

8. Ibid., p. 90.

9. The phrase "death of distance" in relation to the Internet was first used by Martin Dodge and Robert Kitchin, *Mapping Cyberspace* (London: Routledge, 2001), p. 63.

10. John December and Neil Randall, *The World Wide Web Unleashed* (Indianapolis: SAMS Publishing, 1994), p. 927.

11. See *The Economist*, October 19, 1996, p. 23.

12. For a perceptive discussion on the typology of what the authors call "neo-tribes," see Grace J. Johnson, Paul J. Ambrose, "Neo-tribes: The Power and Potential of Online Communities in Health Care," *Communications of the ACM* 49 (2006): 107–113. The authors do not draw a distinction between communities and tribes, but distinguish tribes from neotribes.

13. Jenny Preece, *Online Communities: Designing Usability, Supporting Sociability* (Chichester, UK: John Wiley & Sons, Ltd., 2001). This is one of the first comprehensive textbooks about sociability in online communities.

14. Albert M. Muniz Jr. and Thomas C. O'Guinn, "Brand Community," *Journal of Consumer Research* 27, no. 1 (March 2001): 412–432. They conceived of storytelling as the re-creation of the erstwhile ritualistic tribal tradition of elders telling and retelling stories to newer members of the tribe to ensure an intergenerational transfer of knowledge, myths, societal ethos, and the collective consciousness of the community.

15. Joseph R. Gusfield, *Community: A Critical Response* (New York: Harper & Row, 1978).

16. Muniz and O'Guinn, "Brand Community," p. 414.

17. See Michel Maffesoli, *The Time of the Tribes: The Decline of Individualism in Mass Society* (Thousand Oaks, Calif.: Sage, 1996).

18. Ibid., p. 76.

19. Bernard Cova, "Community and Consumption: Towards a Definition of the 'Linking Value' of Product or Services," *European Journal of Marketing* 31, nos. 3/4 (1997): 300.

20. Robert V. Kozinets, "E-Tribalized Marketing? The Strategic Implications of Virtual Communities of Consumption," *European Management Journal* 17 no. 3 (1999): 252–264.

21. Rob Shields (1996), foreword to Maffesoli, *The Time of the Tribes*, p. x.

22. Cova, "Community and Consumption."

23. Maffesoli, *The Time of the Tribes*, p. 69.

CHAPTER 2

Mimetic Kinship: Theorizing Online "Tribalism"

VERONICA M. DAVIDOV AND BARBARA ANDERSEN

T he term "tribe" is a ticklish one for anthropologists, and one ensconced in layers of its own semiotic mythologies. While "tribes," historically, have been one step on the "ladder of social evolution" diagrams, transitioning between "bands" and "chiefdoms," and a term used as a neutral classification by twentieth-century ethnographers like Bronislaw Malinowski, by the 1970s Morton Fried argued for a discourse of tribes as epiphenomena produced through encounters between powerful colonial forces and indigenous polities. Fried argued that "So-called tribal groups . . . are not social organizations whose integrity receded into a remote past; rather the tribalism displayed is a reaction to more recent events and conditions." Fried highlights the murky exegesis of the concept of "tribe" and proposes a model characterized by fluid boundaries, rather than static structure: "The nature of the concept of tribe has been a confused and ambiguous one from its earlier period of utterance. . . . variations exist in the degree and type of political cohesion in such units insofar as they represent populations integrated for the achievement of diverse internal or external goals, management of the community or warfare."[1] In many ways, Fried's model informed later postcolonial critiques of "tribes" and associated vocabulary. As Leon Sheleff writes, "for many, tribes are really a relic of the colonial age; they originated as no more than figments of imperial imaginings and designs."[2] In his book on British policies in colonial India, Martin Chanock demonstrates the ways in which the praxis of tribalism enabled indirect rule, whereby headsmen and chiefs were designated, through whom control over members of their "tribes" was maintained.[3]

Despite the problematic status of "tribes" as precolonial political forms, in the postcolonial milieu, tribes have emerged as indigenous units formed for the purposes of cultural preservation, lobbying, activism, and advocacy. In the United States, Native American tribes have become political and social units for the purposes of identification, belonging, and personhood among their members. While colonial tensions are present in the noumenon of a native tribe, which is inscribed in the historical context of its own marginalization and resistance, its structure and membership are produced within, rather than imposed from without: "Becoming a member of a particular Tribe requires meeting its membership rules, including adoption. Except for adoption, the amount of blood quantum needed varies, with some Tribes requiring only proof of descent from a Native American ancestor, while others may require as much as one-half."[4] The situation in Canada is somewhat different; the question of who is and is not an Indian (according to the Indian Act) and who is entitled to band membership (and the rights associated with membership) continues to generate conflict and disagreement both within and outside Native bands.[5] Still, self-governance has become a widely shared political goal, and interband political bodies such as the Assembly of First Nations have become influential lobby groups. The Inuit Tapiriit Kanatami, an organization representing peoples across the Arctic region, has managed, in only three decades, to meld the geographically dispersed (and historically "nontribal") Inuit into an effective Nation—so successfully that the Inuit now have a Territory, Nunavut, of their own. Moreover, they have been able to create cultural, political, and social links with other Arctic peoples in Russia, Alaska, and Scandinavia. In South America, indigenous alliances such as CONAIE (of Ecuador) represent distinct tribes on a national level, working on land rights and sustainable development and effecting opposition to oil drilling on lands that are legally designated as indigenous tribal territories. Because in South America class mobility is frequently associated with a sublimation of one's indigenous ethnicity, tribal (as opposed to local/community) membership operates as a political, public mode of self-identification and assertion of belonging.

All this is to say that with intentionality becoming a dominant aspect of affiliations that fall in the category of a "tribe," that category shifts from a descriptive framework enabling the naturalizing of constellations of social relationships and interactions by an outside (colonial, ethnographic) gaze to an actively chosen discourse that simultaneously signifies and reproduces formative/emphasized aspects of personhood. This transformation, where, in a way, social networks play "superstructure" to the "base" of personhood, is similar to the one Marilyn Strathern describes as categories of kinship in English families shifted from biological relationships to "enterprise kinship": "the emergence of personhood itself was taken to be a natural process, the outcome of biological development rather than the person's . . . participation in relationships with other persons."[6] In both cases, the biosocial factors previously determining affinity are deemphasized in favor of the desublimated and personal factors, making social relationships into a medium for an assertion of a chosen personhood. So, in a traditional anthropological heuristic of tribes, the system structures and determines individuals' relationships to each other within the framework of that system; in the context of tribes-as-intentional-communities, individuals externalize their identities into a unifying framework that reproduces their notions of personhood in the public sphere.

Models of affinity are fluid and thus are particularly useful for creation of self-aware communities. So, while there is, increasingly, a growing chasm between the interrogated discourse of "tribe" as an ethnographic and heuristic category and tribes as sociopolitical units that have emerged as postcolonial versions of their colonized selves, what bridges them is a certain degree of *intentionality and agency*. Intentionality and agency are present in both the anthropological understanding of tribes as social units constructed to respond to a particular set of social and historical pressures, and the appropriation of the term, with all of its semiotic mythohistorical nuances, by intentional communities, including the ones in cyberspace.

Consider the statement of intent of tribe.net—an online social network used to promote events, find housing, and make connections with potential friends. It proclaims an "intentional community" and elaborates: "We're about physical 'meatspace' communities—ecovillages, cohousing, residential land trusts, communes, student co-ops, urban housing cooperatives and other related projects and dreams." Furthermore, subgroups formed within that network are also referred to as "tribes" and are intentionally structured in terms of the unifying "theme." The "create your own tribe" instructional template offers several options for tribe membership: public, which anyone may join; moderated, requiring moderator approval for membership; and private, visible only to invited members. Though the language of a cooperatively shared "dream" evokes essentialist and romantic ideas about tribal peoples, functionally such spaces share parallel goals of alliance, affiliation, negotiation, and resistance.

The tribe.net model is an explicit example of intentional social networks adopting the vocabulary and/or the modality of a "tribe"—a tribe not as a noumenon, but as a meme about an idealized past/elsewhere, a cluster of desires and longings externalized into a chronotope.[7] The particulars of this chronotope illuminate a historical imaginary of "tribes" as a social unit signifying utopian ahistorical time—an unspecified bucolic past, characterized by any combination/bricolage of the following: sustainable ecology; barter or gift economy; preindustrial sustenance; matriarchy as a social order; and tribes as small-scale social formations, engaged as a community, rather than alienated from it. A historical past is projected as a utopian blueprint for the future of society at large, but in the present resolves itself into small intentional communities that adopt the "tribal" model. Some of these communities are real and corporeal, marked on maps, but many other intentional communities exist on a part-time or fragmented basis, as temporary alternatives to the late-stage capitalist zeitgeist. One such example is Burning Man, an annual event whose many participants refer to themselves as a tribe, and form an ephemeral community that encourages artistic, spiritual, and personal expression, and functions exclusively in the mode of gift economy. Another example is a Web "tribe," where the term evokes a shared purpose, a community, and its reason for existing. As Michel Maffesoli wrote, "The feeling of tribal belonging can be comforted by technological development. . . . potentially, 'cable,' electronic bulletin boards (playful, erotic, instrumental, etc.) create a communication matrix where groups with diverse configurations and objectives emerge, are fortified and disappear; groups which recall the archaic structures of tribes or village clans."[8]

An example of the ideology expressed through this terminology is found in the "CyberTribe Rising"[9] manifesto, which circulated on the Internet in 1993, advocating a type of alternative/resistance to capitalist reality based on the writings of Hakim Bey and his concept of TAZ (Temporary Autonomous Zone)[10]—an ephemeral, but empowering and liberating intervention—a Full Moon rave in this particular example. The manifesto calls for a technoutopia, where "this technology of control and domination [is mutated] into a technology of sharing and cooperation. What is needed is a new paradigm based upon the cybernetic model, but with the additional ideas from Deep Ecology, Distributed Systems Theory and the 'New Physics.' For lack of a better term, I refer to this as C_5I_2—Community, Consensus, Cooperation, Communication, Cybernetics, Intelligence and Intuition." The intention and agenda of this community are expressed through technological language that simultaneously evokes the tropes of utopian science fiction. In the same vein, the authors continue:

Communication and Cybernetics constitute the areas of opportunity and challenge for our group. The creative and dynamic use of these technologies will make the difference between a "flash in the pan" fad, or a serious contribution to global culture that we could make as the CyberTribe. . . . The CyberTribe exists today. All over the world, thousands of ravers communicate daily via e-mail over an international computer network called the INTERNET. They do everything from exchanging information on the latest _techno_ trax, to planning and organizing raves, to discussing the Scene, politics, and the ultimate meaning of life. E-mail has turned out to be an invaluable tool for keeping in touch with folks in our "family" as well as the worldwide "Family." . . . At no other time in history has a movement had the facilities of high speed communication at their disposal; this is significant, but technology alone is not enough to make a difference. Each and every one of us must strive to become more aware, and more loving.[11]

This manifesto is rooted in the idea of a "tribe" as a utopian meme, tribe as a symbol and index of what Donna Haraway calls the "personal and collective yearning for barely possible worlds."[12] The authors' call for a renegotiation of the social order so that it reflects their values and enables a formation of a meaningful community exemplifies Haraway's observation that computers are the medium "through which potent 'things' like freedom, justice, well-being, skill, wealth, and knowledge are variously reconstituted."[13] This reconstitution is based on semiotically commandeering an imaginary historical trope in the service of an imagined/desired future.

However, the symbolic system established in such formations is more than postmodern nostalgia as imagined history, and more than a utopian fantasy deferred into the future. The fantasy itself is a reality in cyberspace. The virtual communities are not references to "tribal" structures; through their very existence, they enact these structures through a production of "ingroup" personhood for participants through shared language and terminology, the protocol for exchange between the members, the (usually) fluid but codified rules for integration and acceptance. The ensuing personhood is rich in signifiers such as adopted names, representative avatars, signature quotes, and so forth. In a sense, the map is the territory in cyberspace, as the articulation of shared values for a community constitutes a community with those shared values, in and of itself. Slavoj Žižek's thoughts about a different aspect of virtual sociality (cybersex) are particularly applicable here: "What fascinates me is that the possibility of satisfaction already counts as an actual satisfaction. . . . just typing your fantasies is the fascination itself. In the symbolic order the potentiality already gives actual satisfaction. . . . in the computer I see virtuality, in the sense of the symbolic function, collapsing."[14]

At the root of network imaginaries is the concept of the connection. Those who have been involved with the Internet—and its brother, sister, and parent networks, including Usenet and FidoNet—since before the days of ubiquitous computing can recall the way in which connection was an act that was sensory and experiential. The sound of the dial tone, the clicks, the escalating registers of connection, the flood of characters down the terminal screen: it was an *act* that was felt, seen, and heard. Slow modems and dialing queues impressed upon the user the quality of time passing, and the punctuation of empty time with acts of connection invested those acts with much of their meaning. The fact that computer use tended to take place in spaces of personal isolation—before the gaming arcade, Internet café, wireless laptop, or student lab provided alternatives to the bedroom or basement—overdetermined the sense that confinement and solitude were the impetus for acts of connection.

A discussion of the model of personhood emerging from this phenomenology of connection can help us reconsider the way in which "tribalism" appears online. The privileging of "freedom," alongside a "fundamental contradiction in American culture between nature and law," generates a space of self-determination that imagines social participation as always "bought" or "exchanged" for something else.[15] "Connection" has, as such, an unusual double meaning: intimate, even embodied understanding, on the one hand; and a self-interested commodity relationship on the other. A connection is a way to have personal needs met and fulfilled; occasionally, an explicit connection is a metaneed in and of itself. One way of structuring one's social interactions that transforms the abstract notion of a connection into a meaningful, ritualized practice is the model of fictive kinship.

"Fictive kinship," in anthropological theory, refers to the extension of kin terms to people who are culturally recognized as nonkin. Fictive kin practices appear, in some contexts, to be closely tied up with resource availability and the relative position of a person's social group. Sociologists studying kinship in North America have observed that African Americans identify fictive kin more readily than Anglo Americans,[16] and that groups with low social capital or status (prisoners, single mothers, sexual minorities, the elderly) tend to extend kinship terms to nonkin more readily than those with high capital and status.[17] This is because kinship is more than an abstract relationship between persons; it is also a set of obligations implying reciprocity.[18] The specific obligations a person has to a relative—fictive or otherwise—can be affective, material, symbolic, or a combination thereof.

The distinction between "friendship" and "kinship" in middle-class Anglo American conceptions of relatedness is not easily discerned in the abstract. Both terms imply obligations that are chiefly emotional (or "supportive") and presume a certain amount of egalitarianism.[19] Ideally, friendship is consensual, free, and noncommodified—although so, for that matter, is kinship. Close, nonrelated intimates are described in terms of familial tropes: "like family"; "like a sister to me"; "blood brothers." Because of the way in which family relationships are assumed to be accompanied by a sense of "enduring, diffuse solidarity,"[20] they are easily transferred metonymically to other types of relationship.[21]

That people who engage in social relationships online sometimes express feelings of "enduring, diffuse solidarity" is undeniable. That they will play with the idea of being a "family" of sorts, and even track their relationships in ways that suggest affinal and kin ties, is also evident. The fictiveness of their kinship is assumed outright. However, even as "play," fictive kinship is still a functional system that enables the development of ingroup sentiment, resource-sharing, and practices of fission and fusion.

In analyzing the basis of Internet kinship it is important to start with the production of the person in online contexts; followed by an exploration of what it is that persons are expected to need from one another; and finally observing how those needs are managed in online interactions.

When you first started using the modem, what was it you wanted?
    connection.
Did you get it?
    yes.
What other things did you get?
    what else is there?
What did you give?
    connections.
—DRONGO REFLECTING ON HIS REASONS FOR PARTICIPATION IN ONLINE COMMUNITIES

In the early, slow-modem years of cyberspace, when Usenet and the Internet were the exclusive domain of academics, echomail technology enabled small local networks. The original hobbyist echomail network, FidoNet, comprised thousands of nodes, a well-established hierarchical structure, and a distinct amateur culture of debate and discourse. At the same time, individuals with different productive and interactional goals—software pirating, ANSI art, demo production, music, hacking— adapted the echomail technology developed for FidoNet, enabling new, smaller networks to flourish. Because echomail networks were relatively inexpensive to set up and run, teenagers and young adults often ran BBSes out of their bedrooms or basements. One network in the 604 area code emerged out of this context. The group's name, an allusion to the parentage of its two founders, suggested a goal of intentional community and chosen family: the Adopted Bastards Network.

Drongo, one of the two original "adopted bastards," had a reputation for an extremely abstract style of trolling. It amused him to take on the persona of a macro attack,[22] dumping endless loops of random text into message bases. Usually it was to indicate that he felt the conversation was going around in circles; that he'd seen the discussion before; that he thought that talk was pointless. Eventually it became a cute personality quirk, and he would perform his "macro attacks" to indicate a silly mood. The effect was to draw other people to him. Every base would have the same message at the top. Expressions of annoyance, over time, melted into familiarity and recognition. People who didn't understand that it was "just Drongo" were revealed as outsiders. Behavior that would—and indeed did—see him booted off FidoNet was ritualized as a sign of the playfulness and tolerance he wanted to see in the communities he had helped to build. Drongo's parodic imitation of a random string of text was part of what made him real to his community: it reminded them of their origins, and of the practice of technology that had initiated their involvement. The fact that he was acting like a nonperson was, ironically, a sign of his personality.

When users attempt to explain the affiliative logic of Internet social groups in offline contexts, we can see how the act of translation can create offsets. When asked by an outsider, "How do you know so-and-so?" they may downplay the online world, generating explanations like "Oh, I met x through y, who is a friend of k that I met at a party at j's house." Networking imagination vies with community imagination for explanatory force. Though the community provides a link, it does not explain how that link would translate into friendship. The affiliation of users, the relationship they have with one another, requires the interposition of an entity—the network itself—that cannot be explained to people who are not members. It's not that the network is *secret*, but rather that its appealing qualities emerge out of ingroup sentiments.

More novel interfaces have networking imagination built into them. Friendster, MySpace, Facebook, and LiveJournal imagine the individual as the potential building block of a network, and visualize each user as a point of entry into discrete "scenes" or "communities." This explicit visualization of connectedness, however, is an overlay that tells us very little about what people actually do with their networks. Like a family tree, it tells us a lot about formal structure and very little about practice. Judith Donath and Danah Boyd have noted the problematic assumptions underlying these mappings: "that there is a need for people to make more connections, that using a network of existing connections is the best way to do so, and that making this easy to do is a great benefit."[23] The individual's participation in social life is imagined as utilitarian, self-interested, and, above all, chosen. Technically and epistemically, the individual *has* to be prior to the community—and the individual characteristics of users ("interests") become the motives organizing participation. Sharing an interest, like sharing blood, can be a route to connection, but that connection has to be lived through practice in order for it to produce the affective resemblance that characterizes kinship.

Entrée into a community requires the demonstration of a particular set of membership entitlements. The "new user application" is recalled by participants in art, gaming, and hacking scenes as a means for demonstrating the knowledge, skills, or resources that one could bring to the community of practice; as a demonstration of status, applications are ritualized iterations of resemblance as an entitlement.[24] In communities where a prior (offline) identity is the assumed ground of membership, applicants need to demonstrate their entitlement through other means. For example, illness-based Internet support groups often require that users state their diagnosis, length of time since diagnosis, and treatment regimes in their message signature file.[25] However, because membership is also an ongoing practice of relating to others, reciprocal iterations of resemblance and affiliation can be a large part of how group identities are lived. In a sense, the system of rules and tasks and particularized relationships *is* kinship. The very act of learning, internalizing, and attempting to work through these preexisting rules—which are often policed by other members or built into the software—transforms membership from a technical requirement to a cognitive and social norm.

Gay Becker, Anneliese Butler, and Robert D. Nachtigall, discussing the impact of new reproductive technologies on American kinship, point out that "resemblance talk"—the social practice of pointing out the similarity between family members as a way of creating a sense of connectedness—is one of the primary ways in which normative models of descent are upheld on a daily basis.[26] The iteration of similarity through practices of comparison, whether intended seriously or as play, likewise generates the appealing affective features of online interaction. Discovering someone *who* is like you and seeing that likeness revealed and reiterated through conversation, interests, shared friends, and so forth, works to establish that person as a relatable interlocutor. "Memes," quizzes, and other language games—which project, even if humorously, certain categories of being onto the user—simultaneously characterize people for the benefit of others and provide a medium of exchange through which reciprocal relations can be played out. "Tagging" someone with a meme is an act of recognition; answering a meme makes one recognizable in particular ways.

Most online communities are structured around reciprocities of some type. "Question/answer" or "post/response" formats, which comprise the archetypical mode of cybersociality—the text-based discussion forum—help to create the sense that one is talking to someone else who is both real and relatable. In a sense, cyberenvironments map as Karin Knorr Cetina's "object worlds." As spaces where others are frequently invisible or unknown, these object worlds embed individuals through the way in which they encourage position-taking. Looking back at George Herbert Mead's theorizations of social interaction, Knorr Cetina writes:

> Mead devised his famous role-taking formula for an interpersonal sociality, which he thought comes about when a person sees the world from the perspective of the other, includes in his or her perspective-taking the other's attitude toward him/herself, and when the process is mutual, involves both parties in an interaction. . . . The process of position-taking involves the subject's "becoming the object," a sort of crossover through which the subject attempts to see the object world from the inside, to "think" as it does, and to feel its reactions.[27]

The "structural affinity between subject and object" in online social relations—a structural affinity enabled by particular practices of sharing, extrapolation, and play—"provides a sort of backbone for the idea of a reciprocity."[28]

Of course, online likeness is never completely abstracted from offline identifications. The problem of who is treated like a "real person" online has occupied theorists of cyberspace since the beginning. The ways in which early interactive technologies made it possible for people to play with identity opened a space for rethinking authenticity, proximity, and intimacy as products of social interaction. However, as Samuel M. Wilson and Leighton C. Peterson note, "identities are negotiated, reproduced, and indexed in a variety of ways in online interactions, and these often cannot be understood without considering the offline context."[29] Interactive styles, interests, and even understandings of intention are gendered, classed, and raced attributes. The affinity produced through practices of intentional community can reproduce social boundaries, all the more dangerous because of their apparent disembodiment and otherworldliness. Although affinity is pleasurable to those who partake of it, and who find their own chosen "tribe" online, the tribal meme also works to produce a sense of inevitability and cooperation, which can be used to suppress argument and resist change.

Cthulu, a gamer interviewed about his online social practices, started using the modem in order to get "video games on demand." After the initial thrill of cracking, leeching, and trading began to wear off, he noticed that the currency demands of BBSes (which often took time bank deposits in the form of uploads) enabled a new game—"the prospect of interaction with real intelligences, not just artificial ones." Slowly, other players became recognizable:

> In some games (Barneysplat) it was limited to seeing how people performed in the high score table relative to you. . . . others (VGA Planets, Barren Realms) offered limited interaction in a fashion analogous to the venerable "play by mail" wargames. Still others (the Pit) boasted simultaneous gameplay with the SysOp at the other end. Yet another category had players occupying a shared universe with occasional points of intersection (the Inn in LORD), and finally there were the pseudopersistent shared worlds of games like Tradewars and Operation Overkill 2, involving coordinating the actions and virtual resources of groups of players for mutual benefit and success. Playing in tandem with other people was so much fun it took a while to realize that the main appeal there was in the interaction, not actually in the gameplay . . . leading people to the strangest "game" yet—the message bases.

The structured interaction of the BBS games had produced relatable individuals, perhaps with a shared interest in particular types of play, enabling new opportunities for connection. The apparent "newness" of the types of relationship that online interactions offered—from the perspective of a teenage boy whose social world had, up to that point, been limited to the awkward intimacy of family and school—suggested to Cthulu that there was something unusual, strange, or unprecedented about his practices. The utopianism of cyberspace combined with his phenomenological experience of connection to generate feelings of awe and excitement. His sense of a shift away from commodities (the free games that had motivated his initial involvement) as the locus of interaction transformed others from mere "connections" to connective relations and community members.[30]

Reflecting on their early online life together, Cthulu's friend Calvinball dismissed the idea that there was something otherworldly about their interactions:

> As it turns out, that's mostly how socialization works. You find random things to talk about communally and you talk about them. You find random other things to do together—playing computer games, dialing BBSes, watching movies, or hanging out at the mall—and then you do them.

Calvinball's musings on the praxis of friendship illustrate the tension between the "tribalism" found online and the problem of creating appropriate forms of affiliation. On the subject of the mundanity of intentional community, he wrote, "everyone . . . seems to think there's something more to it—that there's this ideal level of social interaction that they can never access, that leads them to think all that totally genuine social interaction they had with people was somehow not the real thing." The Internet has been simultaneously lauded as an expansion of the public sphere, enabling new forms of alliance, action, and identity, and as a regressive space of sociopolitical involution, catering to subgroups who are not interested in (or capable of) an appropriately public form of life. These tensions are ubiquitous in the media commentary on cyberspace, manifested in discussions of domestic and intimate matters—pornography, cybersex, cult membership, body boundaries,[31] "Internet addiction," and the loss of the ability to distinguish between "real" relationships and "virtual" ones. These are anxieties about kinship: about the forms of relationship and engagement that are appropriate to a particular type of person, and about the social formations that individuals ought to reproduce through their chosen affiliations.

The "tribe," as a meme and as a functioning unit of fictive kinship, necessarily creates stratification between insiders and outsiders. Ultimately, all of these alliances and anxieties are negotiated in the context of a fluid structure, characterized by fission/fusion, rather than strict, static boundaries. Despite the fact that the cybertribes of today are steeped in mythology reifying society "as it once was," that imaginary referent is as invented as the previously discussed tribes of the colonial taxonomies. The conceptual ur-tribe that is used as a model—whether in the spirit of inspiration or appropriation—is imagined as a social phenomenon that informs personhood. However, the functional tribe, as a cyber-noumenon, is a social locus that is created and enabled by choice and agenda. As such, it is a mutable social form, even as it pays homage to an idealized monolithic institution in its discourse of its own creation and purpose. An actual/virtual tribe that has successfully imagined itself into being is a creature of Durkheimian externalization, where a group is discursively unified around shared values, ideas, and language, which are enacted and ritualized as symbolic forms of interaction and exchange, reaffirming itself, and summing itself up as a community.

Notes

1. Morton Fried, *The Notion of Tribe* (Menlo Park, Calif.: Cummings Publishing, 1975), p. 5.

2. Leon Sheleff, "Tribalism—Vague but Valid," *African Anthropology* 6 (1999): 228.

3. Martin Chanock, *Law, Custom and Social Order: The Colonial Experience in Malawi and Zambia* (Cambridge: Cambridge University Press, 1985).

4. "Frequently Asked Questions" (Washington State Governor's Office of Indian Affairs), http://www.goia.wa.gov/FAQ/FAQ.htm#q4 (accessed June 26, 2005).

5. Noel Dyck, *What Is the Indian "Problem"? Tutelage and Resistance in Canadian Indian Administration* (St. John's, Newfoundland: Institute of Social and Economic Research, 1991).

6. Marilyn Strathern, *Reproducing the Future: Anthropology, Kinship, and the New Reproductive Technologies* (New York: Routledge, 1992), p. 23.

7. In "The Dialogic Imagination," Bakhtin describes the chronotope as being "characterised by a sudden change" when "time . . . thickens, takes on flesh, becomes artistically visible; likewise, space becomes charged and responsive to the movements of time, plot and history" (Mikhail M. Bakhtin, *The Dialogic Imagination: Four Essays*, ed. Michael Holquist, trans. Caryl Emerson and Michael Holquist [Austin: University of Texas Press, 1981], p. 84) and notes that "The chronotope is where the knots of narrative are tied and untied. . . . [it functions] as the primary means for materializing time in space, [it] emerges as a center for concretizing representation" (Bakhtin 1981, p. 250). So, this iconic time/space zone located in the nonconcrete, mythologized past enables the narrative of the tribes of the present and the future.

8. Michel Maffesoli, *The Time of the Tribes: The Decline of Individualism in Mass Society*, trans. Rob Shields (London; Thousand Oaks, Calif.; New Delhi: Sage Publications, 1996), p. 139.

9. http://ftp.hyperreal.org/raves/spirit/politics/CyberTribe_Rising.html (accessed June 26, 2005).

10. Hakim Bey, *TAZ: Temporary Autonomous Zone*, 2nd ed. (Brooklyn, N.Y.: Autonomedia, 2003).

11. http://ftp.hyperreal.org/raves/spirit/politics/CyberTribe_Rising.html (accessed June 26, 2005).

12. Donna Haraway, *Modest_Witness@Second_Millennium.FemaleMan_ Meets_OncoMouse™: Feminism and Technoscience* (Routledge: New York, 1996), p. 129.

13. Ibid., p. 126.

14. G. Lovink, "Civil Society, Fanaticism and Digital Reality: A Conversation with Slavoj Žižek," *Ctheory: Theory, Technology and Culture, an Electronic Journal* 19 (1996), http://www.ctheory.net/articles.aspx?id=79 (accessed June 26, 2005).

15. Raymond D. Fogelson, "Schneider Confronts Componential Analysis," in *The Cultural Analysis of Kinship*, ed. Richard Feinberg and Martin Ottenheimer (Urbana: University of Illinois Press, 2001), http://www.press.uillinois.edu/epub/books/feinberg/ch1.html (accessed June 26, 2005).

16. Linda M. Chatters, Robert Joseph Taylor, and Rukmalie Jayakody, "Fictive Kinship Relations in Black Extended Families," *Journal of Comparative Family Studies* 25 (1993): 297.

17. Silvia Dominguez and Celeste Watkins, "Creating Networks for Survival and Mobility: Social Capital among African-American and Latin-American Low-Income Mothers," *Social Problems* 50, no. 1 (2003): 111–135.

18. This notion of reciprocity relies, in turn, upon a conception of the individual as a free agent with a stable identity, formed prior to any relationships with others.

19. Daniel Miller, *The Dialectics of Shopping* (Chicago: University of Chicago Press, 2001).

20. David M. Schneider, *American Kinship: A Cultural Account* (Chicago: University of Chicago Press, 1980).

21. Substantive descent—as an outcome of shared "blood" or "genes"—for Anglo Americans, generally becomes an issue in contexts where legal (sex, marriage, inheritance, divorce), moral (sex, reproduction, interracial affiliation), or medical (reproduction, illness, death) frameworks pertaining to kin relationships need to be negotiated.

22. Early telecom software allowed function keys to be programmed with macros—that is, long strings of keystrokes. "Macro attacks," if they contained control characters, could sometimes break the interface.

23. Judith Donath and Danah Boyd, "Public Displays of Connection," *BT Technology Journal* 22, no. 4 (2003): 71.

24. Rene T. A. Lysloff, "Musical Community on the Internet: An On-line Ethnography," *Cultural Anthropology* 18, no. 2 (2002): 233–263.

25. Claire F. Sullivan, "Gendered Cybersupport: A Thematic Analysis of Two Online Cancer Support Groups," *Journal of Health Psychology* 8, no. 1 (2003): 83–103.

26. Gay Becker, Anneliese Butler, and Robert D. Nachtigall, "Resemblance Talk: A Challenge for Parents Whose Children Were Conceived with Donor Gametes in the US," *Social Science and Medicine* 61, no. 6 (2005): 1300–1309.

27. Karin Knorr Cetina, "Postsocial Relations: Theorizing Sociality in a Postsocial Environment," in *Handbook of Social Theory*, ed. George Ritzer and Barry Smart (London; Thousand Oaks, Calif.; New Delhi: Sage Publications, 2001), p. 531.

28. Ibid., p. 530.

29. Samuel M. Wilson and Leighton C. Peterson, "The Anthropology of Online Communities," *Annual Review of Anthropology* 31 (2002): 449–467.

30. The extent to which these relations mapped onto notions of kinship can be seen in how concerns about "incest" within groups he belonged to would later prompt Cthulu to write, "I have resolved that I am not allowed to contemplate a relationship with anyone who is a part of a social group which I am a part of, and no one a further degree away. Naturally, with pondering forbidden, my mind is starting to fill with nothing but images of pink elephants."

31. Communities "promoting" suicide, self-mutilation, and anorexia—especially among young women—have been recently added to the litany of threats posed by cybersociality. (See, for example, "Anorexia Fight Moves to Web" [CBS News, October 11, 2005], http://www.cbsnews.com/stories/2005/10/04/earlyshow/contributors/melindamurphy/main910424.shtml; "The Winner Dies" [Salon.com, July 23, 2001], http://www.salon.com/mwt/feature/2001/07/23/pro_ana/index.html.)

CHAPTER 3

Electronic Tribes (E-Tribes):
Some Theoretical Perspectives and Implications

BOLANLE OLANIRAN

With computer-mediated communication (CMC) media such as the Internet, the barriers of time and geographical boundaries to communication are easily overcome. Thus, the idea of electronic tribe (i.e., e-tribe) is able to take shape where individuals are able to communicate with like-minded people, with the aid of electronic communication media, as if they are within the same geographical area. The flexibility and speed offered by electronic media provide easy access for communicating globally.

This chapter will offer an overview of global communication and e-tribe development. After discussing the use of CMC and their possibilities for global communication, I will move to specific media theories to describe how they attempt to explain communication interactions never possible before CMC and often difficult to observe. In addition, theories are presented to explain subsequent relational development among group members, especially in e-tribes. The chapter will then proceed to discuss the implications of e-tribes and CMC media from organizational, communication, and cultural standpoints. Recommendations will also be provided for external organizations aiming to promote to e-tribes as consumer groups.

Global Communication and E-Tribe Formation

The need for people to communicate and collaborate across their immediate physical environments is pressing. Such a feat is revolutionary, considering that even in academic environments that provide technically suitable venues for scholars who want to discuss similar or specific problem areas, such collaboration is made difficult because few universities employ two or more experts on the same subject.[1] However, with the Internet, scholars have means and access to engage in online—in addition to offline or face-to-face (FtF)—communication. Individuals interested in each other's works are able to communicate and work together while living in different geographical locales. As these scholars familiarize themselves with each other's work, their network becomes "crystallized" as a less amorphous "invisible college" that is defined or characterized by shared interests in the area of specialty and may culminate in social friendship ties. The resulting group is a scholarly "in-group" like an electronic tribe, a unique entity that functions to allow members to assist one another and share with each other in areas of specialization. While some scholarly groups or networks of individuals are able to communicate both through electronic means and FtF (e.g., meetings at conferences), there are hosts of other social networks that are tight in-groups, but their communication is restricted to the electronic media. Electronic groups may or may never extend their communication beyond the confines of an electronic medium, yet their ties are no less than those of e-tribes with FtF possibilities. The focus in this chapter is on those e-tribes without FtF possibilities. E-tribes have an informal and adaptive structure, which allows them to be flexible in exchanging and evaluating information. The lack of a formal structure in an e-tribe suggests that communication depends on the group's frequency of interaction and the quality of social ties.[2]

The Critical Mass Theory

Computer networks facilitating development of e-tribes allow members to exchange information, to collaborate, and to socialize. At times, e-mail is used to communicate with members one-on-one, at other times, to small groups of them (e.g., through listservs); the Web is used for gathering data and in turn circulating data among members. Given the nature of e-tribes as small, dynamic, ongoing groups communicating for the purpose of accomplishing specific goal(s), it is important to examine the use of media by groups and the effects of these media on them. One of the theories addressing this issue is the *critical mass theory*. The critical mass theory distinguishes between the diffusion of innovations for individual versus group use by stressing that diffusion of a new communication medium requires collective participation by two or more people, which is different from the diffusion of commodities such as soaps, which are used independently by each person.[3] On the contrary, a person can only benefit from the use of a new communication medium when others in the network choose to use it. As a result, the critical mass theory predicts that the chances of a person using a new medium depend on the benefits accruing to a critical mass of users rather than to one person.[4]

However, simply aggregating perceptions of group members about a new medium is not sufficient to predict its use. Rather, significant consideration must be given to the degree of influence certain members have on other members. In essence, critical mass theory explains how members influence each other in the decision about adoption of a given communication medium. Members continue to influence each other long after perceptions about the medium have occurred and adoption decisions have been made. The critical mass theory focuses on adoption decision, while neglecting activities beyond adoption.

The Social Influence Perspective

The social influence theory of media use takes over where the critical mass theory left off by focusing on how members who have adopted a communication medium influence other members' perceptions of its use.[5] One may argue that e-tribes' members have already committed themselves to using electronic media chosen collectively by group members. The social influence theory of media use was developed in response to the media richness theory, which advocated that individual perceptions and uses of a medium are determined by objective characteristics of the medium.[6] The media richness theory predicts that individuals choose a medium that is most appropriate for a given task. Hence, a task that has a high degree of equivocality is best accomplished by "rich" media. Traditionally, face-to-face (FtF) communication has been considered the richest medium. However, this use of FtF communication as a benchmark has been called into question, given that technologies such as group decision support systems (GDSS) offer augmented FtF communication, which is considered to be richer than FtF-only interaction.

The social influence theory argues that media are not in and of themselves rich or lean, but, instead, individuals socially influence each other's perceptions of a medium's richness.[7] Individuals can influence one another and foster positive perceptions by (1) stating a personal assessment of a medium, (2) serving as role models with their own use of the medium, and (3) offering feedback to others on their use of the medium. Scholars such as Contractor, Seibold, and Heller are quick to point out that there is nothing in the core formulation of the social influence model that makes judgments about the innate richness of any particular medium.[8] Instead, the emphasis of the social influence model is on methods by which people socially influence one another's perceptions of media richness. Therefore, e-tribes' interaction over an electronic medium can be assessed in terms of the social effects that participants are able to cultivate and negotiate with fellow members.

The Adaptive Structuration Theory

Another theory that shapes perception of communication media is adaptive structuration theory.[9] The theory is based on the assumption that interactions among people are task-related and social in nature. The adaptive structuration theory suggests that rules and resources (i.e., structures) are tools that people use to generate and sustain interactions and practices in a given medium. Some of these structures are: (1) the ease with which group members communicate ideas in their groups, (2) the extent to which members are affected by others' contributions in the group, and (3) the extent to which members do not hesitate to present their ideas to the group. Communication interaction is central to the adaptive structuration theory, to the extent that structures have no existence independent of the interactions they constitute and in which they are constituted.[10]

Structures are formed from related social institutions, "systems traditions," and technological compositions—that is, the norms or specifically rules and resources established in a given context. Electronic mediums and technologies usually based their structures on social institutions with which users are familiar, regardless of whether designers acknowledge those institutions or not. Likewise, e-tribe members can be argued to stress or focus on communication technology to address tasks, including the selection of procedures that guide interactions through features that aid decision-making processes and general interactions. Consequently, group members (i.e., in e-tribes) make conscious and unconscious choices to use and not to use specific features of a technology (i.e., structural potential).[11] As a result, a group constantly develops a version of the structures as part of its "structure-in-use" (i.e., appropriated structure).

Both structure-in-use and structural potential shape users' (members') perception of the technology as they aid intragroup communication and the discussion process, and reduce evaluation apprehension, which affects productivity loss in group interactions.[12] The process by which perceptions are shaped is a key factor in the adaptive structuration theory. As with the critical mass theory and social influence theory, adaptive structuration theory did not subscribe to the deterministic notion of media effects on individuals' perceptions of communication media. Instead, like the social influence perspective, adaptive structuration theory acknowledges that individuals' perceptions of media use are socially constructed. Unlike the social influence perspective, however, adaptive structuration theory does not view media richness as a critical point that shapes individuals' perceptions of media use. Therefore, adaptive structuration theory suggests that people's perceptions of media use are shaped by group members' structures-in-use that are associated with the media.[13]

Specifically, in a test of three different media not directly tied to adaptive structuration theory, it was found that there are differences in attributions people make about communication media and that these differences influence group communication outcomes.[14] Furthermore, the study finds that one's gender, along with a system's attributes and gender composition status (all of which are part of social institutions), affect perceptions. The study also argues that factors such as perceived ease of use of media may be attributed to users' knowledge and experience with the communication media. That is, while there are inherent media characteristics, it is also possible that users' perceptions of them are subjectively and socially constructed. With e-tribes, a chosen electronic medium may not necessarily be the preferred choice for individual members but the most feasible for the group as a whole. Therefore, the chosen medium forces e-tribe members to adapt to the medium's use, consequently influencing members' perceptions of the medium and the ensuing social interactions. For instance, one study indicates that satisfaction with CMC is influenced by individual perception of a communication medium based on ease of use—the degree to which employing a medium is perceived to be free of effort, along with the degree to which the medium is helpful in accomplishing a specified task.[15] Therefore, a given communication medium's perceived ease of use will vary when feasibility of its use is taken into consideration.[16] This variation will result in situations where a given medium is rated as easier to use in one situation and more difficult in another.

The Social Identification/Deindividuation (SIDE) Model

Given the small size of e-tribes and the group dynamics that take place, it is important to address how e-tribes' members come to perceive and communicate or interact with one another. A particular theory that explains CMC partners' behaviors is social identification/deindividuation (SIDE).[17] The theory is based on cognitive social identity/self-categorization theory of group behavior.[18] Using the foundations of social identity theory, SIDE adds the notion of deindividuation that occurs when people interact electronically or without one another's physical presence. The central tenet of the model suggests that in the absence of physical presence (i.e., individuating cues about cocommunicators), interactants judge each other on the basis of group similarity or difference (i.e., ingroup and outgroup). Since CMC provides users relative anonymity, users build "stereotypical impressions" of their partners based on available subtle cues (such as: linguistic, typographic, and contextual cues). The challenge, however, is that CMC participants tend to engage in an overattribution process without mitigating the impressions about their partners derived from insufficient social cues.[19] The overattribution is promoted by the deindividuating nature of CMC due to the lack of nonverbal cues within the medium.

The SIDE model presents expectations based on individual and group identity. The model argues that both sets of identity do not necessarily affect the negative or positive perceptions made by group members. On the other hand, a group identity is believed to intensify conclusions drawn about group members, while individual identity mediates the magnitude or the strength of the effect of group norms on participants' perceptions and behaviors. Thus, when group identity is "salient" in an electronic mediated interaction and not undermined by the individuating information in FtF, then group members are likely to adopt whatever norms developed in the group. In contrast, however, when individuating identity is salient, participants are expected to interpret individuating information in a less polarized manner. As a matter of fact, because most participants are average on medium characteristics, their perceptions of those characteristics are expected to follow accordingly.[20]

Since some members are bound to deviate from the average on media characteristics, the random distributions of positive and negative values are expected to negate one another and result in neutral evaluations by a group. FtF communication is expected to result in the same kind of perceptions as individuated CMC, where partners interact based on personal impressions versus a group-based bias. The SIDE model is significant in describing outcomes both positive and negative (e.g., flaming) in CMC interactions. However, the SIDE model still leaves unclear the ability to specify directions and types of norms that are to be reinforced by group identification in CMC.[21]

The Hyperpersonal Model of CMC

The hyperpersonal model of CMC extends the developmental impressions in CMC groups and reinforces the idea of relational communication proposed by the social information processing (SIP) theory. It recognizes the fact that as CMC participants exchange and interpret social cues within the medium, they come to the realization that the medium allows for the transmission of social cues. Thus, they use the medium to achieve more favorable impressions and a greater level of attraction or intimacy than those in FtF interactions. The tendency to seek information about one another, and toward self-disclosure, in an attempt to reduce uncertainties in a CMC medium through verbal, linguistic, and chronemic behaviors is critical to impression formation and positive perceptions. Notwithstanding, CMC research identifies a major difference between longitudinal and experimental research findings. Specifically, there was an absence of "initial" difference between CMC and FtF in terms of relational warmth in longitudinal versus one-shot group experimental research. The difference has been attributed to the role of "anticipated future interaction."[22] The anticipation of future interaction (AFI) is believed to influence the way communicators interact in terms of how they seek information about each other, whether they act friendly, cooperate in negotiations or conflicts, and self-disclose or in general engage in a positive relational communication.[23] The implied presence of AFI affects social information-seeking and general positive interaction tendencies as participants begin their interaction. Thus, to think that one's interaction will be limited (without AFI) induces strict task orientation, while thinking that interactions will be continuous (AFI presence) induces socially oriented participation.[24]

The hyperpersonal model suggests that relational communication (i.e., affection from partners) is greatest in long-term groups, especially when group identity is salient, whereas it is least in short-term groups. On the other hand, relational communication is moderate in either long-term or short-term groups when individual identity is salient.[25] Similar results were found for perceptions of group members' attractiveness. As a result, the status of the group as short-term or long-term, along with group or individual identities, poses significant implications for different communication scenarios and outcomes. In order to make diversity advantageous in long-term CMC groups, a focus on trust or unity rather than individual differences is a must.[26] The contention is that greater task effort is facilitated by equivalent social orientation. In essence, time spent in social interaction may stimulate task performance, implying that time spent in social interaction does not hinder task performance, especially when participants use asynchronous CMC in multiple sessions.[27]

Electronic tribes present one of those situations where asynchronous CMC offers the most practical means for communication. At the same time, CMC is also an "amplifier" of attitude and communication phenomena. Therefore, it stands to reason that e-tribe contexts, along with the chosen communication medium (i.e., CMC), interact in a way that facilitates the resulting communication outcomes. However, it may help to get an overview of some characteristics of e-tribes that contribute to the interaction process and the eventual communication outcomes.

Understanding the Communication Process in E-Tribes

E-tribes are electronic groups similar to virtual teams that operate for the purpose of accomplishing varieties of tasks. Accordingly, e-tribes are usually ongoing and, in most cases, long-term, with a rigid focus on goals that are neither strictly task-oriented nor social in nature. More important is the fact that members are participating from geographically dispersed locations from around the world. This tendency may introduce the issue of culture, typical in communication encounters, especially those that are multinational. Though participants may come from different cultural environments with different communication practices or preferences, they are brought together by the conscious decision they made to use or interact over a particular CMC medium. Thus, one can argue that participants in e-tribe environments exhibit communication characteristics that deviate from the social norms with which they are familiar. At the least, they are willing to relinquish certain aspects of their individual identity for the new virtual group identity, however temporarily.

An apparent emphasis on goal accomplishment in e-tribe communication interactions is characteristic of the phenomenon. Productivity (i.e., goal/task accomplishments), which is the primary reason for which the participants come together in the first place, is sought. At the same time, the contention of the hyperpersonal perspective[28] cannot be discarded in e-tribes where time spent in social interactions appears not to hinder task accomplishment in the use of CMC, especially in asynchronous mode.[29] This argument seems to have some support in the fact that the projected uniform effects of time on CMC relational development through social information processing (SIP) and anticipated future interaction (AFI) have not materialized in all contexts. Therefore, other social factors appear to impede or interact with communication outcomes in e-tribes and other CMC encounters.

One such social factor that is important to e-tribe interaction is the voluntary and enduring nature of interactions by members. The voluntary participation implies, from a social identity perspective, that individuals adhering strongly to a group will follow the group norm and would find others who do interpersonally attractive. Thus, it could be suggested that e-tribe members, in general, are more apt to display social identity (i.e., group) normative tendencies. However, this is not to say that the social identity normative tendency precludes the display of individual and personalizing identity in the process of communicating electronically. In the process of communicating via CMC, a shift from social identity processing to interpersonal processing does occur.[30] However, the precise point where the shift takes place is not clear. However, one may speculate with regard to e-tribes.

As indicated earlier, the focus in e-tribes is goal accomplishment, which could be task-oriented or social in nature. As a result, the ensuing communication interaction will be affected according to the nature of the goal. It would seem that aside from members' initial self-disclosure statements, for impression information, the group focus is on goal accomplishment, which implies emphasis on group identity. However, over time and as the goal of the group continues to be achieved, it is possible for transition toward relational messages (individuating) to occur and in a way that further helps the group to realize its goals while fostering positive perceptions about cocommunicators and their interaction experiences.

Furthermore, a factor mediating interaction experiences in e-tribes is the fact that members are set apart from the general population of their country of origin. This factor creates, or at a minimum establishes, the need to conform and adopt group norms in e-tribes. The communication implication is that members must develop a new set of norms that is unique to their particular group. In addition, a true consensus-seeking interaction represents the central focus of these groups, which further reinforces the emphasis on social identity tendencies. In other words, a communication process that is neither his or hers but typifies "our" way of communication is fostered.

In e-tribes, as in other electronic mediated communication that uses e-mail, the ease of sending messages to all members at once allows e-tribe members to stay in communication with other participants, without having to adhere to a single dominant person.[31] It is also worth noting that participation in an e-tribe allows for sending messages to focused lists, hence permitting participants to belong to multiple groups/tribes. Moreover, e-mail is useful for developing and maintaining weak ties (i.e., networks with which a participant does not have close relationships of information exchange or intimate friendship).[32] Weak ties, however, tend to be more heterogeneous when compared to homogeneous strong ties.

At the same time, while e-mail is appropriate in e-tribe interactions and may be the preferred mode, one should realize that the choice to use the medium is one that noncompliant individuals cannot influence. Noncompliant members will either use the mode or be excluded from participation. Though e-tribe members do work autonomously from their respective locations, they nonetheless possess and are committed to a common bond. In this respect, participants are expected to make available to one another their expertise, resources, and findings in the process of creating and accomplishing a shared vision.

Compared to traditional groups, e-tribe members are more active and discerning, less accessible to one-on-one processes, and are knowledgeable, with a wealth of valuable cultural information.[33] Robert Kozinets suggested that the members of an e-tribe community are transformed by electronic media, which in turn are responsible for what Marshall McLuhan calls "retribalizing" human society into clusters of affiliation.[34] Therefore, e-tribes bring about significant social changes. Networked computers "empower" people from all over the globe to overcome time and geographic boundaries and meet in groups based on a wide range of interests and social affiliations. Moreover, once users connect and interact with others online and in e-tribal groups, they are influenced by others to the extent that they continue to seek out their e-tribe members as valuable sources of information and social exchange.

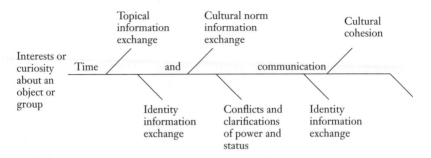

Figure 3.1. Pattern of Relational Development in E-Tribe Adapted from "Developmental Progression of Individual Member Participation in Online Communities of Consumption," figure I in Robert Kozinets, "E-tribalized Marketing?: The Strategic Implications of Virtual Communities of Consumption," 1999.

The indirect implication is that the interactive influence of e-tribes will then filter through to members' immediate cultural environment. As a result, one can argue that e-tribe participants, and to a greater extent electronic media, serve as social agents for cultural transformations in users' various cultures.[35] If virtual communities (to which e-tribes are similar) consist of people who share norms of behavior and actively enforce some moral standards, and who intentionally attempt to find like-minded people,[36] then they could be likened to innovators and early adopters.

This position can be illustrated with the example of an individual from a different culture or country, or from a rural community, who, with a passion for sports memorabilia, can seek out and develop social relationships, in a virtual group, with others who have a similar passion. In turn, the individual might seek out people in his/her community to develop the interest in FtF encounters.

The social influence of virtual communities and e-tribes is not to be taken lightly. Though e-tribes will never replace FtF encounters and other traditional media, they are an important supplement to direct social interactions. Consumers and others are an increasing online presence, gathering information and even becoming social activists. Online interactions and alignments affect their behaviors as citizens, as community members, and as consumers.[37] As a result, these groups present both opportunities and challenges for communities and organizations that need to understand them and their patterns of behavior.

The pattern of relationship development in e-tribes is similar to that in virtual environments. The development usually starts out with interests in or curiosity about something, leading to topical information exchange within a group, and then on to identity information exchange, along with cultural norm information exchange. From this set of normative information arise conflicts and clarifications of power and status relationships, albeit briefly (those not interested or satisfied will drop out), and decisions to accept, adopt, and enforce the norms are made alongside interpersonal impression formation. Taken together, consensus leading to cultural cohesion is developed and continued communal relationship takes place.[38]

In the relational development of e-tribes, four categories of people were identified and are useful for e-tribes. It helps to enumerate them:

1. Tourists—lack strong social ties to the group and maintain shallow interest;
2. Minglers—have strong social ties but maintain token interest in the group activity;
3. Devotees—maintain strong interest and enthusiasm for group goals and have few social attachments to the group; and
4. Insiders—those who have strong personal ties and a strong interest in the group activity.[39]

Given the nature of e-tribes as close-knit communities, one can argue that they are more likely to consist primarily of devotees and insiders. Members exhibit loyalty and heavy usage socially and culturally to reinforce the group activity. Although e-tribes have the tendency to focus initially on factual information exchange, over time the exchange can be expected to mix factual information with social or relational information. For instance, the nature of communication interaction for devotees and insiders is transformational—group participants communicate as a way to accomplish specified tasks focused on longer-term social gain. A case in point is online consumer activist groups over the Internet.[40] Furthermore, group interests inspire devotees to demand and seek positive change inside and outside the group.

Implications of E-Tribes and Electronic Media

There are certain communications implications with regard to organizations and sociocultural community. Some of these implications are addressed in the following paragraphs.

Organization

As discussed above, e-tribes provide a rich opportunity for groups and subgroups to come together in a forum to address or develop common interests. The growing influence and social activities of virtual communities create a way for individuals who have never met and may never meet in the near future to organize themselves and actively develop and empower their concern about areas of collective interest. Thus, e-tribes and their participants have attracted the attention of organizations attempting to better target their activities. For example, one current opinion recommends that virtual consumer groups be recognized by marketing organizations as segmented groups of consumers.[41] Specifically, organizations should embark on communal segmentation strategies—where marketers identify different types of e-tribes and their members by paying attention to the different types of "computer-mediated interactions" in which they participate. In essence, an effective approach toward e-tribes is one where organizations understand the characteristics of e-tribes and interpret or use the information in ways that avoid linear or one-to-one or unwelcome "heavy-handed" marketing and advertising strategies.[42] Another name for this approach is *relational marketing*.

Relational marketing also requires that organizations must effect a mutually beneficial and continuing relationship with consumers.[43] At the same time, relational marketing can foster loyalty from customers when there is a perception that an organization cares and accepts inputs from its customer base in product development, branding, and marketing services. In essence, relational marketing by organizations to e-tribes can become "virtual relationship marketing" in its truest form.[44]

Perhaps the greatest challenge for organizations attempting to exploit e-tribe potentials and customer groups is in sustaining consumer loyalty. It has been argued that e-tribe insiders have the power to influence behaviors of other members. For instance, an insider who is trusted by group members in a particular e-tribe can get others to switch allegiance along the lines of his or her own preference. The collective switching can result in group defections, which can cause problems for e-tribes and organizations attempting to market to them. Similarly, the possibility of divided loyalty in an e-tribe through insiders suggests the need for organizations to identify such individuals and explore their influence capacity and harvest it for mutual gain. By recognizing those insiders whose interactions are high in both informational and social exchanges, organizations can be prepared to handle the consequent divided loyalty or prevent it altogether.[45]

On another note, the issue of access must be addressed. The potential and avenues for accessing virtual community may be easy for organizations due to their online presence. However, the task of successfully analyzing and marketing to e-tribes becomes increasingly complex due to idiosyncrasies of different groups. Therefore, organizations marketing to these virtual communities must be adept in the task of simplifying access, compiling data, and accurately interpreting the data to implement functional yet differentiated strategies for different groups.

The trend, therefore, is involving customers in organizational strategies, which would then result in consumer loyalty through retention. In essence, the days of organizations passively developing products and services with the "if we build it, they will come" mentality are numbered. Enduring loyalty is indeed "retention with attitude."[46]

Consumers, with the aid of CMC, have begun to take a proactive role in demanding what they want, how they want it, and how much they want to pay for it (i.e., all facets of marketing from product development to marketing). In light of the difficult task that awaits organizations in marketing to e-tribes along with other online community members, these organizations stand to benefit when they identify the preferences of different e-tribe factions. Such identification can lead to the development of new products or enhancements, or general realization of new customer segments altogether. The approach would lead to a much richer understanding by both consumers and marketers of the way in which a product/service is viewed or given meaning. This relational marketing can prevent marketing disasters the likes of "New Coke" and "Crystal Pepsi," where consumer behaviors were misinterpreted, costing the respective organizations a fortune.

From an organizational standpoint, e-tribes offer a way to negotiate interorganizational relationships. Organizations can develop a way to monitor interorganizational information about competing organizations, products, services, and general operational environments. Information collected from e-tribes can be integrated into internal organizational strategy with the hope of modifying external information and effecting change in the organizational structure as necessary. In essence, information from e-tribe participants has the capacity to offer a corrective mechanism allowing organizations to institute policy or strategy changes for effective performance in interorganizational fields.

Communication

The activism resulting from e-tribe social interaction is an area that deserves attention. Online social interaction creates a place for groups of individuals (consumers, scholars, etc.) to actively seek and exchange information about organizations, the quality of their products and services, and other ideas. However, whether expressed ideas and group activities are correctly interpreted or not, marketers and societies at large will have to adapt to e-tribes' activism. The groups will use their influence and informational exchange to strengthen their interests. Therefore, the power is shifting away from established structures (e.g., government agencies and organizations) that tend to control the flow of information in traditional marketing to consumers in online marketing.

The implication from such a shift is that as consumers, for example, increasingly adopt and use the Internet, they may use it to exercise their collective power in saying no to programs, ideas, and organizations they found to act contrary to their vested interests. Royal Dutch Shell, for example, found this out the hard way when interest groups used the Internet to call negative attention to the company's environmental practices in the Nigerian Ogoni land.[47] While a variety of e-tribes are formed to better members' knowledge, they are often used to usurp efforts of others who try to profit at their expense.

Traditionally, there is an assumption that communication and marketing online can be done successfully when individuals are isolated into a single grouping. This approach follows what is believed to be a binodal path of communication between organization and individual (as in TV commercials). Online connectivity via CMC is replacing the binodal model with multinodal (many-to-many) communication networks.[48] Virtual communities of interest groups (i.e., e-tribes) establish forums where the intensity of their influence can be exponentially increased as organizations dealing with these groups are compelled to work with them.

Interpersonal Communication

The process of communication influence itself is worthy of attention. Members of an e-tribe work together in such a way that they evaluate ideas or products' qualities together. Therefore, members place significant emphasis on the information provided by group members, especially those considered to be experts (i.e., devotees and insiders). The effort of collectives in reaching decisions creates and mediates behaviors while complicating the relationship between organizations and their market audience. Consequently, online marketing organizations cannot speak to individuals, but must address the group, because its collective decisions supersede individual receptivity to an organization's or marketer's communication. Also, organizing into e-tribes and virtual groups empowers members and seems to elicit members' activist tendencies.[49] Aside from the effects on their consumption behaviors that they experience, group members walk away with a renewed sense of assurance that they have more power than they originally envisioned. Members can also bounce ideas around within their groups to determine strategies for handling situations where they feel powerless.

Howard Rheingold addresses a concern about communication in virtual communities that is applicable to e-tribes when he suggests that being attentive in the Information Age requires paying attention to *where* people are paying attention.[50] Attention by organizations then implies the acknowledgment that human communication interaction in all its forms (especially, human-computer interaction) supersedes time and information as a commodity. In essence, an understanding of the interactions taking place among online members provides multifaceted information that can be analyzed for organizations to discern where their target audiences are focusing their attention.

Culture

The cultural implications of e-tribe participants as members of society should not be overlooked. Communication technology (i.e., CMC) allows increased knowledge acquisition and speedier information dissemination, which prompts a greater awareness of different cultures in communication encounters. In virtual teams, scholarly and relational bonds develop.[51] Thus, it stands to reason that the solidarity and bonds created in virtual online settings transfer to behaviors and communication patterns offline. The direct implication from this view is that the norms developed within electronic interactions may run quite contrary to the expectations of virtual group members' FtF environments (i.e., towns, regions, and countries).

Also, as people permeate national borders, either physically or through CMC, a systemic effect (however minute) takes place and leaves people as cultural change agents for both the host and the expatriate cultures.[52] Examples include the effects of mass media programming in India, where the views portrayed in such American TV shows as *Friends* left trails of discontentment and contradicted traditional roles and be-liefs in that culture.[53] Paul James points to the notion of "disembodied-extended integration"—the level of cultural disarray that occurs in so-cial integration where relationships among people are extended across time and space by communication technologies, a concept that can be applied to e-tribe settings.[54] The emergent disembodied-extended inte-gration heightens new cultural contradictions in the sense that new me-dia remove power from nations and their regulatory agencies in terms of surveillance, monitoring, and administrative and cultural management policies.

Specifically, research findings suggest that CMC interaction mini-mizes or challenges the need to save face because assertiveness is gener-ally the norm for the communication process.[55] M. Love points to the fact that as exposure to different values occurs, those values permeate various cultures, with technology leading the way, and consequently the distinct national cultures are gradually eroded and replaced.[56] For instance, certain effects of communication technology on human com-munication at the public level include those on "face," a common ele-ment in many Asian cultures that shows credibility, integrity, and the ability to function as a member of a group or society.[57]

The notion of face, however, has been described as the positive so-cial value that an individual clings to, relative to others, during inter-action.[58] Face behaviors are potentially problematic in terms of message comprehension, due to cultural differences, in intercultural CMC. Deborah Tannen illustrates that Americans consider directness in com-munication strategies to be "logical" and consistent with power, whereas indirectness is equated with "dishonesty" and submissiveness.[59] Indirect-ness represents the norm of communication in other cultures. Whether intentional or unintentional, the favoritism toward directness is built into communication technology (especially text-based media, where us-ers are expected to code their messages more explicitly); hence a bias is created against cultures that embrace indirectness. Cultural traditions that establish rules and structure or give a community its essence are gradually being dissolved to the extent that the classical nation is being succeeded by a postmodern one.[60] Sorin Matei and Sandra Ball-Rokeach suggest that the Internet may result in cultural assimilation where Western cultural values are promoted unbeknownst to other cultures.[61] Whether this leads to total disengagement from primary local or eth-nic culture is yet to be determined; however, there is no doubt that the outcome of this assimilation has a direct bearing on the primary culture in some form.[62] Similarly, Robert McDougal found in his study that the mind-changing power of communication technology in societies can be seen among Native Americans.[63] Specifically, the introduction of e-mail is perceived as altering what the Mohawk tribe believed to be essential ways of life and ways of relating to the world.

Another area ripe for examination involves the cultural impact of CMC on power and status in a society. It seems that as e-tribe participants become more familiar with the CMC media and their potential, they will begin to adapt them to their primary cultures so that variables such as power, consensus, and other norms are confronted in their immediate environment. Glen Hiemstra indicated that communication mediated by technology may "lead to" and "result from" alterations in the symbols and meanings specified by a culture.[64] Power can be viewed from a cultural standpoint using the notion of "power distance."[65] Power distance involves the extent to which the less powerful members of institutions and organizations accept that power is distributed unevenly.[66] People from high-power-distance cultures view one another differently according to their status, and these cultures often stress the coercive use of power. People from low-power-distance cultures only acknowledge the use of power when it is an expert or legitimate power.[67] Looking at the degree to which a culture acknowledges power distance, it would seem that some cultures may show greater readiness to embrace authority than to engage in a democratic decision-making process. High-context cultures (e.g., Africans and Asians) are consensus seekers that strive for harmony more than low-context cultures.[68] The consensus-building decision-making environment, which prevails in high-context cultures, emphasizes a decision-making structure that minimizes internal conflict and maximizes internal group harmony.[69]

As people realize CMC power in protecting certain group interests, computer-mediated e-tribes can become the norm, and individuals can steer others to become more passionate or vocal about their respective causes, while developing ways to perpetuate their causes even in societies that do not look kindly at such antinormative behaviors. It has been argued that the proliferation of CMC across cultures would result in increased normative violations for high-context cultures that emphasize consensus or group harmony.[70] An anecdotal example of how new technology media challenge or rearrange the power structure and traditional norms was offered by Bolanle Olaniran and David Williams in describing the tactics Ken Saro-Wiwa and his supporters used in furthering their fight for justice against the Royal Dutch Shell oil company and the Nigerian government.[71] In this scenario, Ken Saro-Wiwa and his group, the Movement for the Survival of the Ogoni People (MOSOP), were able to utilize the Internet to bypass the local and traditional media and enlist Greenpeace and other sympathizers to join their cause, while abandoning the traditional norm of seeking harmonious discussion and negotiation. The MOSOP group used e-mail, Web sites, and chat rooms to get international activist organizations to help them bring about changes in Nigeria by presenting pictures of human rights abuses and environmental degradation such that anyone having access to a computer could see and assess the situation, to the ultimate end of joining the cause and enlisting others. While this particular application can be argued to have brought about positive change, the fact remains that technology capable of enabling an advantageous purpose could also be used to bring about negative changes. However, the point here is to stress the fact that new media employed by e-tribes' members will leave traces of change in any society, but more importantly can reinvent cultural norms when considered cross-culturally.

Notes

1. Emmanuel Koku, Nancy Nazer, and Barry Wellman, "Netting Scholars Online and Offline," *American Behavioral Scientist* 44, no. 10 (2001): 1752–1774.

2. Barry Wellman, "Physical Place and Cyber-Place: The Rise of Networked Individualism," *International Journal of Urban and Regional Research* 25, no. 2 (June 2001): 227–252.

3. Lynne Markus, "Toward a 'Critical Mass' Theory of Interactive Media," in *Organizations and Communication Technology*, ed. Janet Fulk and Charles W. Steinfield, pp. 194–218 (Newbury Park, Calif.: Sage, 1990).

4. Noshir Contractor, David Seibold, and Mark Heller, "Interactional Influence in the Structuring of Media Use in Groups: Influence in Members' Perceptions of Group Decision Support System Use," *Human Communication Research* 22, no. 4 (1996): 451–481.

5. J. Fulk, J. Schmitz, and C. Steinfield, "A Social Influence Model of Technology Use," in *Organizations and Communication Technology*, ed. J. Fulk and C. Steinfield, pp. 117–140 (Newbury Park, Calif.: Sage, 1990).

6. Richard Daft and Robert Lengel, "Organizational Information Requirements, Media Richness and Structural Design," *Management Science* 32, no. 5 (1986): 554–572.

7. Fulk, Schmitz, and Steinfield, "A Social Influence Model of Technology Use," p. 126.

8. Contractor, Seibold, and Heller, "Interactional Influence," p. 457.

9. Geraldine DeSanctis and Scott Poole, "Capturing the Complexity in Advanced Technology Use: Adaptive Structuration Theory," *Organization Science* 5, no. 2 (1994): 121–147.

10. Scott Poole and Geraldine DeSanctis, "Understanding the Use of Group Decision Support Systems: The Theory of Adaptive Structuration," in *Organizations and Communication Technology*, ed. Janet Fulk and Charles Steinfield, pp. 173–193 (Newbury Park, Calif.: Sage, 1990).

11. Contractor, Seibold, and Heller, "Interactional Influence," p. 458.

12. Bolanle Olaniran, "Group Performance and Computer-Mediated Communication," *Management Communication Quarterly* 7, no. 3 (1994): 256–281.

13. Contractor, Seibold, and Heller, "Interactional Influence," p. 459.

14. Bolanle Olaniran, "Perceived Communication Outcomes in Computer-Mediated Communication: An Analysis of Three Systems among New Users," *Information Processing & Management* 31, no. 4 (1995): 525–541.

15. Ibid., p. 538.

16. Bolanle Olaniran, "Computer-Mediated Communication in Cross-Cultural Virtual Teams," in *Dialogues among Diversities*, ed. Guo-Ming Chen and William Starosta, pp. 142–166 (Washington, D.C.: NCA, 2004).

17. Martin Lea and Russell Spears, "Paralanguage and Social Perception in Computer-Mediated Communication," *Journal of Organizational Computing* 2, nos. 3–4 (1992): 321–341.

18. Henri Tajfel and John Turner, "The Social Identity Theory of Intergroup Behavior," in *Psychology of Intergroup Relations*, ed. Stephen Worchel and William Austin, pp. 7–24 (Chicago: Nelson-Hall, 1986).

19. Lea and Spears, "Paralanguage," p. 323.

20. Martin Lea and Russell Spears, "Love at First Byte? Building Personal Relationships over Computer Networks," in *Under-studied Relationships: Off the Beaten Track*, ed. Julia Wood and Steve Duck, pp. 197–236 (Thousand Oaks, Calif.: Sage, 1995).

21. Joseph Walther, "Group and Interpersonal Effects in International Computer-Mediated Collaboration," *Human Communication Research* 23, no. 3 (March 1997): 342–369.

22. Ibid., p. 349.

23. Kathy Kellermann and Rodney Reynolds, "When Ignorance Is Bliss: The Role of Motivation to Reduce Uncertainty in Uncertainty Reduction Theory," *Human Communication Research* 17, no. 1 (1990): 5–75.

24. Bolanle Olaniran, "Computer-Mediated Communication and Conflict Management Process: A Closer Look at Anticipation of Future Interaction," *World Futures* 57, no. 4 (2001): 285–313.

25. Walther, "Group and Interpersonal Effects," p. 349.

26. Olaniran, "Computer-Mediated Communication in Cross-Cultural Virtual Teams," p. 159.

27. Laku Chidambaram, "Relational Development in Computer-Supported Groups," *MIS Quarterly* 20, no. 2 (June 1996): 143–163.

28. Joseph Walther, "Computer-Mediated Communication: Impersonal, Interpersonal, and Hyperpersonal Interaction," *Communication Research* 23, no. 1 (1996): 1–43.

29. Chidambaram, "Relational Development," p. 145.

30. H. Giles and P. Johnson, "The Role of Language in Ethnic Group Relations," in *Intergroup Behaviour*, ed. J. C. Turner and H. Giles, pp. 199–243 (Oxford, UK: Basil Blackwell, 1981).

31. Koku, Nazer, and Wellman, "Netting Scholars," p. 1754.

32. Sorin Matei and Sandra Ball-Rokeach, "The Internet in the Communication Infrastructure of Urban Residential Communities: Macro or Mesolinkage?" *Journal of Communication* 53, no. 4 (2003): 642–657.

33. Robert Kozinets, "E-tribalized Marketing?: The Strategic Implications of Virtual Communities of Consumption," *European Management Journal* 17, no. 3 (June 1999): 252–264.

34. Marshall McLuhan, *Culture Is Our Business* (New York: McGraw-Hill, 1970).

35. Olaniran, "Computer-Mediated Communication in Cross-Cultural Virtual Teams," p. 161.

36. Lee Komito, "The Net as Foraging Society: Flexible Communities," *Information Society* 14, no. 2 (1998): 97–106.

37. Kozinets, "E-tribalized Marketing?" p. 252.

38. Ibid., p. 254.

39. Ibid., pp. 254–255.

40. Joseph Zelwietro, "The Politicization of Environmental Organizations through the Internet," *Information Society* 14, no. 1 (1998): 45–56.

41. Kozinets, "E-tribalized Marketing?" p. 256.

42. Arthur Armstrong and John Hagel, "The Real Value of On-line Communities," *Harvard Business Review* 74, no. 3 (May–June 1996): 134–141.

43. J. Capulskyt and M. Wolfe, "Relationship Marketing: Positioning for the Future," *Journal of Business Strategy* 11, no. 4 (1991): 16–20.

44. Kozinets, "E-tribalized Marketing?" p. 256.

45. Ibid., pp. 256–257.

46. Simon Knox, "Loyalty-based Segmentation and the Customer Development Process," *European Management Journal* 16, no. 6 (1998): 729–737.

47. Bolanle Olaniran and David Williams, "Protecting the Environment and People's Well-being in the Nigerian Ogoni Land," in *International and Intercultural Public Relations: A Campaign Case Approach*, ed. Michael Parkinson and Daradirek Ekachai, pp. 320–332 (Boston: Allyn & Bacon, 2005).

48. Donna Hoffman and Thomas Novak, "Marketing in Hypermedia Computer-Mediated Environments: Conceptual Foundations," *Journal of Marketing* 60, no. 3 (July 1996): 50–68.

49. Kozinets, "E-tribalized Marketing?" p. 258.

50. Howard Rheingold, *The Virtual Community: Homesteading on the Electronic Frontier* (Reading, Mass.: Addison-Wesley, 1993).

51. Kerryellen Vroman and Joann Kovacich, "Computer-Mediated Interdisciplinary Teams: Theory and Reality," *Journal of Interprofessional Care* 16, no. 2 (May 1, 2002): 161–170.

52. K. Liu, "Emergent Globalism and Ideological Change in Post-Revolutionary China," in *Rethinking Globalism*, ed. Manfred Steger, pp. 86–107 (Oxford, UK: Rowman and Littlefield, 2003).

53. William Deresiewicz, "A Letter from India," *Yale Review* 92, no. 2 (2004): 29–37.

54. Paul James, "Forms of Abstract 'Community': From Tribe and Kingdom to Nation and State," *Philosophy of the Social Sciences* 23, no. 3 (1992): 313–336.

55. Bolanle Olaniran, "Computer-Mediated Communication (CMC): Misunderstandings in E-Mail Environment," *Journal of Educational Technology Systems* 31, no. 2 (2003): 205–222.

56. M. Love, "The Changing Role of Nation-States and Their Sovereignty," in *The Virtuous Vice: Globalization*, ed. Siamack Shojai and Robert Christopherson, pp. 77–96 (London: Praeger, 2004).

57. Olaniran, "Computer-Mediated Communication in Cross-Cultural Virtual Teams," p. 159.

58. Erving Goffman, *Interaction Ritual: Essays on Face-to-Face Behavior* (New York: Doubleday Anchor, 1967).

59. Deborah Tannen, ed., *Gender and Conversational Interaction* (New York: Oxford University Press, 1993).

60. James, "Forms of Abstract 'Community.'"

61. Matei and Ball-Rokeach, "The Internet in the Communication Infrastructure of Urban Residential Communities," p. 691.

62. Olaniran, "Computer-Mediated Communication in Cross-Cultural Virtual Teams," p. 159.

63. Robert McDougal, "Subject Fields, Oral Emulation and the Spontaneous Cultural Positioning of Mohawk E-Mail Users," *World Communication* 28, no. 4 (1999): 5–25.

64. Glen Hiemstra, "Teleconferencing, Concern for Face, and Organizational Culture," in *Communication Yearbook*, ed. Michael Burgoon, pp. 874–904 (Beverly Hills, Calif.: Sage, 1982).

65. Geert Hofstede and M. Bond, "Hofstede's Culture Dimensions: An Independent Validation Using Rokeach's Value Survey," *Journal of Cross-Cultural Psychology* 15, no. 4 (December 1984): 417–433.

66. Ibid., p. 419.

67. Nabil Kamel and Robert Davison, "Applying CSCW Technology to Overcome Traditional Barriers in Group Interactions," *Information & Management* 34, no. 4 (November 2, 1998): 209–220.

68. John Oetzel, "Explaining Individual Communication Processes in Homogeneous and Heterogeneous Groups through Individualism-Collectivism and Self Construal," *Human Communication Research* 25, no. 2 (December 1998): 202–224.

69. Starr Hiltz and Murray Turoff, *The Network Nation: Human Communication via Computer* (Reading, Mass.: Addison-Wesley, 1978).

70. Bolanle Olaniran, "The Effects of Computer-Mediated Communication on Transculturalism," in *Transcultural Realities*, ed. Virginia Milhouse, Molefi Asante, and Peter Nwosu, pp. 83–105 (Thousand Oaks, Calif.: Sage, 2001).

71. Olaniran and Williams, "Protecting the Environment."

CHAPTER 4

Revisiting the Impact of Tribalism on Civil Society: An Investigation of the Potential Benefits of Membership in an E-Tribe on Public Discourse

CHRISTINA STANDERFER

Many scholars draw a distinct line between tribes and communities regarding whether they contribute to or detract from constructive public dialogue. Tribes are often characterized as ever-narrowing enclaved groups who refuse to interact with people different from themselves. As such, tribes are seen as detrimental to open debate about social issues, and their inability to engage others may result in public policies rarely guided by the voice of the people or democratic action. In contrast, communities often are held up as sites where democratic dialogue may flourish and citizens can come together to create their own solutions to problems that affect a wide variety of people. Few, if any, scholars have posited that tribes and communities do not necessarily represent a dichotomy but rather may work in concert to revitalize community and community action.

In this chapter I argue that while some forms of tribalism may be detrimental to public life in general and public discourse specifically, tribalism in the form of e-tribes—that is, diasporic tribes of engaged citizens who meet in cyberspace—may in fact serve to revitalize American public discourse. Rather than precluding engagement in community, belonging to a virtual tribe may actually promote and support more active community involvement.

My argument begins with a review of the current literature concerning tribalism and communitarianism in the context of maintaining and nurturing a civil society and an engaged citizenry. I proceed to an investigation of the discursive practices of subscribers to one specific electronic mailing list called VISTAnet. VISTAnet subscribers are potential, former, and current members of the national service program AmeriCorps*VISTA (Volunteers in Service to America). I aver that subscribers to VISTAnet constitute a tribe based on certain discursive practices. I further suggest that online public spheres such as VISTAnet serve as potentially ideal spaces in which tribe members can practice productive public dialogue and, though geographically dispersed, can renew and reinforce their membership in a virtual tribe while simultaneously renewing and reinforcing their commitment to civic engagement and social justice in real communities.

Tribes and Communities in the Civil Society Debate

Theorists who decry the state of public life in America often link decline in civic responsibility to what they perceive, pejoratively, as the impact of identity politics on public dialogue. In *Democracy on Trial*, Jean Bethke Elshtain claimed our public language has become overwhelmed by declarations predicated on narrow self-interests. These self-interests are largely derived from our allegiances to some group identity based on race, ethnicity, gender, sexual orientation, mental and physical (dis)abilities, and so forth. She further maintained that this retribalization of the American public into "fixed identity groups" results in a politics of displacement "that dislodges the concerns of the citizen and public life in favor of politicizing all features of who and what we are."[1] In a 1998 address, Dave Frohnmayer, president of the University of Oregon, echoed Elshtain's concerns and used the term "New Tribalism" to describe "politics based upon narrow concerns, rooted in the exploitation of divisions of class, cash, gender, region, religion, ethnicity, morality and ideology—a give-no-quarter and take-no-prisoners activism that demands satisfaction and accepts no compromise."[2] In other words, public debates driven by the politics of new tribalism can degenerate quickly into "us versus them" squabbles that do nothing more than reinforce differences among people.

According to Adam Seligman, this return to what amounts to tribal loyalties derives from a need to have some basis for a sense of self. However, if identity based on group affiliation becomes the foundation for an understanding of self, Seligman argues, "it will herald an end to trust as a form of sociability and interaction making life that much more nasty, brutish, and short."[3] Moreover, the focus on authenticating one's identity through group affiliation can lead to a public discourse charged with overpersonalization. Discussion of public affairs may turn solely on assertions of participants' identities and personal agendas. The upshot of this is that dialogue that might lead to the transcending of differences for a common good is silenced. Attacking others' opinions is equated with attacking their identities: identity-driven ideology usurps democracy and everybody loses. Needless to say, in the context of revitalizing public dialogue and creating a vibrant public sphere, the term "tribe" is beyond problematic: it is a devil term.

While the retribalization or the repositioning of people into fixed identity groups may contribute to the poor quality of public dialogue, some scholars argue that the revitalization of communities represents one of the best means to understand and to improve the public life of citizens. These scholars subscribe to a communitarian perspective on civil society. John Brandl, a faculty member at the University of Minnesota's Hubert Humphrey Institute of Public Affairs, noted that a communitarian perspective is "the conviction that humans are more appropriately understood not as autonomous individuals but as social creatures, whole only in groups and when devoted to those groups."[4] Communitarians also call for what William Sullivan termed a "covenant morality," in which citizens "make an unlimited promise to show care and concern to each other."[5] Harry C. Boyte and James Farr indicated, "Communitarians have helped to reconceptualize citizens as moral selves, fully 'situated' in a community."[6]

From a communitarian perspective, "civil society is the sphere of our most basic humanity—the personal, everyday realm that is governed by values such as responsibility, trust, fraternity, solidarity, and love."[7] While communitarians may overidealize life in real communities, their general argument concerning communities as sites where values are formed, including the valuation of talk that leads to public action, should not be dismissed.

In sum, within the context of debates concerning civil society, the difference between tribes and communities is clear. Tribes are identity-based and encourage discourse that maintains the unique identity of their members at the expense of engaging difference. Communities, on the other hand, may be seen as sites where citizens can "reclaim responsibility and develop the power and learn the skills and knowledge to seriously address public issues and to become 'co-creators of history.'"[8]

The existence of identity-based tribes, then, constitutes an obstacle to be overcome, and the maintenance or revitalization of communities represents a way to ensure the continuation of a vibrant democracy. One problem with this bifurcation is that it frames "tribe talk" as merely "identity (or identity-driven) talk" and assumes "community talk" is inherently democratic. This may not be the case in practice. In fact, the voice of marginalized people may be silenced in communities based on the perception that they belong to "different" or "problematic" tribes because of their race, age, economic status, and so forth. The democratic promise of communities may require the realignment of tribe affiliations. For over forty years, members of national service programs such as AmeriCorps*VISTA have worked to bring about this realignment.

AmeriCorps*VISTA and the Democratic Promise of Communities

In 1965, Lyndon B. Johnson declared a war on poverty, and the VISTA (Volunteers in Service to America) program was born. Although VISTA continued to exist during subsequent administrations, former President William J. Clinton gave new life to VISTA by establishing an overseer agency for all national service programs, the Corporation for National and Community Service (CNCS), and expanding these programs.[9]

In one of his first addresses announcing this expansion, former President Clinton declared that national service participants would "transform the world in which we live, city by city, community by community, block by block." In addition, he called all Americans to service—"young and old, Democrats and Republicans, white, black, Hispanic, Asian and you name it"—in order to "rejoin the citizens in communities of this country, bonding each to the other with the glue of common purpose and real patriotism."[10] In this call to service, Clinton invited all Americans to what Benjamin Barber termed "high citizenship"—a joining together to transform "the market ethic of private voluntarism into a civic ethic of citizenship."[11] The current mission and vision statement of CNCS continues this emphasis on engaged citizenship, the promotion of "partnerships at all levels of society," and the building of "bridges among seemingly disparate groups to improve the quality of life of people in our nation."[12]

People, then, who join national service programs such as AmeriCorps*VISTA are charged with the responsibility of bringing diverse groups of people together to find ways to improve the quality of life in the communities in which they serve. Their mission is to ensure the democratic promise of community life is met and all citizens have a voice in making decisions about public issues that impact their lives. In short, AmeriCorps*VISTA members work to combat the politics of "new tribalism" and to draw enclaved groups into productive (issues-driven rather than identity-driven) public dialogue.

While AmeriCorps*VISTA members may be working to "de-tribalize" the American public arena, *I argue that AmeriCorps*VISTA members who subscribed to the electronic mailing list VISTAnet constitute a tribe in the sense that their talk is often identity-driven, discourages expression not in line with the accepted ideology of the tribe, and positions members as engaged in an "us versus them" struggle.* However, rather than having a crippling effect on the public sphere, the tribe talk of AmeriCorps*VISTA members on VISTAnet works to facilitate members' ability to function effectively in the communities in which they live and serve. I make this claim based on three factors: *(1) the VISTAnet tribe is geographically dispersed; (2) the identity talk of the VISTAnet tribe serves to motivate rather than to isolate; and (3) the "us versus them" talk positions poverty rather than specific groups or people as the enemy.*

I will address the last two factors in the next section. Here I wish to touch briefly on the geographic dispersion of the tribe. While some AmeriCorps*VISTA members may serve in the communities in which they already live, others choose to move to communities new to them. In either case, AmeriCorps*VISTA members do not have many opportunities to gather with other members in a physical space, nor do they have a physical space that may be defined as their own. Moreover, AmeriCorps*VISTA members may have few, if any, colleagues serving in the same organization or even the same community as they do. Although members have the opportunity to gather face-to-face at two CNCS-sponsored training conferences during their year of service, these conferences are organized geographically, so even if Ameri-Corps*VISTA members attend, they do not have the opportunity to interact with members who may be serving in distant areas. Furthermore, the training space is not really "AmeriCorps*VISTA space"—it is "Corporation space" and therefore not necessarily conducive to tribe talk.

The diasporic configuration of AmeriCorps*VISTA members in general presents some obstacles for maintaining a group identity, but it also offers some advantages in regard to the impact of the VISTAnet tribe's talk on public dialogue. Since frequent face-to-face meetings are not an option, the chances of the AmeriCorps*VISTA members becoming enclaved or refusing to interact with nonmembers are minimal. No physical space exists for the members to retreat to. However, given this lack of defined physical space, maintaining connection and identification among AmeriCorps*VISTA members presents a challenge. One means to overcome this challenge is through subscription to and participation on the electronic mailing list VISTAnet.

VISTAnet: Maintaining Tribal Identity and Ideology

While national service may have a history dating back to the 1960s, easily accessible online discussion of issues, concerns, and opportunities within such service is a fairly new development. Although several electronic mailing lists centering on national service exist, only two lists are dedicated exclusively to the ongoing discussion of AmeriCorps, or AmeriCorps*VISTA: AClist and VISTAnet.

AClist is run by the National Service Resource Center and receives funding from CNCS. Job postings, official newsletters, and official announcements dominate AClist. VISTAnet, by contrast, is not formally connected to the Corporation. It is run from St. John's University and was started in 1995 by two former VISTA members.[13] Subscribers to VISTAnet include not only AmeriCorps*VISTA members, but also VISTA alumni, potential AmeriCorps*VISTA members, and some CNCS staff.

Currently 511 people subscribe to VISTAnet.[14] Archives of messages from January 1999 to the present are available at http://maelstrom.stjohns .edu/archives/vistanet.html. I personally have archived messages dating from January 1997 and have monitored the postings to VISTAnet for the past eight years—reading and categorizing literally thousands of messages. I have determined from my research that excluding broadcast announcements from CNCS and training providers, standard postings of available service positions ("Habitat for Humanity positions," "VISTA positions in Louisiana"), posts concerning benefits (how to get health insurance, how to use educational awards), and automated response messages ("I'll be out of the office"), most of the posts on VISTAnet can be sorted generally into five types of messages or message threads: (1) introducing; (2) testifying; (3) requesting/supplying project help; (4) discussing announcements about AmeriCorps*VISTA-related activities; and (5) discussing poverty and poverty issues.[15] In the course of posting and responding to each of these types of messages, list subscribers establish and maintain their membership in and reinforce the ideology of the diasporic VISTAnet tribe.

Introducing

Introducing posts are exactly that: introductions. The subject line for these types of posts is predictably "My Introduction," "Hello!" or something similar. Introducing posts generally take the following form:

> Hi everybody! My name is Katherine Sullivan and I am an Ameri-Corps*VISTA Leader in Aberdeen, North Dakota. My sponsoring organization, the North Dakota Association for Lifelong Learning, was granted 9 VISTA slots with the purpose of increasing the literacy levels of adults in our state. This is my second year of service on the project and I will be terminating in the middle of July. I am new to the listserv so I thought I'd tell you I'm here. Carpe Diem!

The majority of introducing posts begin with some salutation ending in an exclamation point followed by some variation on "My name is" and "I am—" (a new AmeriCorps*VISTA member, a VISTA alum, someone interested in becoming a VISTA). Most introducing posts go on to briefly describe what the person is currently doing and end with a short statement followed by another exclamation point ("I'm glad I found this list!" "Hope you have a great day!").

Welcoming messages generally follow introducing posts. In response to the above message, the following welcoming post appeared:

> Welcome! I have found some great inspiration and information on this listserv and hope you do the same!

Responses to introducing posts also tend to be formulaic: a salutation ending in an exclamation point and some statement that conveys excitement about the list itself and the new member's decision to join.

In form, introducing posts and the responses they generate resemble the standard way people introduce themselves at self-help group meetings ("Hi! I'm John and I'm a——." "Hi, John!"), and they function in much the same way. They allow subscribers to self-identify as a member of the group and receive support for their decision to join. The self-identification offered in these introducing messages almost invariably begins with a declaration that the sender is an AmeriCorps*VISTA or VISTA member, former member, or potential member. The implication of the primacy of such a statement is that such identification serves to legitimize the sender's presence in the group and his or her right to participate. Once subscribers declare their identity as AmeriCorps*VISTA members, former members, or potential members, their presence is sanctioned by one or more people who already subscribe to the list, and the welcoming ritual based on declaration of identity is complete.

As mentioned earlier, civil society theorists have argued that the primacy of identity in public talk is detrimental to public dialogue and creates divisions in society. However, the identity talk on VISTAnet and responses it receives tend to motivate rather than isolate. While the tribe talk of AmeriCorps*VISTA members who subscribe to VISTAnet may start with identity talk, it does not end there. As evidenced by the response above and testifying responses described below, while subscribers' legitimacy in the group is established by declaration of their affiliation or interest in AmeriCorps*VISTA, these declarations also mark subscribers as open to giving and receiving inspiration and information that facilitate their work in the communities in which they serve.

Testifying

Testifying posts present stories of the struggles and triumphs of being an AmeriCorps*VISTA member. As these posts tend to be long, I offer only a portion of one such post as exemplary of testifying messages. This post started with the subject line "Can you sit with me at the computer?" and described "An AmeriCorps*VISTA Personal Journey" to being on the "front lines of the digital divide." The post indicates the sender has a long way to go to be accepted by the community, "having moved here less than three months ago." The sender then proceeds to delineate the hardships of being an AmeriCorps*VISTA member and living on a stipend that amounts to about $3.80 an hour:

> The culture of poverty is horrible and crippling. It forces one to exercise necessary restraint, stay home, pray for a car that runs . . . apply for food stamps . . . and rely on the kindness of strangers. Most people think we are crazy to willingly accept this burden, especially since most of us are college educated and could get a "real" job.

This is the kind of identity talk that many civil society theorists view as creating and maintaining tribal divisions within society. The sender is making a clear distinction between those who have and those who have not, positioning him- or herself in the latter category. Moreover, the sender makes clear that a conscious decision was made to live a life of poverty as an AmeriCorps*VISTA member. The sender also implies those in different circumstances may reject the decision to become an AmeriCorps*VISTA member as "crazy." However, the post continues:

> As I stated before, we take the burden of poverty on willingly, and I wouldn't trade my experience for the world. I get to do hands-on, grassroots work in my newly adopted community. I am learning how to write grants, organize and participate in community meetings, recruit and coordinate volunteers, work with the kids in the computer lab, and plan activities and projects. In exchange I get the experience of a lifetime, doing great work with amazing kids and making a difference. I am living the AmeriCorps motto and working like hell to "get things done." Don't worry, one of these days I'll get a "real" job that pays a living wage. For now I'll settle for real work.

This last segment of the testifying post can be read as both a statement of motivation for other subscribers and as an argument to present to those who might question AmeriCorps*VISTA members' decisions to live in poverty during their year of service. In this sense, it is identity talk that does far more than work to reinforce the identity of the sender: it provides an example of how to engage others who may question one's decision to become an AmeriCorps*VISTA member. It is not rooted in the exploitation of division, but rather offers reasoned explanations for the decision to claim a certain identity: hands-on experience in community development, grant proposal writing, and project management. The tribal identity talk derided by many civil society theorists begins and ends with the statement of identity. The identity talk evidenced in testifying posts on VISTAnet does not.

Requesting/Supplying Project Help

Requesting/supplying project help threads begin with the posting of questions about how best to complete a task (fund-raising, volunteer recruiting) and include responses to the question based on the responders' own experiences. Sometimes the responses are posted in personal e-mail to the original poster, but even if they are, the person who started the cycle often posts a message to the list expressing gratitude for the suggestions ("Thanks to everyone who offered tips!"). As with introducing posts, posts requesting project help usually start with the senders identifying themselves as AmeriCorps*VISTA members. For example, a post for help with how to conduct a community meeting that would include both English-only speakers and Spanish-only speakers began as follows:

> I just joined Americorps Vista in June of this year and I really enjoy it! I have to say that it is all so new for me because along with 2 other Vistas we are new to our sponsor and to the site! I moved from Muncie Indiana to Visalia California and it has been a real change.

The opening of this post establishes the sender as an AmeriCorps* VISTA member and affirms the poster's excitement concerning the decision to join. The post continues with a query concerning the pros and cons of holding separate community meetings, given the languages differences, and ends with "I look forward to hearing from some Vistas past and present!"

Response posts generally start with some indication of the poster's past or present experience with a situation similar to the one indicated in the initial post ("I'm working on a similar project," "When I was a VISTA"). Those who responded to the appeal above suggested holding only one meeting, to "establish a sense of community." One response suggested starting the meeting with an activity that would stress commonality among the group members and "make language differences seem less important." Several noted the need to make everyone at the meeting feel "comfortable" and to "show respect for those in the minority (culture, ethnicity, religion, etc)." Another responding post warned that "splitting them [Spanish-speakers and English-speakers] up only divides the line more."

These responses indicate an ideology that values both respect for diversity and community. Oftentimes when posters request help, another subscriber will ask for more specific information about the population to which the task relates. A post that asked for help with setting up summer camps was followed by a post asking for the ages of the people who would be participating in the camp. When another subscriber asked for help with neighborhood organizing, a follow-up post inquired about "what kind of assessments" the original poster had already done "to find out what the unmet needs" were. This reply indicated that talking to people one-on-one was "a good way to get people talking" and ended with the admonition "Rather than come up with the [community] issues on your own, ask them!"

The work done by requesting/supplying project help posts is similar to that of introducing posts in that the initial poster first establishes identity before asking for help. The responders reestablish their identity by offering advice based on their own experiences as AmeriCorps*VISTA members. Requesting/supplying project help posts go beyond identity talk, however, in that they serve as indoctrination or reinforcement concerning the accepted ideology of the tribe: an ideology based on respect for differences among people, the value of community, and the value of talk. Maintaining this ideology requires certain sanctions on how tribe members should talk and what they should talk about. These sanctions will become apparent in the discussion of the next two types of posts.

Discussing Announcements about AmeriCorps*VISTA-related Activities

While not all announcements about AmeriCorps*VISTA-related activities posted on VISTAnet generate discussion, some do. Announcements about service awards and special event activities (e.g., Martin Luther King Day and National Volunteer Week activities) rarely result in much discussion. Some posts about AmeriCorps activities, however, particularly announcements centering on the president's involvement in these activities, generate heated discussion.[16] Two such announcements were one posted in January 2001 about George W. Bush's proposed faith-based initiative and another posted in June 2004 concerning Bush serving with an AmeriCorps team at the Florida Coastal Reserve during National Volunteer Week (April 18–24, 2004). As might be expected, the discussion generated by these posts ostensibly centers on the pros and cons of the initiative or action but also reflects approval or disapproval of the president in general. Most importantly, these posts indicate how members of the VISTAnet tribe subtly and not so subtly engage in interaction to discourage noncompliance with the ideology of the tribe.

On January 30, 2001, a reprint of an article that appeared in the *Washington Post*, entitled "Bush Unveils 'Faith-Based' Initiative," was posted to VISTAnet by the Corporation for National and Community Service's AmeriCorps*VISTA field liaison officer.[17] This post generated a discussion of the implications of the initiative. Two of these posts included the following:

> I'm certainly not against churches, of whatever denomination helping people, but I could see a lot of problems arising from having government subsidies given to churches.

Think about the little tiny communities—rural communities—where it is not cost effective to have larger program offices—little churches can help provide help in areas that would not otherwise receive services, if funded. Who knows, maybe a VISTA will be able to work in broader social issues (wearing MANY hats) through sponsorship of a rural church—and truly mobilizing a community to help itself?

While these posts represent different points of view concerning the faith-based initiative, they also are similar in that they do not assert opinions closed for discussion. Both messages contain tentative language ("I'm certainly not against," "Who knows, maybe"), and they reflect an ideology based on the values of helping others and communities.

Soon after these posts, another VISTAnet tribe member sent a message that contained the following:

as we all try to figure out what this new federal program means, it might be helpful to be a little careful with the terminology. "churches" doesn't include mosques, temples, synagogues and other faith-based organizations that are also included in this order.

This second post expresses the accepted ideology of the VISTAnet tribe both in content and form. The sender clearly takes issue with the use of the term "churches," which is not an inclusive term, and therefore seeks to correct the previous senders' inattention to respect for differences. However, this admonition is framed in a way that reflects the value of community ("as we all") and, by using the phrase "it might be helpful," does not single out the users of the questionable "terminology." This implies "we all" need to be reminded to respect differences, not just the senders who used the noninclusive term.

While the above posts indicate subtle ways VISTAnet tribe members discourage expression of noncompliance with accepted ideologies, at times the discussion of announcements concerning the president and AmeriCorps*VISTA-related activities turns from the issue at hand to a discussion of how discussion should proceed based on the ideology of the tribe. This was the case when VISTAnet tribe members began discussing the fact that a photo taken in April 2004 of President Bush serving with AmeriCorps members at the Florida Coastal Reserve was still on the AmeriCorps Web site two months after Bush had completed his day of service. The post that started the discussion posed the question: "Wouldn't it be something if the President answered his own 'call to service' and decided to give a year of his life as a VISTA?"

The first tribe member responding to this question remarked: "You might want to keep in mind that even when President Bush signed up, there is little evidence that he showed up." This generated a few posts defending and criticizing the president's service record and the pros and cons of mandatory service for all Americans. It also generated a discussion of who has the right to criticize whom, starting with a post in which one tribe member suggested no one should criticize anyone else's service record unless the accuser's record was "flawless." That post ended with the following:

> I suggest we promote the idea of serving to everyone, regardless of who they are or what their "record" has been. That's at least the kind of civil society I envision.

This post resulted in a response about the right to free speech:

> With all due respect, free speech permits criticism even without a perfect record. That's the American way.

Then came the following exchange:

> Even though freedom permits criticism, it also comes with a certain level of responsibility, perhaps in this case the responsibility of respecting differing view points or engaging in civil discourse. When I became a VISTA (the same year as Steve, I think) I myself had to learn some hard lessons about our "American Way" mentality, which usually means speaking out rather than speaking with. I have strong beliefs, but when I entered my new community I had to hold strongly to believing that others' beliefs were just as valid as my own.

> The purpose of my previous post was not to try and make a case for sitting by silently while world political corruption runs rampant. The point I was trying to make is that service should be promoted to everyone regardless of their rank or record of service, even the President, for the good that it does for the individual and for society.

> Perhaps if your original post hadn't been composed of ambiguous rhetorical doublespeak and seemingly negative insinuations, we wouldn't be engaged in this obviously pointless dialog. Your purpose and your point could have been made much clearer with a little more thought and effort.

Reserve your right to disagree with one individuals' opinion and take issue certainly but commenting on the quality of the argument and the level of articulateness with which the argument is presented is petty and unnecessary.

What these posts do is both reinforce an ideology of respecting difference and valuing community and strongly discourage the degeneration of VISTAnet talk into ad hominem arguments or "pointless dialog," given this ideology. In other words, while it is perfectly acceptable to disagree, particularly if it brings about new ideas and productive dialogue, it is not acceptable to attack another's way of speaking or his or her person or to engage in talk without purpose: stick to issues that matter to the tribe and its mission or be silent.

While this implies a sanction against some types of speech, it is not necessarily a sanction that curtails argument (in the best sense) or leads to "us versus them" talk that may set tribe members in opposition to each other or the administration. For once verbal attacks become too personal, either toward other members or toward the public official being discussed, or the dialogue becomes too off-topic, someone steps in to remind the participants of the value the tribe places on respecting difference, building community, and engaging in productive talk. The imposition of ideology through discouragement of talk not in line with these values serves not only to keep the tribe members themselves "civil" but has implications for their work in real communities. This transfer of tribe talk to community talk is indicated by the post that declared learning the "hard lesson" of "speaking with rather than speaking out" was a requisite to being both accepted within a community and working to better that community.

Discussing Poverty and Poverty Issues

Another common thread of messages on VISTAnet is the discussion of poverty and how best to combat it. Poverty poses a double threat to the tribe: it is a constant obstacle to tribe members' ability to complete their missions in the communities in which they serve, and as such it often leads to outbursts of frustration that threaten the morale of the tribe in general. Tribal discussions of poverty and how to combat it work in much the same way discussions of announcements of AmeriCorps*VISTA-related activities work, in that they discourage expression not in line with the accepted ideology of the tribe. However, they also work to set up tensions among tribe members, often based on the declaration of identities other than AmeriCorps*VISTA identities and disagreements concerning what causes poverty and the best ways to defeat it.

The threads that lead to discussion of poverty usually start with tribe members identifying themselves as former or current Ameri-Corps*VISTA members and making a statement about the relationship of poverty to war, wealth, government programs, structural or societal constraints, and so forth. Besides offering a theory about the reasons why poverty exists, these posts generally indicate some level of frustration on the part of the senders in regard to how effective they are at bringing about positive change within the communities in which they serve. One such exchange took place on VISTAnet in January 2003. In the initial post, the sender identified as "a current VISTA" and as a "socialist-feminist agnostic." This declaration of identity was followed by a long rant on the detrimental effects of the Patriot Act and other homeland security measures on AmeriCorps*VISTA work specifically and democracy in general, the lack of socialized health care in America, and the rape of the environment by "rich, white men."

What followed were posts from various tribe members who identified as current and former VISTAs. Some of the posts took issue with the original sender's position, some agreed with the sentiments expressed. However, what could have been a discussion that drove tribe members apart in terms of political and religious differences was tempered by continued reference to the common enemy, poverty itself, and its power to frustrate and complicate the work of the tribe. For example, a sender who identified as "a cooperative anarchist," "religious believer," and "a man who supports gender equality, rather than a feminist" could have attacked the original sender based on differences in perspectives, but instead, after declaring those differences, commented that he could relate to the original sender's "feeling, thoughts, and concerns." He also agreed "that our fight against poverty as VISTAs is unfortunately, often, and even hypocritically, undermined by political and business leaders"; however, he never identified the offenders by name and his post included the following:

> When John F. Kennedy put forth his famous statement, "Ask not what your country can do for you, ask what you can do for your country." He expressed the kind of thinking that we as VISTA's have the opportunity to live out in our actions.

Another tribe member who identified as a "Christian and social democrat" remarked, "I understand your frustration" and went on to say that as a Christian she was drawn to the antipoverty goals of VISTA. She agreed that the work of AmeriCorps*VISTA members could be hampered by bureaucracy and that angered her; however, this tribe member added:

> I can also see in the faces of the women I work with that they are overjoyed that someone is paying attention to them and their needs and THAT is what makes my frustrating volunteer work worth it, though they may be few in numbers. Keep fightin, sista!

While discussions of poverty and poverty issues potentially could set tribe members in opposition to each other based on different political and religious perspectives, they generally do not. In the end, tribe talk that reinforces tribe members' AmeriCorps*VISTA identities, discourages talk that violates an ideology of tolerance of difference, and positions tribe members in a struggle against the common enemy of poverty works to keep the tribe intact. It also has implications for the communities in which these tribe members serve.

The Implications of VISTAnet Tribe Talk on Community Talk

In *Vernacular Voices: The Rhetoric of Publics and Public Spheres*, Gerard Hauser argued that the discursive dimension of civil society is best understood as reticulate, consisting of webs of interactions. Thus, the publics that participate in the deliberations within these webs cannot and should not be viewed as constituting a "general" or unified public. Instead, attention must be paid to the discursive conditions that facilitate civic judgment among people with differing opinions. Hauser held that "a *well-ordered* public sphere is inherently tied to the quality of its rhetorical exchanges" (emphasis in original).[18] The quality of these exchanges can be measured based on at least five rhetorical criteria: permeable boundaries (conditions that allow social actors to move among publics), activity (ability and means to engage others), contextualized language (symbolic action not colonized by technocrats or epistemic elites), believable appearance (the ability to interact with and gain the trust of those different from oneself), and tolerance (the ability to engage difference without necessarily relinquishing one's own position).

I argue that these criteria may be more easily met when e-tribes such as VISTAnet exist. Among themselves, tribe members practice the rhetorical skills they need to be effective in the communities in which they serve. Through tribe talk, members reinforce their identities as AmeriCorps*VISTA members. Tribe talk also encourages an ideology of tolerance of differences while building solidarity among tribe members by identifying a common enemy: poverty. Given their geographic dispersion and their mission to build better communities, VISTAnet tribe members work in the interstices among various publics. In so doing, they may be able to cross borders of existing publics more easily and encourage other citizens to become active in public issues by "forging the trail" for future border crossings by others.

The geographic dispersion of tribe members also guarantees patterns of critical publicity within the larger public sphere. Members of the VISTAnet tribe serve both as carriers of information and opinion between publics and, when interacting in the communities in which they serve, as embodiments of an ethic of civic participation that respects differing perspectives. E-tribes such as VISTAnet facilitate not only a *well-ordered* public sphere, but a public sphere in which civic judgments based on widespread understandings of various perspectives can be made.

Conclusion

As evidenced by the existence of e-tribes such as VISTAnet, the line between tribes and communities may not be as distinct as some civil society scholars argue; nor are tribes and the talk they foster necessarily detrimental to the American public sphere. E-tribes such as VISTAnet have the potential to generate bridging social capital[19] more than most voluntary associations or publics. In other words, the discourse of VISTAnet tribe members, both online and in real communities, can change the terrain and dynamics of many public spheres and in turn help fulfill the democratic promise of communities.

Notes

1. Jean Bethke Elshtain, *Democracy on Trial* (New York: Basic Books, 1995); quotation from p. 36.
2. Dave Frohnmayer, "The New Tribalism" (Eugene: University of Or-

egon, 1998), http://president.uoregon.edu/tribalism.html (accessed March 17, 2004).

3. Adam B. Seligman, "Trust and Sociability: On the Limits of Confidence and Role Expectations," *American Journal of Economics and Sociology* (October 1998). Retrieved from Infotrac database March 8, 2002.

4. John Brandl, quoted in Everett C. Ladd, *The Ladd Report: Startling New Research Shows How an Explosion of Voluntary Groups, Activities, and Charitable Donation Is Transforming Our Towns and Cities* (New York: Free Press, 1999), p. 12.

5. William Sullivan, quoted in Harry C. Boyte and James Farr, "The Work of Citizenship and the Problem of Service-Learning," *Campus Compact Reader* 1, no. 1 (May 2000): 4–10; quotation on p. 6.

6. Boyte and Farr, "The Work of Citizenship and the Problem of Service-Learning," p. 6.

7. Bill Bradley, "America's Challenge: Revitalizing Our National Community," in *Community Works: The Revival of Civil Society in America*, ed. E. J. Dionne, Jr. (Washington, D.C.: Brookings Institution Press, 1998), p. 108.

8. Harry C. Boyte, "Populist: Citizenship as Public Work and Public Freedom," in *Building a Community of Citizens: Civil Society in the 21st Century*, ed. Don E. Eberly (Lanham, Md.: University Press of America, 1994), p. 349.

9. Generally, the differences among these programs relate to types of service performed and age requirements for membership. For information about the programs go to the AmeriCorps Web site (http://www.americorps.gov).

10. William Jefferson Clinton, "Remarks by the President in Address to the Community of the University of New Orleans on the President's National Service Initiative" (April 30, 1993), http://www.access.gpo.gov/nara/nara003.html (accessed January 26, 2003).

11. Benjamin R. Barber, *A Place for Us: How to Make Society Civil and Democracy Strong* (New York: Hill and Wang, 1998), p. 59.

12. Corporation for National and Community Service, "Our Mission and Our Vision," http://www.nationalservice.org/about/role_impact/mission.asp (accessed June 26, 2005).

13. Several years ago, I had the opportunity to visit with Brian Geoghegan, one of VISTAnet's founders, when we were both graduate students at the University of Colorado–Boulder. He indicated that from his own experiences as a VISTA in the field, he personally knew how isolating and frustrating that position could be. He and his cofounder (also a former VISTA) envisioned VISTAnet as a low-cost way for VISTAs to network and share their common concerns and frustrations. As Geoghegan stated, "VISTAnet has its own ecology—it is virtually self-regulating." He and his cofounder took a "hands-off" approach to censoring messages when they moderated this list (and that "hands-off" approach continues today).

14. Corporation for National and Community Service, "AmeriCorps* VISTA," http://www.americorps.gov/about/programs/vista.asp (accessed July 18, 2005). According to CNCS, currently "almost 6,000 people are serving as AmeriCorps*VISTA members." Thus VISTAnet subscribers represent between 9 and 10 percent of the total AmeriCorps*VISTA population.

15. I have included only a few representative sample posts from the last five years to explicate these different types of posts. Readers interested in viewing more posts are encouraged to visit the VISTAnet archives at http://maelstrom .stjohns.edu/archives/vistanet.html.

16. This was true during the Clinton administration as well. Announcements about the 1997 President's Summit on Volunteerism generated numerous posts both praising and questioning the president's motives and involvement.

17. The AmeriCorps*VISTA field liaison officer posts between seven and fifteen messages a month. These posts include AmeriCorps*VISTA-related press releases and articles from mass media, announcements about service awards, and copies of *National Service News*, the Corporation of National and Community Service's biweekly eNewsletter that "spotlights people and programs from across the country that are making a difference" (http://www.nationalservice. org/about/newsroom/nsn_archive.asp).

18. Gerard A. Hauser, *Vernacular Voices: The Rhetoric of Publics and Public Spheres* (Columbia: University of South Carolina Press, 1999); quotation from p. 77.

19. Robert D. Putnam, *Bowling Alone: The Collapse and Revival of American Community* (New York: Simon & Schuster, 2000). Bridging social capital is evident in social networks that span diverse populations.

PART II

SOCIAL CONSEQUENCES OF ELECTRONIC TRIBALISM

CHAPTER 5

Theorizing the E-Tribe on MySpace.com

DAVID R. DEWBERRY

Distance is often an impediment to relationships. In 1963, Edward Hall classified distance based on measurement: public space was 144 inches to the limits of visibility, social space was 48–144 inches, personal space was 18–48 inches, and intimate space was 0–18 inches.[1] Angela and I operated within each one of these zones, but it was the two extremes that seemed to be the most fun and disheartening for both of us. I was a graduate student in Arkansas and she was a graduate of the University of Oklahoma. At certain times, we were very close and more often than not we were very far apart. The former was great; the latter, well, not so much. Just because we did not see each other or have any contact with one another did not mean that we were not thinking about each other. One of my close friends, Lyndsay, would often act as an intermediary between the two of us, as she traveled frequently between Oklahoma and Arkansas. When I moved to Denver, I lost my connection with Angela until Lyndsay urged me to keep in touch with Angela on MySpace.com.

Angela, Lyndsay, and I were members of what Ethan Watters dubbed an "urban tribe." In a *New York Times Magazine* article, Watters claimed that single individuals between the ages of twenty-five and thirty-nine who were college-educated and living in a city were a part of an urban tribe, which was "a tight group, with unspoken roles and hierarchies, whose members think of each other as 'us' and the rest of the world as 'them.'"[2] This description seemed to fit Angela, Lyndsay, and myself, as well as other members of our tribe, including Rachel, Brahm, and Tom. Though Angela lived in Oklahoma, the majority of the tribe maintained itself in Fayetteville, Arkansas. However, in the past few years this dynamic has changed—Angela is now in Texas, Lyndsay is in Oklahoma, Rachel is in Indiana, Tom is in Chicago, I am in Denver, and Brahm is still in Fayetteville. We do not all live in the same city or even the same time zone, but we maintain the tribe of friends on MySpace.com.

In *Urban Tribes: A Generation Redefines Friendship, Family, and Commitment*, Watters further developed his concept of the urban tribe. Watters refined his argument of "the tribe as 'tight-knit' and 'us-versus-them,'" which he realized was only partially correct. Urban tribes are "quite fluid in their membership," and "despite changing membership, at any given moment in time these groups could give the feeling of exclusivity, of being clearly defined."[3] He gives the example of Burning Man, in which various individual urban tribes from all across the country come together to form one giant urban tribe in the Nevada desert for a week-long festival.

Watters's conception of an urban tribe was synonymous with the connection my friends and I had, but I found one small problem with his idea: I operated more as a member of an urban tribe that was electronically connected rather than geographically based. My friends are literally all around the United States but exist virtually as an urban tribe on MySpace.com. I had just finished Watters's book as I arrived at Yale University during the summer of 2006, where I met and worked with Professor Tyrone Adams, who introduced me to the concept of the e-tribe. As we talked, I argued that my urban tribe on MySpace.com was an electronic or e-tribe. This chapter relates my arguments concerning the urban tribe as it exists electronically.

Thus, the purpose of this chapter is to theorize the e-tribe by expanding upon Watters's conception of an urban tribe by using Jean Lave and Etienne Wenger's community of practice model. Examining the urban tribe through a community of practice lens reorients the focus of the urban tribe from being geographically based to relationally based. Examining the community of practice through an urban tribe lens reorients the focus from the master/apprentice relationship to informal exchange of gossip amongst friends. Thus, by comparing and contrasting the two theories, we can better understand the nature of the electronic tribe. In fulfilling this purpose, this chapter draws Watters's concept of the urban tribe into the scholarly forum by expanding it through a community of practice approach. Moreover, this chapter expands Lave and Wenger's community of practice by focusing on gossiping among friends and acquaintances as a form of learning.

In what follows, I will first address the major weakness of Watters's conception of the urban tribe and then demonstrate how the community of practice framework addresses the assumptions behind that conception. Also in this section, I will address the educational focus of the community of practice approach and how focusing on noneducational settings can benefit the theory. In the second major section, I will rely on the theoretical framework of the community of practice to examine an urban tribe resettled in cyberspace and to theorize the nature of the e-tribe using MySpace.com as an example.

MySpace.com is a popular social networking Internet Web site similar to facebook.com, Friendster.com, bebo.com, and Classmates.com. While this is not an exhaustive list of social networking Web sites, MySpace.com is the most prolific and salient. According to figures on the Web sites' homepages in July 2006, MySpace.com has over 95 million registered profiles, whereas the total combined number of registered members on facebook.com, Friendster.com, bebo.com, and Classmates.com was just over 100 million. Although the number of registered profiles does not necessarily indicate consistent involvement and participation from every registered member on the Web site, MySpace.com still maintains prominence. Reuters proclaimed MySpace.com was the most visited Web site in early July 2006, beating Yahoo's e-mail service and Google's search engine.[4] Due to its current popularity, I will focus predominantly on MySpace.com to illustrate, through the community of practice approach, how the urban tribe exists electronically. Also, I have maintained my own MySpace.com profile for over a year, giving me a great deal of experience that will provide examples in the following explication of e-tribes, while other examples should probably never be put into print—anywhere.

Theoretical and Empirical Problems and the Interdependent Solution

Uncovering one of Watters's assumptions, which is not a fatal flaw in his work, allows for recognition of the basic precept of the e-tribe. Watters assumes the urban tribe is geographically focused, as in this recollection of when he and his friends approached the Burning Man festival: "There it was, gathered *around a campfire in the desert:* an Urban Tribe" (emphasis added).[5] Watters also claims, "My sense of living as a single person *in a modern American city* was that of belonging to an intensely loyal community of people" (emphasis added).[6] Watters and his friends would often get together at "the biggest *apartment* or most centrally located *home* [of the members of his urban tribe], where the group naturally gathered" (emphasis added).[7] These three examples are indicative of the focus upon the geographical locality of the urban tribe: physical locations such as the campground, apartment, or the city.

The assumption of geographical proximity is also evident in two examples relating to separation of members from their urban tribe and separation from parents. Reflecting on individual members' decisions to move, Watters writes, "We've all reached the same conclusion: the tribe has become *too central to leave behind*" (emphasis added).[8] Also, as tribe members' parents became ill, tribe members were incapable of caring for them, as "distance [from the parents] was often a wall to responsibility."[9] Whether mentioning a physical location or distance, Watters's description rests on the assumption of the urban tribe as being geographically oriented.

We can look to Lave and Wenger's communities of practice for a solution to the limits of Watters's concept of urban tribe. Penelope Eckert claims community studies, much like Watters's explanation of the urban tribe, have defined communities "on the basis of location and/ or population."[10] A community of practice is not "defined by a location or by a population. Instead, it focuses on a community defined by social engagement—after all, it is this engagement that language serves, not the place and not the people as a collection of individuals."[11] Although members of a community of practice are not the focus of study, it is the relationships among the members that are relevant. As Penelope Eckert states, "A community of practice is different as a social construct from the traditional notion of community, primarily because it is defined simultaneously by its membership and by the practice in which that membership engages."[12]

Although we can use the theoretical framework of a community of practice to understand the urban tribe in cyberspace, Watters's conceptualization of the urban tribe not only benefits from Lave and Wenger's theory, but also serves it. Lave and Wenger's community of practice theory has received praise for abandoning the traditional understanding of learning as a process within an individual's head and suggesting that learning operates between individuals; the community of practice, however, is not without its critics.[13] While the five case studies Lave and Wenger offer do not investigate traditional pedagogical settings, they still refer to master and apprentice relationships in coparticipatory learning. A Yucatec midwife learns with her mother or grandmother, Vai and Gola tailor apprentices learned while working with a more experienced tailor, and new Navy Quartermasters learned with higher-ranked and more experienced Quartermasters. While meat cutters do attend school, there is a "mix of trade school and on the job training."[14] In Alcoholics Anonymous there is no master/apprentice phase similar to the previous four case studies, but there is a distinction between "old-timers," who tell stories, and "newcomers," who come to create their own life story to eventually become "a recognized old-timer."[15] Although traditional teaching interactions are not the subject of all five of the case studies, the studies still reveal the implicit hierarchy of master/apprentice and old-timer/newcomer that is similar to the teacher/student relationship. Consequently, using the context of the urban tribe opens up the community of practice approach to recognizing more egalitarian relationships.

Moreover, while I am using the theoretical approach of the community of practice to examine the online urban tribe—the e-tribe—this is not to say that Watters's conceptualization is flawed. Watters's description of the urban tribe echoes, although not explicitly, the underlying components delineated by Lave and Wenger. Recognizing these similarities serves to justify the symbiotic theoretical relationship presented here between the community of practice approach and the urban tribe idea.

When two concepts are nearly identical, exploring their similarities allows for a more in-depth and substantial understanding of both frameworks, which Lave and Wenger as well as Watters recognize. Watters had a moment of reflection just before he was to be interviewed on national television: "I suddenly wondered, there in the greenroom of *Good Morning America*, why we, as a culture, inflate writers into 'experts.'"[16] As a writer, Watters may be an "expert" on urban tribes, but we must, nevertheless, test his ideas against established theory. Also, exploring the similarities benefits Lave and Wenger's theory, which they themselves realize: "The concept of 'community of practice' is left largely as an intuitive notion . . . which requires a more rigorous treatment."[17] In short, examining the similarities between a community of practice and an urban tribe allows not only for a more comprehensive insight into the composition of both concepts, but also offers a bedrock for theorizing about the e-tribe. In the following sections, I will explore MySpace.com as a site for e-tribal interaction based on three main theoretical similarities between the community of practice and urban tribe: participation, definition, and group politics.

Participation

First, participation is inherent in the two concepts. Relating his experience at Burning Man, Watters claims, "This was the ethos of the place—bringing something to share and make friends" and "Burning Man and moshing are not expressions of antisocial behavior but of a heartfelt desire *for connection and community* in the cool guise of rebellion" (emphasis added).[18] In other words, participation in the urban tribe is *active* participation. At Burning Man, as in the urban tribe, passive observation is unacceptable; that is, one cannot just sit idly by. One must actively engage, one must actively participate. Lave and Wenger echo this sentiment, "For newcomers then the purpose is not to learn *from* talk as a substitute for legitimate peripheral participation; it is to learn *to* talk as a key legitimate peripheral participation."[19] For members of the urban tribe and the community of practice, active participation is essential and passivity is discouraged. This is evident on MySpace.com. Nonregistered visitors to the Web site are allowed to visit a few profiles, but are quickly prompted to sign in or register if they are not members to continue exploring the site. Thus, MySpace.com encourages participation by allowing visitors to explore but only as an enticement to subscribe as members.

To better understand the difference between active and passive participation, we must examine participation in contrast to nonparticipation. Within a community of practice, there is no such thing as a nonparticipant; rather, participation is held in degrees. You can only be a nonparticipant if you are not a member of the community of practice. For example, newcomers, such as Navy Quartermasters (who are in the Navy—the community of practice), are not considered full participants until they have worked with old-timers to learn their trade. Eventually, the "new" Quartermasters become "full participants and reach the point at which they are ready to work with newcomers."[20] In other words, full participants are "old-timers," participants on the periphery are "newcomers," and both groups are participants within the community of practice.[21] Thus, members of the community of practice (i.e., the Navy) actively engage in peripheral participation as newcomers, but as they become trained and experienced become full participants, or as Lave and Wenger put it, "peripheral participation leads [to] full participation."[22] Without actively participating, Navy Quartermasters would find themselves in some very hot water.

Friends, unlike Navy Quartermasters, do not operate under demanding conditions. Watters addresses this distinction using Stanford

Professor Mark Granovetter's notion of weak ties. Weak ties are an individual's "acquaintances," who are less "socially involved with one another than our close friends *(strong ties)*."[23] Watters characterizes networks of strong ties as "core groups" and "outliers" as weak ties.[24] Weak ties serve an important function for an individual. While weak ties may not have regular social interaction with an individual, they have their own dense network of friends. An individual's weak ties are, therefore, not just a "trivial acquaintance tie but rather a crucial bridge between two densely knit clumps of close friends."[25] Thus, there is "'the strength of weak ties,' as Granovetter calls it."[26] This is evident in groups of friends, but not in groups such as Navy Quartermasters, for the command and control structure of the military is one of unity and not one conducive to outliers.

Nevertheless, there is participation in both strong and weak ties. Consequently, Wenger argues that one key dimension of a community of practice is mutual engagement: "That is what defines a community. A community of practice is not just an aggregate of people defined by some characteristic. . . . it is [a community] because they sustain dense relations of mutual engagement organized around what they are there to do."[27] As Watters relates, urban tribes exist to facilitate and foster gossip, and the organization of the tribe is furthermore maintained through gossip. Watters's tribe did more than gossip; its members "came together to tackle group projects such as painting a living room, critiquing someone's rough cut of a documentary, or caring for someone who had fallen ill."[28] Nevertheless, these practices rely on geographic locality; Wenger, however, argues geographic proximity is neither sufficient nor necessary for development of a community of practice.[29] Thus, when describing the e-tribe we must focus on the communicative engagement of tribe members. And for Wenger, mutual engagement extends into establishing engagement, diversity and partiality, and reciprocity, which all serve to define the e-tribe.

Wenger writes, "Whatever it takes to make mutual engagement possible is an essential component of any practice."[30] That is, wherever urban tribe members live and work (e.g., Angela in Texas, Tom in Chicago, etc.), they must be able to interact with one another. Given that e-tribe members are not constrained to their geographical locality, e-tribe members must be able to access a Web site such as MySpace .com via an Internet connection, which is nearly commonplace in the United States. Obviously, without Internet access, individuals cannot become members of an e-tribe, for they are incapable of creating profiles on social networking Web sites. Nevertheless, when members of an e-tribe are temporarily disconnected from accessing their MySpace .com accounts for whatever reason—such as not enough time, away from their computer, connectivity issues, or faulty Web site operation— they are still members of their e-tribe. And depending on their degree of inactivity, members may lose strong relational ties due to centrifugal tensions from lack of access, which, again, may be intentional or not. To establish engagement in an e-tribe requires "community maintenance," not only from e-tribe members who connect to MySpace.com, but also from the webmasters and staff of MySpace.com.[31]

The second aspect of mutual engagement is recognition of diversity and partiality of members. A homogenous community involves members who are similar and possess similar knowledge. Like communities of practice, members of an e-tribe operate from a "unique place and [gain] a unique identity, which is both further integrated and is further defined in the course of engagement in practice."[32] While members' identities and positions change, they are "interlocked and articulated with one another through mutual engagement, but they do not fuse."[33] Lyndsay, Tom, Angela, and I are all able to engage in gossip with one another, and it is inherent in gossiping that people speak from unique positions with unique information. For example, Angela, Lyndsay, and I were each able to write about situations, with varying interpretations, regarding events about ourselves and others in our tribe through MySpace.com. In any given situation, each member has a partial explanation that can contribute to a combined understanding.

And not only do tribe members speak from different positions, but MySpace.com allows for individuals to become e-tribe members who would be incapable of being urban tribe members, increasing diversity in our e-tribe. Both Tom and I have made friends with individuals throughout the United States whom we would have never been able to meet in person. Moreover, I have met Denver residents on Myspace .com who would become members of my tribe despite our never meeting in person. It is recognition of diversity and partiality that creates and maintains engagement through novelty and desire for completeness.

The third issue of mutual engagement is the existence of mutual relationships. Wenger believes the word community is usually held to be a positive term, and recognizes that "peace, happiness, and harmony are not necessary properties of a community of practice. Certainly, there are plenty of disagreements, tensions, and conflicts among [members]."[34] While my e-tribe is peaceful and certainly a happy group, other e-tribes of which I am an outlier maintain constant disagreement over political issues, and the comments between the members, as well as responses to members' blogs that are publicly available, indicate that disagreement keeps the groups together and is also an implicit norm for the groups. Wenger claims, "As a form of participation, rebellion often reveals a greater commitment than does passive conformity."[35] While several conservative group members may disagree vehemently with the liberal majority of one of these e-tribes, it is this constant disagreement that maintains the tight cohesion of group members, who once were members of the same debate team and are now spread across the United States. MySpace.com and other similar social networking Web sites allow participation from these group members to continue despite their physical separation from other members, and the resulting question now becomes: How do we demarcate members of the e-tribe?

Definition

The second similarity is definition. Patently, Lave and Wenger's conceptualization of definition, which is akin to the boundary or limits of membership, differs from Watters's conceptualization. Recognition of the difference, however, demonstrates that both formulations arise from the nature of time and are not contradictory despite being different. Lave and Wenger argue a community of practice is an ongoing process where participants may become more or less participatory in the tribe over long periods of time, an argument reflected in their belief in peripheral participation.[36] Thus, they claim, "Nor does the term community imply necessarily co-presence, a well-defined, identifiable group."[37] Drawing an example from one of their case studies, an individual may be a member of the Navy Quartermaster corps for a four-year enlistment but when the end of the enlistment results in his replacement, the individual is no longer a member and the community of practice itself continues. In other words, there will always be a Navy Quartermaster corps, but the members are in constant turnover, so membership, according to Lave and Wenger, would be not well defined.

Watters, on the other hand, conceptualizes tribal definition as temporal or as being very narrowly focused. He writes, "Despite changing membership, *at any given moment* in time these groups could give the feeling of exclusivity, of being clearly defined" (emphasis added).[38] Continuing with the above example, at any given moment there is a specific roster of who is in the Navy's Quartermaster corps. This roster clearly lists who is a member on any given day. Patently, there are two conceptualizations of definition: the community of practice is "not necessarily . . . well defined," while the urban tribe is "clearly defined." On a closer reading, Lave and Wenger understand definition as occurring over time, whereas Watters explains the limits of membership as well defined "at any given moment." In short, Watters views time with a micro lens, whereas Lave and Wenger use a macro lens; thus, it is not so much a difference in conceptualization of definition as it is a difference in the frame of time, which offers two different frameworks that are not contradictory.

Taking the two perspectives together, it is evident that the limits of definition are static within a specific time frame and dynamic over long periods of time. Using both of these frames allows for a better understanding of the e-tribe. Just as in the Navy, MySpace.com has members come and go; moreover, members are allowed to add new friends and delete friends, which results in a well-defined group *at any given* moment. But the list of friends in a group is in constant flux over long periods of time. While a member may have, for example, nine friends when initially registering with MySpace.com and then have nine friends a year later, those nine friends may be completely different individuals.

E-tribes are further defined on MySpace.com by who are depicted on a user's profile. The total number of friends a member is allowed to have is limited only to other registered members, which currently stands at over 95 million members. Nevertheless, users can choose from four to twenty-four friends to be "Top Friends." Top Friends have their picture with a link to their profile displayed on the main page of a user's profile. A viewer can choose to see all of a user's friends, but the viewer must access a subsidiary page via a link on the profile. Just as important as who is a "Top Friend" is the ordering of those friends. I have felt, as have many others, the sometimes painful sting when reduced in rank on a friend's profile. Naturally, it is a difficult decision to determine who gets the coveted number one Top Friend rank. Some MySpace.com members periodically change who is the primary Top Friend; Tom and I both place fictitious profiles as our number one Top Friend—it switches between Jim Jones and Darth Vader.

A group's definition is also demarcated by the language used by its members. According to Wenger, another element of the community of practice is its shared repertoire, which includes "routines, words, tools, ways of doing things, stories, gestures, symbols, genres, actions, or concepts that the community had produced or adopted in the course of its existence, and which have become part of its practice."[39] Watters claims his urban tribe formed their life philosophy together from "song lyrics, sacred texts, our college social psychology classes, our parents, our bosses and coworkers, *The Simpsons*, snippets of wisdom forwarded to us in e-mails and things we overheard on the bus."[40]

However, nonverbal aspects of language are much more limited in computer-mediated communication than in face-to-face interaction. For example, I once received a message from Angela that read, "Dave . . . Chances are high in your favor. Your wish shall be granted." This was all I got. To be honest, and given the circumstances, I did not know what it really meant. Consequently, interactions between e-tribe members are often ambiguous and in need of continual refinement through continued interaction. Wenger writes, "Computer users count on each other to cope with the intricacies of obscure systems," an observation recalling the quality of partiality in the e-tribe.[41] Over the next few days, Angela and I sent several messages back and forth until things were, at least to me, made clear; we then stopped sending messages for a while. That is, in e-tribes, members only need to engage directly in metacommunication when "mismatched interpretations or misunderstandings . . . interfere with mutual engagement," but e-tribal communication calls for more direct and frequent clarification, given the nature of computer-mediated communication.[42]

As I mentioned earlier, Watters and his friends would often get together at "the biggest apartment or most centrally located home, where the group naturally gathered."[43] Yet, as I have argued, Watters assumes a geographical locality and proximity of the urban tribe, which does not integrate into the theorization of the e-tribe; consequently, we must look to benefits from the community of practice approach. In a community of practice, "There is no place . . . designated 'the periphery,' and most emphatically, it has no single core or center. Central participation would imply that there is a center (physical, political, or metaphorical) to a community with respect to an individual's 'place' in it."[44] In other words, when discussing the e-tribe we need not focus on the physical location or definition, but the metaphorical location in cyberspace, as I have done to this point. Now, I will turn to the political aspects of the e-tribe.

Group Politics

The last major similarity of the community of practice and the urban tribe that helps in conceptualizing the e-tribe is group politics. Here, politics involves not only who is allowed to participate in the group, but also to what extent an individual is allowed to participate within the group. At any given moment in the urban tribe there is a single core group, and Watters observed that some "groups had ways of clearly stating who was a core member and who was not."[45] MySpace.com's "Top Friends" option is a clear example of this, but how those members are selected by a user requires more explanation. Lave and Wenger advise, "Because the place of knowledge is within a community of practice, questions of learning must be addressed within the developmental cycles of that community, a recommendation which creates a diagnostic tool for distinguishing among [members within] communities of practice."[46] As groups evolve over time, individual membership may ebb and flow as a member of the core group withdraws and becomes an outlier, or an outlier develops into the core group. Development into the core group is marked by "centripetal participation in the learning curriculum of the ambient community."[47] That is, by learning the participatory norms of the core group and engaging in them, an outlier may be incorporated into the core group, and failing to do so may lead to a reduced status from core group member to outlier.

Just as not adhering to the specific practices of the core group can lead to a reduced status, so too can not following the practices of the entire community lead to separation from the group, whether it be voluntary or involuntary. Thus, while there are no nonparticipants *within* a community of practice or *within* an urban tribe, there are nonparticipants *outside* the community of practice. For example, a neighborhood might have a walking group, but not every member of the neighborhood is a member of the group. The neighborhood is a community—an aggregate of individuals—and the walking group is a community defined by the practice in which they engage. Similarly, the Navy Quartermasters' community, from the earlier example, would not include Navy pilots, since pilots, while part of the same community, learn and talk differently than Quartermasters. Not only do what members talk about and how they talk about it differentiate members of one community of practice from another, but also whom the members can talk to distinguishes who is in a specific community of practice from nonmembers.

Watters relates an argument from British anthropologist Robin Dunbar to show how individuals distinguish who is in their urban tribe.[48] Drawing from his studies of primates, Dunbar maintains that primates maintain group cohesion, which is necessary for protection from predators, through grooming. Dunbar hypothesized that "humans had replaced grooming with talking—gossipy talking in particular."[49] Dunbar writes, "I am suggesting that language evolved to allow us to gossip."[50] But not everyone can gossip with everyone. As examples from military units suggest, the range "of participants" could be anywhere from 106 to 224, but generally "150 was the maximum size at which a group might maintain adherence to its rules solely through the use of peer pressure."[51] Thus, nonmembers of an urban tribe or community of practice are those who reside outside the limits of peer pressure.

A frequent posting on MySpace.com bulletin boards is critical of users who have hundreds of thousands of friends, who are not typically seen as friends but just as the harvest from attempts to gain as many friends as possible. Many of these profiles with hundreds of thousands of friends are not genuine profiles. For example, *Star Wars'* Yoda has a profile with 10,317 "friends," and his profile claims, "Friends I seek, Friends." There is also a profile for "God," who has 6,137 friends, whereas J.J. from the 1970s television show *Good Times* has 7,180 friends and his profile is nothing more than popular lines from the show such as "Dy-no-mite!" Obviously, these profiles are fictional ones, but many celebrities including popular musicians have their own profiles with thousands of friends. Nevertheless, many actual users who represent themselves have e-tribes of 25–250 friends.

Watters contemplates why urban tribes and similar groups had escaped recognition despite their size and ubiquity, and Dunbar offered the answer, "they would escape the notice of others because the very thing that bonded them—the use of gossip—was all but meaningless to those not in the group."[52] Furthermore, "If grouping through gossip was instinctual, then it made sense that we needed no lessons to behave in this manner. . . . these groups would naturally form around us, no blueprint necessary. We were doing what came naturally."[53] In contrast, the community of practice engages in discourse and activities (i.e., their "practices") that are specialized to their community and are capable of being publicly identified as being different from those of other communities.

Politics does not exist solely between two groups but also between the group and the larger structure under which the group operates. Wenger claims a major precept of a community of practice is joint enterprise, which comprises not only the personal and interpersonal notions of members but also the instrumental aspects. These aspects affect all communities of practice, which are "not self-contained entities. They develop in larger contexts—historical, social, cultural, institutional—with specific resources and constraints."[54] E-tribes operate within the limits of MySpace.com, and MySpace.com operates within the limits of the Internet. Each level creates specific restraints on what is allowed. For example, MySpace.com allows members freedom to design their profile in any manner they wish, but each profile contains the basic components: pictures, communication tools, comments, blogs, and general information about the individual. More specific restraints exist for other social networking Web sites, such as facebook.com, that require a verified e-mail address from a recognized high school or university. Nevertheless, while e-tribe members are restrained by conditions of MySpace.com and other Web sites, e-tribe members are able to operate quite effectively under these mild constraints.

Joint enterprise does not only focus on the relationship between e-tribe members and the webmasters of MySpace.com, but also focuses on the relationships between members within individual e-tribes. Wenger claims there must be mutual accountability, including for "what to talk about and what to leave unsaid . . . what to display and what to withhold."[55] On MySpace.com members can communicate in two ways: publicly through posting comments and posting to the bulletin board or discreetly through private messages, which operate as an e-mail system within MySpace.com. Many of the social networking sites explicitly prohibit posting pornography; however, many members will publicly post compromising or embarrassing pictures of friends, which may be technically allowed by MySpace.com but not necessarily approved by the member's friend, resulting in a contentious situation. One reason for this conflict is that rules governing conduct between e-tribe members are not explicitly delineated. As Wenger writes, "While some aspects of accountability may be reified—rules, policies, standards, goals—those that are not are no less significant. Becoming good at something involves developing specialized sensitivities, an aesthetic sense."[56] Thus, deciding what is posted publicly and what is discussed via private messages is a joint enterprise that is communally negotiated.

Summary and Conclusion

This chapter sought to theorize the nature of e-tribes as they exist on MySpace.com by relying upon Lave and Wenger's community of practice and Watters's urban tribe. I have argued that the community of practice approach and the theoretical framework of an urban tribe possess numerous similarities such as participation, definition, and group politics. Examining these theoretical similarities, and acknowledging that a community of practice and an urban tribe are not synonymous empirically, allow for the identification of the electronic tribe. Specifically, the focus of the urban tribe is geographic, whereas the community of practice is broader in scope, which allows for the recognition of an e-tribe that is not bound by geography. On the other hand, the community of practice approach focuses on relationships between masters and apprentices in learning, whereas the urban tribe addresses relationships between peers and near-peers in gossiping. While examining the assumptions of Lave and Wenger, as well as the assumptions of Watters, to identify the e-tribe, I must also recognize the assumptions of this chapter.

Throughout this chapter, I have referred to e-tribes existing on social networking Web sites, which are composed of tribal members on computer networks, but I have also held e-tribes to be a means of communication of gossip. When exploring an e-tribe in terms of "a more tractable characterization" of interaction, an e-tribe can be understood as a process and a phenomenon. Like an urban tribe, an e-tribe is a phenomenon comprising real individuals who operate through electronic mediums such as MySpace.com on the Internet from computers. On the other hand, akin to communities of practice, e-tribes are defined as a process of interaction and dissemination of gossip. These definitions, however, are not mutually exclusive. Without individual e-tribe members, there cannot be interaction, and without interaction, there can be no tribe, whether it is electronically or locally connected. When theorizing social network Web sites as a site for e-tribes, it is imperative to recognize that they are manifestations of urban tribes that are widely dispersed across massively diverse geographic locations and connected through specific practices, which differ based on the community—specifically the particular social network Web site and more generally the restraints and freedoms of the Internet. That is, there are e-tribe communicators and e-tribal communication.

As I began this chapter, I claimed that distance is often an impediment to relationships. Relationships, both platonic and romantic, often suffer more the greater the distance between individuals. However, social networking Web sites are potential sources of tribal interaction that maintains the urban tribe electronically, the form of urban tribe I have held to be an e-tribe. Angela is now in Texas, Lyndsay is in Oklahoma, Rachel is in Indiana, Tom is in Chicago, I am in Denver, and Brahm is in Fayetteville. Certainly in a few years' time, the cities we are all in will change, but that will not affect us as long as the possibility of electronic tribal interaction is possible and we engage in that interaction. We have all formed new urban tribes at our new homes—in Chicago, in Texas, in Oklahoma, and in Denver—but when we do move away from those places, from those urban tribes, we will not leave our new friends behind as long as there is the e-tribe.

Notes

1. Edward T. Hall, "A System for the Notation of Proxemic Behavior," *American Anthropologist* 65 (1963): 1003–1026.

2. Ethan Watters, "In My Tribe," *New York Times Magazine*, October 14, 2001, pp. 6, 25.

3. Ethan Watters, *Urban Tribes: A Generation Redefines Friendship, Family, and Commitment* (New York: Bloomsbury, 2003), p. 57.

4. "MySpace Gains Top Ranking of U.S. Web Sites" (Reuters News Service, July 11, 2006), http://today.reuters.com/news/newsArticle.aspx?type=technology News&storyID=2006-07-11T154250Z_01_N11382172_RTRUKOC_0_US-MEDIA-MYSPACE.xml (accessed July 21, 2006).

5. Watters, *Urban Tribes*, p. 23.

6. Ibid., p. 39.

7. Ibid., p. 46.

8. Ibid., p. 44.

9. Ibid., p. 27.

10. Penelope Eckert, "Communities of Practice: Where Language, Gender, and Power All Live," in *Language and Gender: A Reader*, ed. Jennifer Coates (Oxford: Blackwell, 1998), p. 489.

11. Ibid., p. 490.

12. Ibid.

13. D. Edwards, review of *Situated Learning: Legitimate Peripheral Participation*, by Jean Lave and Etienne Wenger, *British Journal of Psychology* 84 (1993): 554–555; Edwin Hutchins, review of *Situated Learning*, by Lave and Wenger, *American Anthropologist* 95, no. 3 (1993): 743–744; Elana Joram, review of *Situated Learning*, by Lave and Wenger, *Applied Cognitive Psychology* 7, no. 1 (1993): 88–90; Eugene Matusov, Nancy Bell, and Barbara Rogoff, review of *Situated Learning*, by Lave and Wenger, *American Ethnologist* 21, no. 4 (1994): 918–919; Chris Street, review of *Situated Learning*, by Lave and Wenger, *Mentoring and Tutoring* 11, no. 1 (2005): 151–153.

14. Jean Lave and Etienne Wenger, *Situated Learning: Legitimate Peripheral Participation* (orig. 1991; reprint, Cambridge: Cambridge University Press, 2003), p. 77.

15. Ibid., p. 80.

16. Watters, *Urban Tribes*, p. 6.

17. Lave and Wenger, *Situated Learning*, p. 42.

18. Watters, *Urban Tribes*, p. 22.

19. Lave and Wenger, *Situated Learning*, p. 109.

20. Ibid., p. 99.

21. Ibid., p. 80.

22. Ibid., pp. 36–37.

23. Mark Granovetter, "The Strength of Weak Ties: A Network Theory Revisited," *Sociological Theory* 1 (1983): 201.

24. Watters, *Urban Tribes*, p. 51.

25. Granovetter, "The Strength of Weak Ties," p. 202.

26. Watters, *Urban Tribes*, p. 106.

27. Etienne Wenger, *Communities of Practice: Learning, Meaning, and Identity* (Cambridge: Cambridge University Press, 1999), p. 73.

28. Watters, *Urban Tribes*, p. 37.

29. Wenger, *Communities of Practice*, p. 74.

30. Ibid.

31. Ibid.

32. Ibid., p. 76.

33. Ibid.

34. Ibid., p. 77.

35. Ibid.

36. Lave and Wenger, *Situated Learning*, pp. 64, 101.

37. Ibid., p. 98.

38. Watters, *Urban Tribes*, p. 57.

39. Wenger, *Communities of Practice*, p. 83.

40. Watters, *Urban Tribes*, pp. 7–8.

41. Wenger, *Communities of Practice*, p. 7.

42. Ibid., p. 84.

43. Watters, *Urban Tribes*, p. 46.

44. Lave and Wenger, *Situated Learning*, p. 36.

45. Watters, *Urban Tribes*, p. 51.

46. Lave and Wenger, *Situated Learning*, p. 100.

47. Ibid.

48. Robin Dunbar, *Grooming, Gossip and the Evolution of Language* (Cambridge, Mass.: Harvard University Press, 1996).

49. Watters, *Urban Tribes*, p. 66.

50. Dunbar, *Grooming, Gossip and the Evolution of Language*, p. 79.

51. Watters, *Urban Tribes*, p. 68.

52. Ibid., p. 69.

53. Ibid.

54. Wenger, *Communities of Practice*, p. 79.

55. Ibid., p. 81.

56. Ibid.

CHAPTER 6

Don't Date, Craftsterbate: Dialogue and Resistance on craftster.org

TERRI L. RUSS

My name is Terri and I'm a craftaholic. Miscellaneous crafty items have taken over my office, displacing those trivial things like books and journal articles. Stuff that most people consider garbage is squirreled away in my inspiration closet—with just a little bit of duct tape, that empty Triscuit box could be turned into a cute purse. Yards of fabric spill off of my bookshelves, covering the beads that I stopped counting when I reached five thousand. I lust over the Janome Memory Craft MC 4400 sewing machine and have fully rationalized the $1,500 cost as a sound investment in my future. Until just over a year ago, I lived a double life—serious scholar by day and mad crafter by night. Despite my advanced degrees, I never found a way to explain how my love for a traditional feminine art meshed with my postmodern feminist sensibility. All this changed, though, the night I stumbled upon the craftster.org (Craftster) Web site and realized that I wasn't alone in my crafty obsession.

No Tea Cozies without Irony

One night during the summer of 2004 I decided that I must expand my repertoire of craft skills and teach myself how to make purses. The fact that I didn't own a sewing machine and hadn't touched one since my junior high home-ec class was no deterrent. I jumped online and searched for patterns or other how-to information. Along with a plethora of helpful tips, I found a virtual fix for my crafting addiction. Five hours later, after overdosing on inspiration and explanations, I set out to find a hardback book that could be turned into a funky yet functional clutch purse and made plans to purchase a sewing machine the next day.

Launched in August 2003, Craftster is a "repository for hip, crafty, diy (do it yourself) projects."[1] The site was created and is still operated by Leah Kramer, a part-time multimedia programmer and self-proclaimed craft addict. Since its inception, twenty-one craftsters have added their volunteer services to regularly assist in various aspects of the site's operation and maintenance. Craftster's goal is to provide an organized and easily searchable forum for "people who have crafty urges, but who are not excited by cross stitched bunnies and crocheted toilet paper cozies."[2] Many outsiders still associate crafters with the grandma who knits hideous sweaters and then guilts her grandchildren into wearing them. Crafts themselves are commonly assumed to be the stuff of little old ladies or preschool pastimes and are thought to be the useless and ugly tchotchkes that litter the shelves of thrift shops.

Craftster is not the only online craft forum aimed at the young hipster crowd; it is, however, decidedly different in appearance, form, and content. Other craft forums provide a free-form or blog-form approach to craft tips and discussion. While these sites may provide a multitude of useful and interesting entries, they are usually presented in a haphazard manner. Craftster attempts to transcend this free-form model by providing a more structured and organized forum. At this time, there are over 51,500 separate posts, with more added daily. These are housed within twenty-one major categories that include crafting topics like: purses, clothing, jewelry, and knitting. Other major topic areas include less crafty diy pursuits such as: crafting for good/evil, cooking tips, and miscellaneous topics. Members can post completed projects, ask questions about future topics or techniques, comment on existing posts, or simply lurk and look. Searching through these categories, one finds myriad options, with everything from how to make a bracelet out of pop tabs to what kind of yarn is best to use while learning how to knit. Unique among the Craftster posts are the tutorials, or "tutes," provided by members. In a Craftster tute, members share detailed instructions, often with step-by-step pictures, on how to make the item in question. These same members then respond to questions, provide clarifications, and encourage others to try to make their own version of the project.

Since its initial launch, Craftster has expanded to over forty thousand members, with approximately one thousand new members joining each month. Within the first year, Craftster became a full-fledged virtual community, and its popularity increased to the point that managing the site switched from being Leah's side project to a full-time job. Harold Rheingold asserts that a virtual community develops "when enough people interact for long enough with sufficient feeling to form webs of personal relations in cyberspace."[3] Even though they lack a physical presence, virtual communities provide us with a sense of belonging that often seems to have disappeared in the postmodern world. We turn to virtual communities to connect with like-minded others and escape from the harsh realities of our everyday lives—with a few clicks we can escape—at least momentarily. In the virtual community we can be whoever we want to be whenever and however we want.

One of the appeals of virtual communities is that we control when we want to be a citizen of them. In the 24/7 world of the Internet, our virtual communities are always there waiting for us. Likewise, if we tire of the community we can choose never to visit again—to deny it the privilege of our citizenship. I can't ignore my campus community, refuse to participate in it, or pretend to be too busy without facing immediate and possibly severe sanctions. I am in the campus community in a physical sense, so my presence is known to and expected by others. The lack of physical presence in the virtual community creates a lower sense of responsibility. Because I can't be seen and because I can mask my identity, I can come and go as I please without fear of sanction.

Craftster is clearly a virtual community by Rheingold's standards; however, it is not just any virtual community. Craftster members share a love bordering on addiction of all things crafty that exists even before they join the community. As Craftster Moi[4] explains, "I feel that there is not only a shared interest with other Craftster members, but a whole freaky DIY vibe that we share." This "freaky DIY vibe" has helped turn the Craftster community from virtual community to *virtual tribe*. Greg Leichty defines a cultural tribe as an "interpretive community that shares a particular bias."[5] Mihaela Kelemen and Warren Smith point out that tribes "reflect our will to live."[6] In other words, tribes are a community *plus*, with the plus being a certain bias or Weltanschauung that keeps members bonded to each other. For the Craftster tribe, this bias is embodied, at least in part, in its mission statement:

> Special emphasis is placed on projects that involve recycling, reusing and repurposing existing objects. The thinking is that whenever an object can be reused rather than buried in a landfill, it's a worthy venture—not to mention an interesting challenge![7]

As a tribe, craftsters view the world and everything in it as potential. The latest Miu Miu dress is not something to be purchased, but a challenge to figure out how to re-create it for a tenth of its original cost. All of those free AOL CDs cluttering the desk drawer are votive candleholders in waiting. All they need is to be melted, molded, and embellished with glitter. Guitar picks become jewelry, cassette covers become journals, and juice pouches become purses. For the Craftster tribe, everything can turn into something better with just a little creative enhancement. The tribe lives to craft and crafts to live.

Living to craft may be the initial factor that brings individuals to the Craftster Web site. Once there, a second component helps to reinforce the sense of tribal belonging, though. Craftsters enact a high level of responsibility to each other and to Craftster. As Jane Jane observed, "from bunnies to skulls, from beginners to seriously skilled, from 12 year olds to 200 year olds, from those with little or no formal education to PhD—all are considered valid as posters." Noticeably absent from Craftster are flaming posts, in which individuals are personally and vehemently attacked. This is not to say that Craftster is some sort of technological utopian tribe where everyone is happy and smiles all the time. Members regularly disagree with each other and express divergent opinions. On occasion, a moderator will need to post a gentle reminder to members that the purpose of the forum is for crafts and craft-related discussions. When discord does occur, it is generally handled with a strong sense of care and concern for the other. Examining these interchanges further, it becomes apparent that craftsters do more than simply post words in the cold, distant world of the Internet; they also engage in dialogue to a degree usually thought impossible to achieve online.

Crafty Hipsters Share Clever Ideas

In recent years, dialogue as a concept and term has been watered down and overused to the point where it is usually thought to be synonymous with everyday conversation. However, as Nicholas C. Burbules highlights, "dialogue is not something *we do* or *use*; it is a relation that *we enter into*."[8] Conversation, or merely talking with another individual, does not make a dialogue. While conversation is an inherent part of dialogue, individuals participating in dialogue engage with each other at a higher emotional and interpersonal level than that which occurs in everyday talk. As an area of study, dialogue comprises two schools of thought—the prescriptive, based on the work of Martin Buber, and the descriptive, based on the work of Mikhail Bakhtin.

Dialogue, according to the *prescriptive* view, is a way of being with another. It is an ideal to be achieved through ethical interaction with others. The goal is to transcend our usual way of relating to others as partial beings (I-It) and instead relate to them as whole beings (I-Thou).[9] To relate to each other on the I-Thou level, we must "withhold nothing" and give all of our self.[10] We must accept the other as is without attempting to impose our will or desire on her. Instead of focusing on ourselves or our own interests, we allow her to be as she wishes to be. While the true Buberian I-Thou relationship is achievable only in a spiritual sense, it still remains something that we should strive for in all relationships.

Dialogue in the *descriptive* school is a way of talking with another. It is a "pervasive, defining feature of humanity that simply needs to be identified and accurately characterized."[11] According to Bakhtin, "to be means to communicate," meaning that we live through our communication with others.[12] Bakhtin's focus is on the "answerability" that we owe to others and to ourselves.[13] When we participate in dialogue, we engage in responsive understanding in which each side responds to and interacts with the other, while maintaining its own integrity. For Bakhtin, dialogue occurs as a product of the interaction of our language and the context in which we speak. When I participate in dialogue, my utterance enters the metaphorical space between you and me, where it combines with your utterances. Even though I speak the words, they gain relational meaning only through your hearing them and combining them with your words. Our dialogue, then, is not my words or your words, but our words, intermingling and combining.

The descriptive and prescriptive approaches to dialogue provide a nice, concise method for us to study it; however, dialogue as a lived discourse is not so neatly and easily categorized. With this in mind, I approach the study of dialogue using elements from each school and consider dialogue itself to be a relational discourse involving commitment and openness to each other and to the self. When we enter into dialogic relations with another, we share more than mere facts with that person, we also share elements of our self. Through dialogue we enter a dialogic space and together create and re-create a meaningful discourse. The dynamic of dialogue is not polarized and focuses on "collaboration instead of opposition."[14] A successful dialogue "involves a willing partnership and cooperation in the face of likely disagreements, confusions, failures, and misunderstandings."[15] Dialogue allows for the tension of disagreement, and from within this discord, "common understanding [or] resolutions may be created that could not have been foreseen."[16]

When we participate in dialogue, we invest emotionally in the other.[17] This emotional factor, when present in dialogue, helps bind us to the other and moves us closer to relating to each other on the I-Thou level. We enact concern for the other and try to understand the dialogue from her point of view. We listen closely, ponder what she says, and respect her opinion to a greater extent than in everyday conversation. Through enacting concern, we begin to invest in the other and take the time to genuinely communicate with her. In dialogue, we work to remain true to our thoughts and convictions, while allowing the other to do so as well. We must take the risk that for the dialogic moment the other will suspend judgment and that beyond the dialogic moment she will maintain our secrets. Not only must we value the uniqueness that the other brings to the exchange, but we must also express a love for her that creates a sense of expectation that keeps both of us coming back for more. We see in dialogue the possibility of reaching new heights and greater understanding of our individual self and of the other. We don't abandon dialogue when the going gets tough or discord and conflict enter the scene.

When we achieve dialogue with another, it helps us develop our sense of self, our identity: "I am conscious of myself and become myself only while revealing myself for another, through another, and with the help of another."[18] Our dialogue develops so that "what I say arises as you and I genuinely relate to one another."[19] Dialogue occurs when we allow all of our self to be in the moment with the other. We stop trying to seem like something that we are not. We put aside all of those *shoulds* and face games and be just as we are. When we achieve this level of dialogue, we enter into dialogic relations that take on lives of their own, moving "beyond a particular point" such that "no one may be consciously guiding or directing it, and the order and flow of the communicative exchange itself takes over."[20] From this we learn that "dialogue constitutes a relation in which spontaneity and creativity are possible. In the to-and-fro of exchanged comments and response, dialogue builds upon itself to reach new and unexpected results—and this can give us pleasure and delight."[21]

Since online communities are virtual communities with no real physical presence, achieving dialogue would seem to be a difficult or impossible proposition. Member identities are usually masked through the use of screen names that may have little or no resemblance to the individual behind them. Since presence is virtual, not physical, individuals can be whoever they want. Men can be women. Young can be old. Conservative can be liberal. This ability to mask the self at will changes the usual dynamic of interpersonal communication and is one of the many reasons why flaming occurs. With the mask of screen names, social decorum and rules of conduct are often forgotten or pushed to the side. Despite these same limitations, dialogue regularly occurs on Craftster.

What Have You Crafted Lately?

To study the dialogue on Craftster, I analyzed posts in at least five topics from each category in order to obtain a holistic understanding of the site. Additionally, in January 2005, I turned to the Craftster community for input on why they return to Craftster. I posted four questions that generated a total of sixty-three responses through both regular posts on the site and personal messages or e-mails to my private account.[22] To illustrate my analysis, I have chosen examples that display the emotional care that allows dialogue to develop.

My discussion is framed with Burbules's "Three Rules of Dialogue": participation, commitment, and reciprocity. Though labeled "rules," these components act more as norms or expectations of successful dialogue. Referencing Ludwig Wittgenstein, Burbules positions these rules as "signposts, indicating a general direction," that leave open for each individual the possibility of negotiating how that direction is pursued and allow for a "diversity of approaches."[23] We enact and expect these rules intuitively. No one has spelled them out for us. Through our past experiences of dialogue, we have learned them. All three rules interact with each other, and any dialogic exchange will contain elements of each. For purposes of clarity, I keep them separate with the understanding that any one discussion may contain elements of the other rules as well.

Participation

For dialogue to occur, there must be *participation*, or opportunities for "engagement, questioning, trying out new ideas, and hearing diverse points of view."[24] All concerned individuals must have the option of participating in the dialogue without coercion or force. With full participation, individuals can raise any topic that is important to them and others can challenge it, raise questions, or even agree with it without fear of the dialogue breaking down.

Participation is evident throughout Craftster posts such as this typical crafting question from Kittycatalina:[25]

> After watching my baby throw his blocks with alarming velocity, I have decided to craft up some soft blocks out of felt. I'm planning on adding the alphabet, and thought some cute appliqués would be nice too. Problem is, I'm stuck on a few letters. I've polled the friends and family, with some good ideas, but non crafters think it's a breeze to appliqué complicated illustrations (Jungle? Noodles? Where would I even start?). Anyone got some ideas for J or N that would render themselves well in appliqué felt format?

Kittycatalina's question elicited numerous prompt suggestions. In addition to providing lists of possible items for the letters, members also discussed possible ways to portray the suggested items. A representative example is this one from Bond Girl: "For the J for Jelly you could just have the shape of the jelly when you take it out of the mould. By the way I'm Australian so when I say jelly I mean jell-o—I think! *confused* It might work in a bright red or something." Some posters provided detailed responses like Bond Girl; however, many more provided only one or two possible words. All responders, though, were welcomed into the dialogue and allowed to participate as they saw fit.

Equal participation in a discussion about felt baby blocks is rather easy to do, since the topic is the type expected on the site. However, this same level of participation is evident in more difficult and surprising topics such as the "Embarrassing woman-ness question" thread initiated by Aly 421:[26]

> Ok . . . this is uber embarrassing but when i get my period, i have to poop a lot. and not always regular poop . . . the muddy waters kind . . . i also get REALLY bad cramps. worse than when i was younger. so, i was wondering if anyone has heard of this or has any super cramp remedies?

When I first happened upon Aly 421's post, I was a bit surprised, since Craftster is a craft forum and her question seems rather far removed from the world of crafts. However, the fact that she feels comfortable enough to ask such a question demonstrates the depth of emotional trust and availability of full participation enacted on Craftster. Even though Aly 421's question differs from the usual business of crafty discussions, it is not dismissed as off topic, nor is Aly 421 flamed for raising such an uncomfortable topic. Her question was quickly addressed with posts such as these:

> Kitchwitch: "Aly: nothing to be embarassed about I also have the 'runs' when I get my period. My groin-o-cologist says that this is quite common. . . . Just drink a lot to keep yourself good and hydrated. As for the cramps. If they are laying you up for a day or two, see your doctor. She might prescribe a painkiller or recommend you go on the pill—sometimes that helps lessen the effect of menses. It worked for my sister . . ."

> Sagethyme: "I read recently that whatever it is that makes the blood thin (it's mostly mucous, you know) also can get in the intestine and make the bowels thin and mucousy, too. So that's normal . . ."

In addition to providing practical advice, Kitchwitch and Sagethyme express a deep empathy and concern for Aly 421. They reassure her that she is "normal" and that her situation is "quite normal."

One of the most surprising developments of this thread was the response of a male member, since the majority of craftsters are women. In a rather long post SnailMaleRaftCraft also expressed empathy for Aly, "Whatever you lot [of] lasses do, I hope it works. I dread to think what it must be like." He reassured her, "And it's not embarrassing, it's natural." Finally he provided suggestions such as exercise and application of heat based on advice from his "mum who used to work in the medical practice and has plenty of books on cramps." SnailMaleRaftCraft's comments were equally welcomed into the dialogue, despite his lack of personal experience and different gender. This type of nondiscriminatory and open participation is encouraged throughout Craftster and is one of the things that helps to maintain it as an environment where dialogue is welcome.

Commitment

The rule of commitment concerns the "pursuit of intersubjective understanding, which may or may not result in agreement."[27] When commitment occurs in dialogue, each individual joins with the other without losing any aspect of her individual self. To be successful, commitment must be threefold—to the dialogue, to the other, and to the self.

Commitment to dialogue on Craftster is especially apparent when difficult issues are raised, as in the following thread from Miscellaneous Discussions entitled: "Funny present, or sick? (Birthaids!)":[28]

MADness 323: "Alright, so, my sister was talking about how one of her new friends, whom she barely knows, came along one day and said, 'My birthday is Friday! Get me something, k?' and that got her thinking, what would be a good present for people you don't really know? Or who are hard to shop for? Something really original and funny . . . and of course, she asked me what I think. Which was a bad idea, because I tend to have a sick mind. my idea, Birthaids. A vial of fake . . . bodily fluids . . . with a label saying 'AIDS'. I KNOW. It's sick. and wrong . . ."

Not surprisingly, many subsequent posts expressed disdain, such as this from Smarmyclothes: "hmmmm . . . i'm going to say that this is not funny. i don't mean to rain on your parade or anything, but i just don't think that aids is something people will find funny and i don't think it's something to treat as a joke." However, other posts were more supportive, such as this from Era Vera: "Ha, I think it's funny. And I wouldn't be offended." In keeping with the nature of this being a crafting Web site, a few individuals provided helpful tips: Kirbay831: "Maybe instead . . . get lil jars and put plastic babies in . . . along the theme of 'Give a friend a fetus' . . . less likely to get in trouble, less offensive, more funny?"

In the face of a highly controversial and potentially offensive topic, all of these posts remain true to the dialogue. Clearly, with an issue like this, individuals are going to have strong opinions that would make it easy to either ignore the topic and move on to something less controversial or to respond with some sort of flaming attack. However, even those individuals who are offended or differ in opinion allow for all avenues of dialogue to occur.

Yet another unique facet of the dialogue on Craftster is the commitment that members enact over time. One of the most popular posts is for the *Jordy bag*, a tutorial for how to make a basic square-bottom purse.[29] Originally started in January 2004, the thread is still going strong and boasts nearly 900 responses and over 175,500 views. Additionally, the main thread has spawned a number of related threads that present alternate versions of the original design. Throughout all this activity and time, the original poster, Jordy, has demonstrated commitment to the dialogue by continuing to respond to questions and offering general comments.

Reciprocity

Since dialogue occurs in relation to an other, it must occur with a sense of reciprocity, or a "spirit of mutual respect and concern, and must not take for granted roles of privilege or expertise."[30] The rule of reciprocity asserts that while participating in dialogue, we must be willing to give as we take so that the relationship does not become fully one-sided. Just as we have a desire to speak, so too do we have a responsibility to listen and respond.

Reciprocity is apparent throughout this discussion of copyright and copying other works.[31] The thread began with this series of questions from YYZ:

> What can/do you do when something original you made to sell is clearly being copied by someone who is profitting from making something afterwards practically the same (I mean undeniably copied, right down to the size, pattern and colour)? Without getting into patents and nastiness, what can be done? Is it something you just accept? Do I have the wrong attitude about it? I am in no position or frame of mind to bring in legal measures, but damn it feels rotten to be in such a situation.

Maintaining the integrity of an original design is of pivotal importance to people who create—especially since many of them rely on their talents as their primary means of support. At the same time, copying original designs is inherent in the Craftster mission. The tension created by these two competing views could, and in many cases would, preclude the enactment of reciprocity. However, the following post does a good job of achieving balance:

> LRS: "As a crafter, I copy and I know people copy me. . . . If I come up with a way to turn yesterday's newspaper into a prom dress (no! I haven't done it), I expect to see it everywhere next year. The way to get the most value out of an innovation is to hit the market hard and fast with it. Your goal is to get your name on it, so that people want the genuine article (like Jordy's bag). If it's good, it will be copied. Chances are, someone will even improve it. That's life!"

As these two examples demonstrate, the dialogue revolves around how to protect your original design, knowing that it will inevitably be copied. In her response and based on her own experiences, LRS could dismiss YYZ's concerns. Instead and in the spirit of reciprocal dialogue, she provides practical advice and comfort.

Scream-a-little expressed different sentiments with a bit more of an edge:

> i'm one of those [people] that take the backside of copyright infringement . . . it's out of control . . . everyone is fighting for their penny of the share . . . to be honest, it's now at a point of ridiculous . . .

Later in her post, she presented an interesting and important analogy:

> i belong to a writing group where we share poetry & short stories . . . some of the [people] copyright each piece that they write . . . i refuse too . . . i honestly believe that takes away some of the originality and the essence of the work . . .

Even though Scream-a-little shares a more cynical perspective on the role of copyright, her comments still allow for divergent approaches. She adds a new twist to the dialogue without shutting it down. Because participants enact reciprocity like this, the dialogue continues to grow and expand, which adds to the overall discussion.

Uncork the Possibilities

Ever since my initial stumbling upon the Craftster site, I have felt welcomed by the tribe. It is comforting to know that I am not the only one channeling the "freaky DIY vibe" and that the vibe is not wrong or weird. This same vibe that helps transform Craftster from virtual community to virtual tribe also facilitates the development of dialogue throughout the site. Repeatedly, I have heard from members that the DIY aspect of the site is what first attracted them to Craftster, but what keeps them coming back is the care and concern, the feeling that they are part of something larger than just another online community.

Through this dialogue, the Craftster tribe resists the dominant norm of crafting as that thing that grandmas and toddlers do. As Craftster continues to grow, more enriching dialogic possibilities develop as well. For example, a fairly recent addition to the site is the "-alongs"—sewalongs, beadalongs, writealongs, embroideralongs, and quiltalongs. During the -along, members work on the same project and provide assistance and support to each other along the way. Any individual -along allows for questions on technique, materials, or anything else related to the project to be answered by others working on the same project. There is no limit on skill level, so many members wishing to learn a new technique use the -along to learn from more experienced members. Craftsters are also beginning to enhance their virtual tribe with the creation of actual tribes. Across the country, members have participated in Craftster get-togethers, where they meet up to communicate and craft together. Moving from the virtual world to the real world, the tribe continues the dialogue initiated on the Web site and further spreads the message of no tea cozies without irony.

Notes

1. "About Craftster.org" (craftster.org), http://www.craftster.org/about .html (accessed June 10, 2007).

2. Ibid.

3. Harold Rheingold, *The Virtual Community: Finding Connection in a Computerized World* (London: Secker and Warburg, 1994), p. 5.

4. All quotes from the Craftster site are referenced by the chosen screen name of the member quoted. I have attempted to remain true to the poster's original grammar and spelling, making only those changes needed to provide greater clarity and understanding.

5. Greg Leichty, "The Cultural Tribes of Public Relations," *Journal of Public Relations Research* 15, no. 4 (2003): 278.

6. Mihaela Kelemen and Warren Smith, "Community and Its 'Virtual' Promises," *Information, Community & Society* 4, no. 3 (2001): 374.

7. "About Craftster.org."

8. Nicholas C. Burbules, *Dialogue in Teaching: Theory and Practice* (New York: Teachers College Press, 1993), p. xii. Emphasis in original.

9. Martin Buber, *I and Thou* (orig. 1937; reprint, Edinburgh, Scotland: T & T Clark, 1999), p. 58.

10. Ibid., p. 23.

11. John Stewart and Karen Zediker, "Dialogue as Tensional Ethical Practice," *Southern Communication Journal* 65, nos. 2/3 (Winter 2000): 225.

12. Mikhail Bakhtin, *Problems of Dostoevsky's Poetics* (Minneapolis: University of Minnesota Press, 1984), p. 287.

13. Mikhail Bakhtin, *Art and Answerability* (Austin: University of Texas Press, 1990), p. 2.

14. Bruce Hyde and Jeffery L. Bineham, "From Debate to Dialogue: To-

ward a Pedagogy of Nonpolarized Public Discourse," *Southern Communication Journal* 65, nos. 2/3 (Winter 2000): 212.

15. Burbules, *Dialogue in Teaching*, p. 19.

16. Hyde and Bineham, "From Debate to Dialogue," p. 212.

17. My discussion here is based loosely on Burbules's discussion (*Dialogue in Teaching*, pp. 35–46) of the emotional aspects of dialogue. Burbules identifies six emotional factors in dialogue: concern, trust, respect, appreciation, affection, and hope.

18. Bakhtin, *Dostoevsky's Poetics*, p. 287.

19. Abraham Kaplan, "The Life of Dialogue," in *Communication: A Discussion at the Nobel Conference*, ed. J. D. Roslansky (Amsterdam: North-Holland, 1969), p. 98.

20. Burbules, *Dialogue in Teaching*, p. 21.

21. Ibid., p. 50.

22. The posted questions are:

1. What keeps you coming back to Craftster?
2. What is it that makes Craftster unique or unlike other online communities?
3. When you think of Craftster, what do you think of?
4. Are there any parts of Craftster that you think deserve special attention? Of course I'm also interested in anything else that you have to say—or add.

The original post can be found at: "Please help with Craftster article" (craftster.org, January 19, 2005), http://www.craftster.org/forum/index.php?topic=23046.0 (accessed June 10, 2007).

23. Burbules, *Dialogue in Teaching*, p. 79.

24. Ibid., p. 80.

25. "A is for apple, N is for ?" (craftster.org, August 2, 2005), http://www.craftster.org/forum/index.php?topic=46191.0 (accessed June 10, 2007).

26. "Embarrassing woman-ness question . . ." (craftster.org, April 17, 2005), http://www.craftster.org/forum/index.php?topic=32317.0 (accessed June 10, 2007). Since the original writing of this chapter, this thread has been removed from the Craftster site by the original poster.

27. Burbules, *Dialogue in Teaching*, p. 80.

28. "Funny present, or sick? (Birthaids!)" (craftster.org, October 1, 2005), http://www.craftster.org/forum/index.php?topic=56075.0 (accessed June 10, 2007).

29. "Jordy Bag—Square Bottomed Lined Bag Tutorial" (craftster.org, January 10, 2004), http://www.craftster.org/forum/index.php?topic=32204.0 (accessed June 10, 2007).

30. Burbules, *Dialogue in Teaching*, p. 83.

31. "When copycats profit . . ." (craftster.org, January 25, 2004), http://www.craftster.org/forum/index.php?topic=1969.0 (accessed June 10, 2007).

CHAPTER 7

Guild Life in the World of Warcraft: Online Gaming Tribalism

THOMAS BRIGNALL III

Introduction

Massively multiplayer online role-playing games (MMORPGs) enable an unlimited number of people to simultaneously play, interact, and socialize in an evolving virtual world by means of the Internet.[1] MMORPGs are distant relatives of paper-and-pencil role-playing games such as Dungeons and Dragons and multiuser domain/dungeons (MUDs). One of the latest MMORPG games, World of Warcraft (WOW), has a large fan base and is the current sales leader among MMORPGs. According to Blizzard Entertainment, on the first day of WOW's release, it sold an estimated 250,000 copies and over 200,000 players created accounts.[2] In June of 2005, over 2 million paying subscribers were playing WOW.[3]

I became interested in studying hard-core online MMORPG players (those who play at least thirty-five hours a week) after reading about Everquest players getting married, failing classes, and experiencing marriage problems.[4] One parent attributed her son's suicide to Everquest.[5] I decided to study Blizzard's WOW because the release was near the end of the fall semester, and I would have all Christmas break to play uninterrupted. The opportunity to conduct a participant-observation at the beginning of a MMORPG's release was an opportunity to watch the social evolution of the game unfold. I focused the study exclusively around hard-core players and the frequency of tribalistic behaviors. From my preliminary research, hard-core players are the driving force behind the creation and sustained popularity of complex MMORPG communities. I also chose hard-core players because it would be difficult to observe players who were not consistently online, or who were less likely to make frequent or significant contributions to the WOW social structure.

Literature on Player Motivations

Richard Bartle suggests that there are certain types of people who are attracted to playing online role-playing games.[6] Nick Yee believes Bartle's motivation types overlook the complexity of individuals by excluding overlap in motivational characteristics, changes over time in the players, or game situations.[7] According to Yee, a better way to understand player motivations is to view them as flexible components rather than fixed types. Yee expanded Bartle's preliminary model and empirically tested the model via player surveys.[8] Yee classified MMORPG player motivations on five components: socialize, achieve, explore, escape, and grief.[9]

Socializers are attracted to the elements of socialization in an MMORPG. Achievers like to meet goals, accumulate items, and/or are interested in the accumulation of power. Explorers are driven by game mechanics and understanding everything about the game. Escapists use the game for stress relief, to escape their everyday world, and/or to role-play different identities. Griefers like to manipulate, dominate, exploit, deceive, annoy, and/or taunt people. They are interested in causing as much chaos as possible. Each individual player has a score for each component, and a researcher can approximate what parts of an MMORPG appeal to the player. A player can have overlapping motivations, scoring high on several components. Yee believes these five components are a starting point to understanding player motivations.

Online Communities' Propensity for Tribalism

One can argue that online communities are not alternate realities but new tribes. Online communities offer individuals the ability to find and interact with people who share a common identity, often amplifying tribalistic behavior. The validity of declaring that Internet interactions amplify and foster tribalism depends on the definition of tribalism utilized.

One definition of tribalism is the occurrence of groups and subgroups within existing social structures that divide into smaller subgroups, or tribes.[10] Tribes frequently form because of the desires of members to be among others with shared identities. One of the criticisms of the effects of tribalism, so defined, is it detracts from the unity of the general population. Further, because of the breakdown of the general population into smaller, more isolated groups, tribalism frequently creates inner struggles, competition, and an us-versus-them mentality within a civilized society. Eventually, various tribes within the social structure become openly hostile toward other tribes.[11] Those critical of tribalism frequently view civilization as the cure for tribal feuding, where tribes dissipate and are replaced by citizens with one shared common identity.

Primitivism is a philosophy in which individuals promote a return to humanity's social roots. Primitivists believe civilization is the primary threat to the future of humanity. Philosophers like John Zerzan and Daniel Quinn believe the solution to the problems wrought by civilization is the pursuit of New Tribalism.[12] The New Tribalism movement revolves around what Quinn sees as the defining characteristics of tribal life: openness, egalitarianism, and cooperation.[13] Quinn argues civilizations replaced tribalism with hierarchalism, which works for rulers and the wealthy but does not work for the masses who are ruled.

Zerzan argues that humanity's fall from grace started with the embrace of symbolic culture.[14] Culture is not the great emancipator of humanity. Language, numbers, art, and music are simulacra of reality. Technology is not a neutral tool; instead, it reinforces the basic values of the social structure. Zerzan contends the solution to humanity's problems is the rejection of civilization, signs, technology, and materialism and a move toward New Tribalism.

Although Zarzan and Quinn reject technology, they still use it. Quinn rejects the supposition that New Tribalists who use forms of technology such as Web sites are hypocrites.[15] Quinn argues that those who are truly concerned about the world must use technology in order to spread New Tribalist ideas. People can use technology to learn that the source of their exploitation is technology and civilization. Eventually, when people are enlightened, they will abandon technology and civilization.

Another perspective is that MMORPG communities may facilitate the development of a neotribalist movement. There are authors who believe the Internet may help flatten hierarchies, dilute the power of traditional elites who monopolize information, permit new and interesting forms of community, make citizen activism easier and more effective, and encourage a generally self-reflective society.[16] Internet technology is the great emancipator of a neotribalist movement.

Signs and Simulacra

Peter Berger and Thomas Luckmann argue there is a tie between social realities and the creation and interpretation of signs and sign systems.[17]

Signs and sign systems have little inherent meaning outside of the collective social understanding of a particular group. Berger and Luckmann believe individuals understand signs and sign systems by engaging in everyday activities. Because all human activity is subject to habitualization, any action repeated frequently becomes a ritualized pattern. Once a person attaches a pattern to a sign in order to understand and label it, a person can reproduce, discuss, and teach it, and incorporate it into the social structure's common sign system. The sign or simulation acts as a stand-in for the original.

Some theorists are concerned about the role of signs and simulations used to explain original behavior patterns, events, or locations. Jean Baudrillard argues that simulations are "the generation by models of a real without origin or reality: a hyperreal."[18] Simulations no longer try to imitate, duplicate, or parody the original. Instead, simulations are the substitution of the signs of the real for the real. All interactions within a simulation reinforce the consumption of objects. Gilles Deleuze contends not all simulacra are copies in search of being an equivalent to the original.[19] Often the simulacrum becomes an entity creating a new space for the simulacrum's own proliferation, undermining the distinction between copy and model. A simulacrum's resemblance to the original is similar to mimicry in nature. A praying mantis that mimics a leaf does not wish to become one with the leaf. It engages in mimicry to kill and consume prey.

Methods

I conducted a participant-observation study of hard-core WOW players. During the study, I conducted informal interviews exclusively with thirty-four hard-core players. The study spanned approximately fourteen weeks. At one point, for eight weeks straight, I played the game ten to fourteen hours every day so that those I was observing would view me as a hard-core player.

Each time there was a break in game play I took field notes of my player interactions, common themes, and game observations. When I stopped playing for the day, I summarized the day's field notes. I maintained confidentiality because all players in WOW are anonymous. I never revealed my identity or the existence of the study to other players. When I studied or talked to anyone, I referred to the player in my notes by his or her screen name. I did not include in my notes any events or information that could be attributed to one particular individual.

I ordered the field notes chronologically, with the date, time, and place on each entry. I split the field notes into five categories: direct observation, inference, analysis, informal interviews, and personal information. I entered each category of notes into separate sections. The separation of inference from direct observation notes allowed me to distinguish my observations from my interpretations. I entered my field notes and interviews into the computer program Hyper Research. I then compared and contrasted the separate data sets and coded the data based on common occurrences, themes, and interview responses.

The Importance of Time

Time spent playing WOW was a dominant and important attribute of hard-core players. Within a week, hard-core players quickly separated themselves from the casual players. Twenty of the players I interviewed reported playing five to six hours a day on weekdays and at least ten hours a day on weekends. Fourteen of the players reported playing between eight to ten hours a day. Several of the players reported that on occasion they played the game for twenty-plus hours straight.

When I asked players how they could spend so much time playing WOW, the most frequent reason reported was being a student on Christmas break. Other reasons included underemployment, sparse homework, being a college dropout, and playing WOW at work. Two players told me they had taken vacations in order to play the game uninterrupted. When discussing time spent playing WOW, hard-core players often conveyed their respect for other hard-core players. For some hard-core players, playing more than thirty hours a week was a sign of a player's commitment, dedication, and reliability.

The Social Aspects of WOW

When I asked players their thoughts regarding the social aspects of WOW, twenty-five of the thirty-four reported they preferred socializing in WOW to offline socializing. Reported reasons included a feeling of strong friendship, group unity, the ability to role-play an alternate identity, hanging out with people who had similar likes, social anonymity, and the ability to ignore disliked people. A majority of hard-core players reported living in isolated areas with a limited potential for finding friends. A common response was it was easier to meet people in WOW. A few reported they had recently moved and did not know anyone. WOW was a way to hang out with their old friends. Several players reported they felt more important in the game, they were able to freely express themselves, and friends online often understood them better than their offline friends did.

When I asked the players if their social lives had changed since they started playing WOW, a few said no. The majority commented that WOW had become, for the time being, their primary source of socialization. Frequently, players insisted that WOW took the place of other leisure activities like watching television or playing other video games. Several of the players insisted WOW was a passing phase and they would eventually quit. After the first month of WOW, it was common for players I observed to express to others how they were spending too much time playing the game and would eventually quit the game.

Several players reported meeting people offline whom they first met via the game. They told me they went to dinner, parties, and movies. In a few cases, players reported they "hooked up" with other players to engage in sexual activities. One player quit playing WOW because their partner left them for another person the partner met online while playing WOW. Some of the players reported they were losing track of their offline friends. Three of the players told me their spouses were getting frustrated with the amount of time they were spending playing WOW. Three of the players I interviewed informed me they could no longer play WOW because they were flunking high school.

Examples of Tribalism and Neotribalism

Based on my observations and interviews, there were frequent instances of tribalistic behavior within WOW communities. WOW's rules and social dynamics made tribalistic behavior hard to avoid. There are two major factions in the game, the Horde and the Alliance. These factions are at war with each other, and it is impossible to communicate with or understand what rival players say. Players join guilds for various reasons, including socialization, quest assistance, and protection from rival faction members. WOW rules encourage players to attack rival faction members whenever possible.

After a few months, Blizzard implemented an honor system rewarding players with honor points when they killed rival faction players. Everyone involved in a quest party (group) received a share of the points. Once Blizzard implemented the honor system, many players became extremely competitive. Some guilds promoted partying exclusively with guild members to maximize the accumulation of wealth, prestige, and honor points for the guild. Honor points allowed players within the guild to gain unique and powerful items.

A frequent player complaint about WOW was how cliquish some players were. There were guilds created for Christians, gays, lesbians, evangelicals, males, specific age ranges, playing styles, and various in-game races. As the game progressed, several guilds (including mine) fragmented or folded. The player who started the first guild I joined left the guild, as did most of the hard-core players. The most common reason reported for leaving the guild was a desire to associate with players who had shared identities and playing styles. The player who created the guild claimed he/she no longer wanted to deal with the frequent guild problems. He/she reported having to constantly break up fights between friends in the guild. Playing with offline friends created too many occasions where feelings were hurt. A majority of the hard-core players who left the guild reported resenting other guild members. They believed some guild members did not contribute enough to the guild, complained too much, acted juvenile, or did not play WOW seriously. Some of the breakaway members asked me to join them because they viewed me as a player who took WOW seriously.

Player Cooperation

While I observed many examples of factionalization and lack of player cooperation, I witnessed and experienced numerous examples of player cooperation. A majority of the WOW players I interviewed reported they played frequently because of the feeling of group unity, friendship, cooperation, and accomplishment. Some of the players I grouped with promoted unity among faction guilds and actively argued against faction infighting. They believed there was a need for cooperation to successfully fight the rival faction. Frequently, I encountered parties that consisted of members from various guilds because they thought guild rivalry was a waste of time.

In the beginning, I relied on the assistance of my guild members. Within a few weeks, however, I started partying predominantly with three players from other guilds. Eventually, this new group developed into my primary source for assistance. We exchanged items and helped each other with quests. I started to "feel" a close bond developing among us. These players "felt" like my closest friends. For example, in WOW level 40, players can buy a mount. A mount allows a player to travel rapidly, and if another player does not have a mount, it is impossible for the mountless player to keep up. When the members of my group reached level 40, they all bought mounts. I was short of money, and it would have taken some time before I could afford a mount. In an amazing example of altruism, without my asking, one of the members gave me enough money as a gift to buy a mount. The level of group unity, cooperation, and trust made playing the game more enjoyable.

Based on previous MMORPG experience, some hard-core players did not join guilds. One player told me he/she wanted to avoid the guild social politics that he/she encountered while playing other MMORPGs in the past. Many of the players who were unwilling to commit to a guild chose to play with a core group of other players. I partied on several occasions with one group where none of the members belonged to a guild. When I asked the group why they were not part of a guild, they told me they did not want the responsibilities or problems that came with guild membership. It was better for them to work together and avoid any formal structure. Absent guild membership constraints, all were free to do what they liked.

Player Motivations, the Social Structure, and Tribalism

Yee's study[20] accurately reflected many of the reported reasons why the players I interviewed played WOW. The motivational components for numerous players I observed appeared to fluctuate constantly. Many functioning guilds met their demise because of fluctuating player motivations. Tribalistic restructuring of guilds occurred as players desired to separate from players they disliked and no longer thought could help them achieve their goals. The frequent abandonment of one group for another resulted in a social environment conducive to a form of neotribalism.

The structural environment of WOW seemed to cultivate some of the negative aspects of tribalism such as quick judgments, stereotyping, and prejudicial behavior. The lack of a shared system of signs, the ease of avoiding others, and the competitive aspect of the game facilitated the quick judgment of others by many of the hard-core players I observed. The WOW world contained what some might argue are prejudicial overtones. The female characters had exaggerated proportions and tighter-fitted clothing. Players could type the command "joke," and their character would tell a joke. Some of the jokes for female characters were sexual in nature (specifically the undead female I played). The Horde race had trolls with Jamaican accents; ogres that danced like MC Hammer; and bull-looking Taurens that lived in tepees and displayed several cultural characteristics resembling "Native Americans." The only choice of skin color for the human, dwarf, and gnome races was white.

Prejudicial conversations were commonplace in WOW. Some players talked about "raping female enemy characters," or emulated sex with the corpses of dead female enemies. Frequently the chat channels were teeming with racist comments. There also seemed to be a propensity for quick judgments. Frequently, Horde players perpetuated the myth that most Alliance members were teenage jocks, griefers, and unintelligent. While many players told me "it is just a game," the conversations about rival faction players frequently were hostile and extremely personal.

Another aspect of WOW that may promote negative tribalistic behaviors is the lack of repercussions and social responsibility within WOW. A player can incessantly taunt and harass someone he or she does not like, and that is an acceptable part of the game. When I asked players how they dealt with people they did not like, they reported they kicked them out of the party and ignored them. I found that the most effective way of dealing with players I disliked was to ignore them. In WOW, a player can add someone he or she dislikes to an ignore list, after which a player will no longer see communications from the individual he or she wishes to ignore.

Not all aspects of WOW were negative. Several guilds frowned on prejudicial behavior. Not everyone used prejudicial language, and my guild kicked out players because of their continual offensive behavior. Many of the top-ranked guilds helped new members rise in level quickly, and promoted the notion that guild members must share everything. I encountered players who were altruistic, helped newer players complete quests, and shared everything with their companions. The camaraderie among many of the players I met made it difficult for me to quit the game. The game was highly addictive, and I enjoyed my overall experience. Debatably, there are positive and negative aspects of most social environments.

Conclusions

Virtual worlds are not free from real-world stereotypes and prejudices. Stereotypes and cultural identities follow players into the game. Anonymity allows individuals to avoid the negative consequences of being prejudicial to other players. According to Blizzard Entertainment's rules on its Web site, the company enforces policies that forbid prejudicial language. Blizzard Entertainment has not published how frequently it enforces this rule. In a world where individuals can behave as they choose, and avoid people they dislike, hard-core players often employed tribalistic techniques in order to associate only with players they liked. Some groups displayed high levels of unity and cooperation. However, there were frequent occurrences of groups fragmenting into smaller subgroups. When our guild's population fragmented into smaller isolated groups, competition and resentment ensued.

Others may argue WOW's lack of social boundaries is emancipating and a positive sign of neotribalism. Why associate with others who do not share a common identity? A player who does not like another player can ignore him or her, reciprocate the behavior, go to another server, or quit the game. Players can choose to reject all social formalities with people they do not like and focus exclusively on social exchange with players of similar beliefs. What I frequently witnessed was that when hard-core players surrounded themselves with players they liked, an open, egalitarian, cooperative community occurred.

I wonder how any form of neotribalism can originate from a simulacrum, such as WOW, and inspire a cultural revolution in offline communities? Could technology and material consumption inspire individuals to give up technology and material consumption? I argue that the commodification of the Internet produces online inequalities that are central in reinforcing the offline constructs of power. From what I witnessed, the simultaneous creation and existence of utopian and dystopian tribal formations are possible. For all the positive aspects of neotribalism, there were plenty of negative. I believe many of the social components within WOW facilitated the adoption of neotribalistic behaviors by many players. There are features of WOW that are enjoyable, but as Yee suggests, individuals are attracted to different game aspects. Making friends, socializing, cooperation, and the creation of new tribes are all components of WOW. However, WOW is part of the gaming industry, and created for entertainment purposes. Make no mistake, WOW's game dynamics center around competition. Without a radical rebellion of players within WOW demanding players have the ability to cooperate and communicate with any person regardless of faction, the current game dynamics favor dystopian forms of neotribalism. Is it possible that cooperation and new in-game discourses will foster a movement among MMORPG players to get along with other players and participate in a neotribal revolution promoting the rejection of technology? Perhaps, but this seems highly unlikely given the fact that an individual must purchase a computer and software, and often pay a monthly fee, to participate in virtual communities. Instead, for the foreseeable future, from a primitivist's perspective, MMORPGs reflect and perpetuate capitalist exploitation. There are neotribalistic elements within WOW, simulacra of freedom, cooperation, war, anarchy, and rebellion. However, can simulated rebellion, cooperation, and freedom transcend cyberspace and radically revolutionize offline forms of social interaction?

To proclaim that equity comes from a structure where players must pay to participate in neotribalism seems a contradiction. One must be a capitalist in order to possess the level of economic resources necessary to support any online neotribal interactions. The United States has a capitalist economic system, so one could convincingly argue that neotribalists must work within the framework of the system they want to reshape. Asking gamers who participate in the role of consumer to simultaneously engage in and reject the technology that facilitates the neotribalistic message is a difficult paradox. I believe the game will prove too distracting to any movement toward the rejection of technology. This paradox will inhibit, not inspire, a mass movement of players adopting neotribalistic philosophies. A more likely scenario is that MMORPGs will amplify traditional forms of tribalism among some hard-core players.

The social structural dynamics of WOW allow groups to promote unity and shared identity. If what I witnessed is any indication of the majority of player social interaction experiences, MMORPGs will also amplify, among many players, a discourse of separation, competition, and antagonism against those who are different. I suppose like offline life, MMORPGs will have positive and negative impacts in shaping how players interact socially.

MMORPGs are simulacra, alternate worlds in which players can do anything they want and have a vacation from their everyday, mundane lives. If one purpose of WOW is the temporary emancipation of players from their otherwise mundane existence, and it seemingly works, what would compel them to focus their energy in creating an exciting offline life instead of playing WOW? More importantly, what does this say about the level of hopelessness some of these players feel, if in fact they play to escape their everyday life? Whether intentional or not, WOW could develop into a hegemonic tool used for the self-suppression and acceptance of one's current place in life. Why bother being proactive and attempting a radical assault on an offline lifestyle, when an individual can shoot up virtually and feel good about his or her online reality?

Is it possible that, at some point, individuals who engage in social interactions within a simulacrum identify that space as real? At what point does it become difficult for players to separate the online and offline realities? If a hard-core player role-plays a cyberbully in the game, habitually terrorizing other players, is it possible this in-game persona will project itself into offline relations? Some may argue that playing the game is catharsis, experimentation, or a relaxing diversion. After playing the game thirty-five-plus hours a week for six months, it is possible that aspects of the online persona will have an effect on the offline identity.

From what I observed, it appeared many of the players felt WOW was real. For some, the consequences of playing the game were real. Some of the hard-core players wanted to meet me offline, would talk to me about personal problems, and call me their friend. For many, WOW became the preferred space and platform for their everyday social interactions. The game was a real and important part of their life. All the players I interviewed insisted they were able to separate and manage the two realities. However, the hard-core players expressed the sentiment that WOW life was better, or at least wished offline socialization was similar to WOW's.

I believe there is a need, as with understanding any social change, to further study the impact of MMORPGs on offline behavior. I also believe it is important to study MMORPG social interactions, because the future of Internet communications may be based on MMORPG technology. People already use the Internet to communicate with friends and family, and to meet new people. Using MMORPG innovations, individuals could walk in their virtual city and talk to local clerk avatars about a product, wander a virtual library to browse through a few books before buying them, or search other cities for items they cannot find in their current physical location. People interested in finding new friends or dating could go to virtual bars where they could talk, exchange pictures, and reveal personal information to others before deciding to meet them offline.

There are obvious limitations as to how far I can generalize about hard-core players based on the methodology employed. Player anonymity may also be a potential problem, because I had to assume those I interviewed were honestly representing themselves. There is no way to tell from my research methods whether the majority of WOW players share my perception of WOW. Perhaps, a majority of WOW players thought the behavior I observed was normal. Other players may perceive the frequency of prejudicial language as part of the role-playing experience. Players choose which computer server they play on, and it is plausible that every computer server has a unique social dynamic and that my observations, experiences, and interviews were therefore unique to the server I played on. However, the results and interpretations derived from this project are similar to those of Yee's study, the discussion about game play on the WOW message boards, and conversations with other WOW players I have met since the study.[21] In the future, I will build upon the results of this study and conduct several surveys of MMORPG players, addressing specific issues I encountered in this project.

Notes

1. "MMORPG," http://en.wikipedia.org/wiki/MMORPG (accessed July 1, 2005).

2. "Blizzard Entertainment Media Alert" (Blizzard Entertainment, November 24, 2004), http://www.blizzard.com/press/042427.shtml (accessed March 5, 2005).

3. "World of Warcraft Achieves New Milestone with Two Million Paying Subscribers Worldwide" (Blizzard Entertainment, June 14, 2005), http://www.blizzard.com/press050614-2million.shtml (accessed July 11, 2005).

4. "Aranath Pops the EverQuestion: The Coupling of Aranath and Syrah Marks EverQuest's First Marriage" (IGN, December 29, 1998), http://pc.ign.com/articles/066/066251p1.html (accessed July 11, 2005).

5. David Becker, "When Games Stop Being Fun," *CNET News*, April 12, 2002, http://news.com/2100-1040-881673.html (accessed April 10, 2005).

6. Richard Bartle, "Hearts, Clubs, Diamonds, Spades: Players Who Suit MUDS" (Muse Entertainment, April 10, 1996), http://www.mud.co.uk/richard/hcds.htm (accessed July 12, 2005).

7. Nick Yee, "Facets: 5 Motivation Factors for Why People Play MMORPG's" (Terra Incognita, March 1, 2002), http://www.nickyee.com/facets/home.html (accessed July 12, 2005); "Documenting Sources from the World Wide Web" (Modern Language Association, February 3, 2000), http://www.mla.org/style/sources.htm (accessed February 17, 2000).

8. Nick Yee, "A Model of Player Motivations" (Daedalus Project, March 13, 2005), http://www.nickyee.com/daedalus/archives/001298.php (accessed July 20, 2005).

9. Ibid.

10. "Tribalism," http://en.wikipedia.org/wiki/Tribalism (accessed July 1, 2005).

11. Ibid.

12. John Zerzan, *Running on Emptiness: The Pathology of Civilization* (Los Angeles: Feral House, 2002); Daniel Quinn, *Ishmael: An Adventure of the Mind and Spirit* (New York: Bantam/Turner Books, 1992).

13. Daniel Quinn, *My Ishmael* (New York: Bantam Books, 1997).

14. John Zerzan, *Future Primitive & Other Essays* (Brooklyn, N.Y.: Autonomedia, 1994).

15. Daniel Quinn, "Questions and Answers" (Ishmael Community, January 4, 2004), http://www.ishmael.com/Interaction/QandA/Detail.CFM?Record =137 (accessed June 5, 2005).

16. Lee Sproull and Sara Kiesler, *Connections: New Ways of Working in the Networked Organization* (Cambridge, Mass.: MIT Press, 1992); David Moore, "Political Campaigns and the Knowledge-Gap Hypothesis," *Public Opinion Quarterly* 51, no. 2 (1987): 186–200; Amitai Etzioni and Oren Etzioni, "Communities: Virtual vs. Real," *Science* 277, no. 5324 (1987): 295; Ed Schwartz, *Netactivism: How Citizens Use the Internet* (Sebastopol, Calif.: Songline Studios, 1996).

17. Peter Berger and Thomas Luckmann, *The Social Construction of Reality: A Treatise in the Sociology of Knowledge* (New York: Doubleday, 1966).

18. Jean Baudrillard, *Simulacra and Simulation*, trans. Sheila Glaser (Ann Arbor: University of Michigan Press, 1995), p. 1.

19. Gilles Deleuze, "Plato and the Simulacrum," *October*, no. 27 (1983): 52–53.

20. Nick Yee, "A Model of Player Motivations" (Daedalus Project, March 13, 2005), http://www.nickyee.com/daedalus/archives/001298.php (accessed July 20, 2005).

21. Ibid.; "World of Warcraft Player Forums" (World of Warcraft, July 27, 2005), http://forums.worldofwarcraft.com/ (accessed July 27, 2005).

CHAPTER 8

At the Electronic Evergreen:
A Computer-Mediated Ethnography of Tribalism
in a Newsgroup from Montserrat and Afar

JONATHAN SKINNER

Date: Sat, 20 May 2000 22:14:09 -0800
From: Geoff Dandy <dandyg@candw.ag>
Sender: owner-mni-info@troy.seeker.com
Subject: THIS IS how this news group got its name.....!
To: MNI News Group <mni-info@nationalradio.com>

For the few of you that might not know.......This News
Group that is in some circles called the "Electronic
Evergreen"......is all because of a TREE !

This little Square in the middle of the Capital City
of Montserrat.....Plymouth had a little "Square" like so
many other Towns, that was located in front of Lawyer
David Brandt's Chambers...that was a "location" that
people met and talked politics.......and all about
everything else that concerned Montserrat.

When Jenny & I moved to Montserrat just over 7 years
ago, that tree was "Knocked-Down" by Hurricane HUGO
in 1989.

But the important part of this message is that this
"News-Group" got its real name from that Park with THAT
EVERGREEN TREE on the Northern Corner.

It was THE place that everyone went to get the latest
Local News (gossip included)...and socialised.

As this is something that many people that are members of this Group...are more knowledgeable than >I <
Please guys.....share with this group of Interested people......what being there was like. Freddie...? Ashman...?

```
http://24.3.18.12/montserrat/photos/072/originalevergreen.
jpg
Blessings...

Geoff & Jenny
```

This e-mail arrived in the mailbox file held by my computer whilst I was online. When I read the message, immediately, I was back on Montserrat, back at the Evergreen, where I worked as an ethnographer, listening, recording, and joining in with the latest island gossip. I could feel the heat, smell the scent from the tree mingling with the smell of the beer bottles we all carried. With this e-mail, I was there in a flash—another flashback. These flashbacks come with the e-mails. They can also be triggered by sounds and tremors, such as when my washing machine moves onto spin cycle and the floor shakes, my pulse races in reaction to another volcanic earthquake. Seconds, or even minutes, later and I am back in front of my computer screen. Curiously, though I can prevent my e-mails from initiating these accompanying experiences, I don't.

E-mail newsgroups operate in virtual spaces, places where text-mediated interaction takes place. The above is a good example of an e-mail posting to the Electronic Evergreen e-mail newsgroup (names and addresses have been changed). This e-mail takes the form of an informal letter and is addressed to all of the members. The e-mail refers to the folk memory, and a digital photograph, of a large tree near the center of Plymouth, capital of the Caribbean island Montserrat, a town now completely destroyed by volcanic debris. It explains the informal naming of the newsgroup after the Evergreen meeting-point tree for those that don't already know. Implicit in the e-mail is a sense of group identity, a sense of community that is held by the authors of the e-mail, and that they assume is also held by the readers of the e-mail. The subject of my chapter is newsgroup interaction such as Evergreen's, and how this maintains and fosters a strong sense of community and how it splits and breaks down.

Computer-mediated Ethnography

According to computer guru Howard Rheingold, "virtual communities" are "computer-mediated social groups," "social aggregations that emerge from the Net when enough people carry on those public discussions long enough, *with sufficient human feeling* to form webs of personal relationships in cyberspace."[1] These relationships are formed and maintained in a conceptual space. These ideational groups cut across the traditional geographic, political, and cultural boundaries; the Electronic Evergreen, for example, is just such a group of "like-minded" e-mail posters and readers, a tribe linked by cognitive sympathy, empathy, and interest. They are the informants of a traditional ethnography I was conducting that went virtual. This transition from face-to-face ethnographic research to computer-mediated ethnographic research is an example that further establishes computer-mediated ethnography as a legitimate ethnographic focus, and, because it embodies the transition, this example is important because it differs from other newsgroup ethnographies, most of which concentrate exclusively upon the online.[2]

Members of the Electronic Evergreen such as the authors above, Freddie and Ashman, who are described and self-ascribed as regular readers and members of the newsgroup, and other readers known and unknown, communicate collectively—if indirectly—through their typed messages; they are members of a "virtual commons."[3] Their text-based messaging creates a narrative, or net world. Starr Hiltz, Kenneth Johnson, and Murray Turoff[4] consider computer-mediated communication (CMC) a great leveler, freeing the literate from the bonds of the body. Critics of this communication thesis—skeptics of the strength of this narrative world network[5]—have pointed out that communication through text alone reduces the coordination of communication because we have lost all nonverbal behavioral cues; depersonalized, socially and racially anonymous, or even masked communication is no substitute for traditional face-to-face (FtF) communication. Furthermore, Lucas Introna and Edgar Whitley[6] suggest that levels of obligation between CMC communicators are considerably lower than between FtF communicators: computer communication lacks background or context, what Jürgen Habermas referred to as the "lifeworld" of the utterance, and so is less binding or formal—what they create is an insincere environment, a "pseudocommunity."[7]

Similarly, there are also both advocates and critics of CMC research in the anthropological and sociological communities regarding whether CMC groups are legitimate communities for consideration or virtual spaces where participant-observation is not possible. Recently, the physical "fieldwork fetish" has come under great scrutiny by the *Writing Culture* and *Siting Culture* "new ethnographic critics."[8] The former initiated an interrogation of ethnographic literature, whilst the latter developed this into an examination of culture locations, the anthropologists' place *of* and *upon* the field. They raised the question of how anthropology might keep pace with a decolonized and deterritorialized world, one of transnational cultural flows, shifting migrations, displacements, and dislocations. This question is especially pertinent to the predicament facing the Montserrat place and Montserratian people, where multisited fieldwork may be necessary following a recent exodus from the island.

Seeking to get away from the static and worn notion of "fieldwork as dwelling," James Clifford suggests that fieldwork can be viewed as a "travel encounter,"[9] one involving displacement for the anthropologist in whatever form or fashion. Electronic travel would count, then, as a kind of *dépaysement*, notes Clifford, who goes on to cite David Edwards's traditional village study in Afghanistan, which continued into Pakistan, neighboring international refugee camps, and eventually on into distant Afghan computer newsgroups[10]—all of which was an in-depth, in-detail, and long-term ethnographic undertaking. With hindsight, Nigel Rapport argues that ethnography is processual and accumulative over a period of time, and that, crucially, the sense of displacement in the ethnographer, the cognitive and experiential, is more important than the physical.[11] It is this form of ethnographic openness that I would like to extend in this chapter, a rebuttal of recent and unexpected assertions made by prominent and progressive anthropologists such as Kirsten Hastrup and Peter Hervik (ethnographic fieldwork is experiential and performative and thus cannot be communicated in dialogue; it requires physical presence) and Judith Okely (fieldwork is a "total," unbounded experience).[12]

According to Benedict Anderson, "[c]ommunities are to be distinguished, not by their falsity/genuineness, but by the style in which they are imagined."[13] This notion of community takes us away from the type of understanding of social interaction based upon geographic area, and leans us instead toward an understanding of community as a complex of ideas and sentiments. Christine Hine rightly points out that this type of computer-mediated communication research has now moved on from an observation of how it feels like a community for its participants[14] to an examination of the ways in which that perception is created and sustained. *Contra* the claims of Ziauddin Sardar and other critics of CMC and computer-mediated ethnography,[15] I would concur with Hine's position that CMC can and does contain personal commitments, authentic identities, temporal continuities, and embedded contexts of interaction.

Newsgroup etiquette—"netiquette"—is, for some commentators on e-mail use, one of the defining attributes of community on the Internet or amongst the various e-mail groups. Netiquette reveals a communal commitment to discursive standards of behavior that reflect "real" life cultural codes and customs.[16] On the Electronic Evergreen newsgroup, all the addresses are listed in the address box, leaving members with a strong idea of themselves, all listed together in a self-constituting way. Nevertheless, the virtual ontological nature of such an organization still begs the question of what commitment is begat by such new interactions and communications where people can engage and disengage with each other with ease: "What are the consequences of differences between temporary and persistent worlds?" as Steven Jones frames it.[17] Community, I would suggest, *is* apparent in cyberspace: meetings may be temporary and dialogues fleeting and readers silent ("lurkers"), but this is also the case offline. People group together at the Electronic Evergreen, interact as a group, and think of themselves as members of a group (consider the collective nature of Geoff's general comments and appeal to other readers in the Electronic Evergreen). These group, newsgroup, or chat areas are "places" where people meet face-to-face, but with different understandings of the words "meet" and "face."[18] They make a convincing community, one worthy of investigation as an ethnographic object.

Montserrat and the Electronic Evergreen

```
I suppose like a teenager who has just developed new
cognitive skills, I thought this medium could change
the world--well, maybe the Montserrat world--that it
might empower people, a pure one-man one-vote demo-
cratic marketplace of ideas, which could help overcome
some of the hidebound secrecy of the way things are
run on Montserrat, that it might become some sort
of real virtual global village reflecting the real
'village' it is focused on.
```

This was the vision for the Electronic Evergreen expressed by the newsgroup moderator Arthur Smith in an e-mail interview I conducted with him in September 2000. Arthur was talking about 1995, when the newsgroup began to coagulate, a new medium giving on to new social possibilities and interactions, a tool with the potential to precipitate great social change through collective action. The Electronic Evergreen, however, did not turn out the way it was expected to.

Montserrat is a small British Overseas Territory in the Eastern Caribbean. Eleven miles long and seven miles wide, an extinct volcanic island, Montserrat had, up until 1995, a population of approximately ten thousand black Montserratians and three hundred expatriates. British and yet black, Montserrat is too small to have a large enough airport runway for mass tourism, but is quiet enough to market residential tourism. I was on Montserrat from 1994 to 1995, a social anthropologist interested in colonial relations between Montserrat and Great Britain, carrying out traditional participant-observation, mucking in, when, in July 1995, we were suddenly hit by waves of earthquakes. The central peak on the island suddenly started rumbling, belching out ash and sulphur; the volcano was no longer extinct. I was subsequently evacuated from the island alongside many Montserratian families and American and British expatriates. I returned to Scotland, whereupon I began writing up my doctoral thesis about life before the volcano. Because I left Montserrat so suddenly, I felt a sudden loss of community: I was desperate to keep in touch with many close friends whom I had made; news and social interaction were what I sought, especially given the natural disaster taking place.

During my time in Scotland, I came across an e-mail group under a "society Caribbean" heading. People from all over the world were "chatting" to each other about Caribbean issues and topics, from hanging to reggae, slavery to tourism. Naturally, some of the conversation turned to what was happening on Montserrat: in the early days, there was a lack of information, both on and off the island, as to what was happening (where the safe areas were on the island, who had been evacuated, and who was still living in an enclave in the north of the island). For information, Montserratians and expatriates on Montserrat posted to the group press briefings from the government in Montserrat, reports from the local radio there, and information based upon their own observations. These reports and descriptions were read avidly by Montserratians living off island, by "friends of Montserrat," and other concerned members of the public who sometimes replied with news cuttings typed in from their local or national papers. I might, for example, type out part of an article from *The Times* and send it to the moderator for passing on. After a short period of time, we began to build up a simple and fast exchange system for pooling information, hearsay and trivia, gossip and chat about Montserrat. Though the communication was asynchronous, less than immediate in the speed of the interaction, space/distance was compressed to such an extent that it became practically immaterial: technological globalization allowed those in the United Kingdom or other islands off Montserrat to feel that they were there with their community, particularly with the regular and repeated nature of the correspondences. For me, it felt as though fieldwork had never finished.

Several months into the volcano crisis on Montserrat, and there were a dozen or so members of this Caribbean newsgroup, regularly posting messages, dominating the topics of conversation. Because we were not interested in reading or responding to talk about tourism or problems on other Caribbean islands, it was suggested that we break off from the "soc.Caribbean" pages to create our own autonomous newsgroup. Approximately twelve addresses were linked together by Arthur Smith, a British academic living in Canada who had spent twelve years living on Montserrat and still felt an affinity for the place and the people. Arthur was our online moderator: he organized and ran the new newsgroup, adding addresses to the list. He also had the interesting idea of adding details about the people he added to his mailing list, such as where they came from, even who they were related to if they were from a Montserratian family. And he asked the new members to introduce themselves to the group. During the early days of the growth of the newsgroup, most of the people from the island knew (of) each other; certainly many of the surnames were recognizable, and distinctively Montserratian in many cases. The number of the group rose to fifty in the first two months of operation, and conversation moved to island gossip interspersed with news information about the volcano. We were an interesting group: many of the members knew each other from real time, whether Montserratians on the island or Montserratians off the island, tourist visitors, or concerned researchers like myself—any doubts about identity were more personal and existential than projections upon other members. Our Electronic Evergreen newsgroup had the advantage that it was able to move quickly past the pleasantries of salutation—though it remains a place to continue old relationships as well as to forge new ones ("how can I get in touch with Daisy Irish who I last saw in St. Patrick's before it was evacuated?"; "does anyone have the address or telephone number for Gabriel Harris?"); a chance for extended long-term field research for myself; an addictive opportunity to reiterate and substantiate the self for others.[19]

I have remained a member of this newsgroup ever since its inception in July/August 1995, following the debates, the flow backwards and forwards of messages: the poetic, political, existential, religious, antagonistic, placatory, the news article cuttings, and the personal rants about slavery and racism. Every day, there are at least five or six postings; several thousand over the years, postings consisting of people talking about identity, their roots, and their lost lands. One poignant observation about members of the group evacuated from the village of St. Patrick's, just before it was destroyed by the volcano, was that they still lived a village life with each other on the group, writing to each other in dialect and swearing as they usually did (until other members objected on the grounds that it was too exclusive between them, and too offensive for those who could follow the communications). These computer-mediated interactions were by no means moderated by the computer medium or the filter of the moderator (though many were aware that their e-mail could be copied and reposted): moderation came from a consensus of opinion against irrelevant and unacceptable postings, repeated discussion strings (one reason why Freddie Ashman may not have taken up Geoff and Jenny's e-mail), and continually provocative postings (ironically, this is one of the symptoms of newsgroups where people are more likely to write in opposition, and to remain silent when in agreement, thus giving rise to the erroneous perception of a newsgroup always in dispute).

As the volcano covered the island, destroying village after village, plot of land after plot of land, there arose a discussion that set expatriates—who felt that they were or had been at home on the island—against Montserratians. Expatriates felt that they were being excluded from the group, that some of the references to color were racist against them (substantiating Kolko, Nakamura, and Rodman's thesis about the embedded nature of Internet communication, one which repeats offline categorizations such as race).[20] Cudjoe Bailey, a local political figure, is a vociferous and antagonistic character. I was working with him on Montserrat before I left. Cudjoe, as he is known to most, is an anticolonialist, a nationalist, and a Pan-Africanist who wants Montserrat to become a black-only socialist island. Cudjoe is eager to engage with Montserratians, expatriates, and tourists to point out the continuing slave position of the black man in the Caribbean and further afield, slaves to the white man, to capitalism, and to colonialism. On several occasions, Cudjoe offended members of the Montserrat newsgroup, provoking public replies to "get professional help." Sanctions against Cudjoe's behavior (ignoring his postings; deleting his postings unread; setting up a "kill file" to automatically delete them; publicly and privately replying to his postings in the same style; or deliberately trying to take the upper hand by replying more formally) were less damaging than the police and colonial harassment he regularly faces on the island.

At present, Cudjoe is no longer a member of the Electronic Evergreen. Since the mid-1990s, the newsgroup has grown to several hundred members, more and more unknown people, some unwilling to introduce themselves; and many of the postings have become business adverts, simple requests for information about tourism to the island, or basic questions about the island that have been covered extensively in previous discussion threads. One spat in 1998–1999 between Cudjoe and an expatriate became particularly bitter and led to Cudjoe's departure: Cudjoe received and reposted some personal replies to his public messages. In other words, his comments to the entire group were replied to at just his own address, but his reply to the unfortunate expatriate was just as public as his original posting. This was tantamount to reading private mail, according to the expatriate writer and many Evergreen readers—a serious and deliberate breach of netiquette.

```
Via MNI-INFO......................................................
i don't make threats. i say what i have to say in the
EE public forum. Any of you have anything to say about
what i say. Place it here. On the EE. Send it to my box
and I'll place it up for you
Cudjoe Bailey

---- Original message ----
From: Alison Graves <a2032@starway.net>
To: Shaka zulu <zulu@hotmail.com>
Sent: Friday, May 21, 1999 21: 23 PM
Subject: Re: Fw: the infamous "LIST"

Your threats don't bother me at all. I sent it to you
privately out of respect to you. It is obvious that you
don't respect anyone unless they agree with you. To me
that shows what little class you really have...
>
zulu wrote:
>>
>>Via MNI-
INFO.............................................................
>>This is a message to all expats. Any time you all in-
vade my mail box
```

```
>>privately from now on I'm going to post it.
>>i could na really care less what your opinions of
me are.
>>i say what i want, and where it drops it drops. Who
like it fine. Who
>>don't also fine.
>>Cudjoe Bailey
```

Such exchanges polarized the regular contributors to the newsgroup into two loose camps or tribes: those who supported Cudjoe, or thought that anyone had the right to voice his or her views in the group, no matter the consequences; and those who thought that Cudjoe should stop posting such critical, aggressive, and controversial "letters." This exchange, amongst others, resulted in Cudjoe leaving the Electronic Evergreen and setting up his own Montserratian newsgroup where discussions could be made by "descendants of the Afrikan Holocaust" about discontinuing colonial mentalities, bureaucracies, and practices without incurring cursory "white comments" such as the above, or the following message from Jim Delvechio:

```
Oh Cudjoe,
Get a life, why don't you. I am so sick of hearing
you whine all of the time. So there were injustices
in the past. There will continue to be injustices in
the future. Why can't you let go of the past and em-
brace the present? I can assure you, you would be a
much happier person, instead of the unhappy one that
you are now.
```

At the end of May 1999, Cudjoe sent his "Last Post" message—"It is full time that Montserratians assert themselves here. The EE is for Montserratians to address issues that relate to every aspect of OUR lives. Past, Present and Future"—inviting "Montserratians to join an alternative Email group called MNIFuture," a collection of Montserratians who can "begin a dialogue about the things WE consider relevant without Outside interference or objections."

In this way, Cudjoe and several other members left the Electronic Evergreen, founding a rival newsgroup, a select grouping of Montserratians who subscribed according to Cudjoe's approval—an action that met with many criticisms about censorship on the Internet from indignant members of the Electronic Evergreen, the same censors of Cudjoe! Individual comings-and-goings are expected on the Internet, but groups' fissionings and fusionings—communication breakdown, vicious tribalism echoing offline social patterns—were not expected or anticipated. Significantly, in this newsgroup case study, some members can maintain allegiance in both newsgroups. Daniel Riley was one member who left for Cudjoe's service, leaving the following anti-tourist/expatriate parting shot in his wake (it includes a dig at the island's controversial tourist slogan):

```
I will join Mr Galway's group because I know he and
others will engage in serious discussion about the fu-
ture of Montserrat from a Montserratian perspective.
A lot of people on the EE only care about Montserrat
from the perspective of 'Montserrat, The Way It Used
To BE' For them, a few cosy bars and restaurants, some
exotic cheeses and Diet Coke from Rams, perhaps a golf
course and access to their villas would be quite suf-
ficient. [...] I look forward to a group where I don't
have to put on gloves when I write, for fear of upset-
ting someone's sensibilities.
```

In our e-mail interview, Arthur and I discussed and lamented this bifurcation of the Montserrat newsgroup. For us, the action highlighted the difficulty involved with applying the "community" label to fluid e-mail newsgroups. Yet we both felt that this was an example of community breakdown.

Computer-mediated Community and Tribalism from Montserrat and Afar

```
Dear Group,
At the suggestion of some folks in the EE group, I went
into Plymouth with my wife yesterday to try and find
some way to get a slip, seed or something from the
Evergreen tree that could be raised up and eventually
planted in Little Bay or some appropriate park that
generations to come could sit under....

George Jackson
```

The Electronic Evergreen split around the members' ideas of "Montser-ratianness" (blackness) versus expatriacy (whiteness). This e-mail news-group case study shows that there is a physical undercurrent to virtual relationships, an embeddedness of relations, which goes against Gid-dens and Castells's characterization of modernity as disembedded.[21] Per-ceptions of physical identity are maintained and symbolically brokered through many e-mail interactions; if anything, Montserratian versus outsider perspectives about events on Montserrat were intensified by the Electronic Evergreen exchanges: *in-your-face* exchanges which could have retained some context of diplomacy and decorum, some social signs and cues to read for any irony, were lost to the invasive *in-your-head* reading affronts on the self.

In both settings—face-to-face and computer-mediated—communi-cative interaction is virtual and imaginative (in Anderson's sense of the word), as well as part physical: there is the presence of computers and sentences, and the presence of bodies and speech, all of which are re-ceived and interpreted internally. Internally, the words and reactions are added to memories and senses of identity and feelings of belonging. On Montserrat, "belonger" is the local term for one associated with the is-land. It is more than a legal status granted to outsiders after marriage to a Montserratian or several years' residence on the island. The term is ascribed to those who have been accepted socially on the island, as members of the Montserrat "community" as it is conceived. Problems and confrontations arise when this belonger status is assumed and self-ascribed by some, actions that lead to criticism and discontent amongst others: Daniel Riley echoes Cudjoe's "Montserratian perspective," which is in disharmony with Alison Graves and Jim Delvechio and their expa-triate or North American "belonger" perspective.

The Electronic Evergreen is a community of the mind. Like all communities—part cognitive illusion and part affective delusion—it is the members' beliefs about community and subsequent community behaviors that create the community—and make it accessible for the ethnographic researcher. A community is more than a collection of in-teractions. A community is social space collectively owned and sustained by performance and practice; it is a feeling of communion; and it is in people's heads whether text-based or not. These feelings affect and alter people's behavior, their practices, and the ways in which they interact. The netiquette of the Electronic Evergreen is one key manifestation of community, the inclusive content and style of the e-mails is another. In this case study, a large proportion of the Electronic Evergreen e-mail

virtual community have a strong sense of community and nostalgia derived from their strong and long physical and emotional associations
with the Montserrat place and the Montserratian people. Members from
Scotland, Canada, England, the United States, a range of European and
Caribbean countries, and Montserrat all come together to create this
special-interest, folkloric space.

I would like to suggest in this chapter that one of the Electronic Evergreen's initial social strengths, the background knowledge and physical relationships of members with respect to other members, eventually
became one of the newsgroup's weaknesses, a centrifugal force impel-
ling it toward fragmentation. Disagreements over the Internet were exaggerated by physical identity, by embedded relations and histories, and
not just a Goffmanesque presentation of self online. Everyday expressions of opinion and identity contributed to what seemed like a virtual
polarization of the newsgroup "community," a collection of assumed
and unknown readers from Freddie and Ashman to Riley and others
such as Cudjoe.

The members of the Electronic Evergreen, a virtual tribe, created
a new home for themselves in the absence of a physical sense of place.
The evergreen tree became the label for the newsgroup, a conscious attempt to replace real activities with the virtual, a symbol of Montserrat
as people remembered and wanted others to remember: the place where
one socialized and gossiped, "limed" (hung out). The naming of the
newsgroup and Jackson's cutting from the evergreen are not arbitrary
actions. Trees have often been used to represent people and places: the
oak as an emblem for the British people, for example, and Jackson's cutting from the evergreen tree, a root from Montserrat's past. In this case
study, the arborescent root metaphor is particularly appropriate, sym-
bolizing the re-creation of the place, the people, and the time before
the volcano when interactions (and ethnographic research) were face-to-
face and not computer-mediated. Now the imagined environment and
imagined community are sustained and facilitated by Microsoft Outlook subdirectories, for me at least.

Conclusions

When Nicholas Fox and Christopher Roberts carried out their cyber-
ethnography of male GPs' (General Practitioners') online conventions
in their "*gp-uk*" newsgroup, they carefully considered the ethics of their

research and the status of online ethnographers.[22] After weighing up the pros and cons of participant-observation (to lurk as covert researchers versus the "distortion" of active newsgroup membership), informed consent (public versus private distinctions, as well as between that which is publicly *accessible* and that which may be publicly *disseminated*), and the "dis-inhibiting" effect of online communication media, Fox and Roberts surprisingly decided, respectively, to lurk as well as to contribute actively to the newsgroup for twelve months. My relationship with the Electronic Evergreen has been more immersive, traumatic, and more long-term than theirs. What began as a mutual information and support list became an extensive and divisive newsgroup over the space of almost six years. At the start, I was an active poster and could reckon to know and be known by all in the group. Once the newsgroup members swelled, my voice became one of many (I never formally introduced myself because I had always been a member, and so I may be an unknown name to new members). For me, the newsgroup has been a support group helping me to deal with my departure from the island and the culture shock of my return to Scotland. Our messages are, so I believe, public material because they are available to anyone who joins the "open" group.

I also believe that I was "hanging out" when I was on Montserrat, liming at the Evergreen; and, similarly, I believe that I am hanging out when I am online, liming at the Electronic Evergreen. In both instances, I have immersed myself as an ethnographer, a participant-observer with more than enough "sufficient human feeling"—perhaps even too much, as the start of this chapter might suggest. Clifford notes that ethnographic practice (Rosaldo's "deep hanging out"[23]) needs to change to reflect and be able to engage with the social and technological effects of the new information communication technologies (ICTs). Yet, rather than become "multi-sited," in the words of George Marcus,[24] Clifford echoes Hine when he advocates a "mobile" form of ethnography;[25] this is because multisited fieldwork is an oxymoron: it compromises ethnographic notions of "depth." A mobile ethnographic approach problematizes reality as a text account of a text-based community (both have the same epistemological basis), and the ethnographic convention of using travel to demarcate the field site; it reorients the notion of the *field as site* to the *field as flow*.

Ethnographic practice should follow these navigators of a new space. It should examine social and technological (and biological) changes, and look at the new and complex ways in which people are coming together.

Communication is taking place in new computer-mediated *forms*, with new patterns—even if the *content* is similar to the more traditional face-to-face interaction and the standard letter. New *forms* of connection with the island Montserrat are being fashioned despite the similarity of their *content* with the old. People such as the Cudjoes and the Delvechios are coming together, meeting and joining or rebounding from each other over the Internet, particularly in the newsgroups such as the Electronic Evergreen, a collection of individuals from Montserrat and afar—one tribe that went to war and became two tribes.

My brief example has been one of newsgroup communication and community. It is part of my traditional ethnography of Montserrat, which went online along with my subjects. This research had a natural development to it, responding to circumstances on the island, and the needs of a naïve anthropologist to retain a sense of connection with a place and a people. It is ethnography: descriptive and analytical writing based upon the repeated, sustained, immersive interaction and observation of individuals in league with each other, their moments of interaction, their moments of being, and their moments of difference and splitting—their tribe and their tribalism. The place Montserrat, and the people Montserratian, have changed considerably over the last ten years of my subscription to the Electronic Evergreen, as, indeed, has the newsgroup itself (now lumbering and unwieldy, it is too large to convey information quickly, to sustain dialogues among members; it now has rival newsgroups). This study was not conceived at the time of membership, but is a by-product of concern and the printing of significant—according to my judgment—messages and exchanges. Rather than sympathize with Cohen's argument about discrete fieldwork periods following discrete fieldwork periods,[26] I conclude from my fieldwork experiences that fieldwork never ceases; in this example, new and unexpected avenues of the same field of research opened up, cyberspace avenues of social life. As a cyberethnographer, I am fortunate to be able to avoid some of the old "ethnographer at home" problems because all are now equally "the Other,"[27] but it would be closed-minded of me to maintain that there are no old anthropological and sociological debates apparent in these new and open systems.

Notes

1. Harold Rheingold, *The Virtual Community: Finding Connection in a Computerized World* (London: Minerva, 1995). See pp. 1 and 5; my emphasis.

2. See Nancy Baym, *Tune In, Log On: Soaps, Fandom, and Online Community* (London: Sage Publications, 2000); and Harold Rheingold, "Community Development in the Cybersociety of the Future," in *Web.studies: Rewiring Media Studies for the Digital Age*, ed. David Gauntlett, pp. 170–178 (London: Arnold, 2000).

3. Frank Bioca, "Communication within Virtual Reality: Creating a Space for Research," *Journal of Communication* 42, no. 4 (1992): 5–22. See p. 5.

4. Starr Hiltz, Kenneth Johnson, and Murray Turoff, "Experiments in Group Decision Making: Communication Process and Outcome in Face-to-Face versus Computerized Conferences," *Human Communication Research* 13, no. 2 (1986): 225–252.

5. Sara Kiesler, Jane Siegal, and Timothy McGuire, "Social Psychological Aspects of Computer-Mediated Communication," *American Psychologist* 39, no. 10 (1984): 1123–1134.

6. Lucas Introna and Edgar Whitley, "Thinking about Obligations in Electronically Mediated Communication" (manuscript, n.d.), pp. 1–11. See p. 2.

7. James Beniger, "Personalization of Mass Media and the Growth of Pseudo-community," *Communication Research* 14, no. 3 (1987): 352–371.

8. See George Marcus and James Clifford, eds., *Writing Culture—The Poetics and Politics of Ethnography* (London: University of California Press, 1986); Karen Olwig and Kirsten Hastrup, eds., *Siting Culture: The Shifting Anthropological Object* (London: Routledge, 1997); and Akhil Gupta and James Ferguson, eds., *Anthropological Locations: Boundaries and Grounds of a Field Science* (Berkeley: University of California Press, 1997).

9. James Clifford, "Spatial Practices: Fieldwork, Travel, and the Disciplining of Anthropology," in *Anthropological Locations: Boundaries and Grounds of a Field Science*, ed. A. Gupta and J. Ferguson, pp. 185–222 (Berkeley: University of California Press, 1997). See p. 198.

10. Clifford, "Spatial Practices," 192; see also David Edwards, "Afghanistan, Ethnography, and the New World Order," *Cultural Anthropology* 9, no. 3 (1994): 345–360.

11. Nigel Rapport, "The Narrative as Fieldwork Technique: Processual Ethnography for a World in Motion," in *Constructing the Field: Ethnographic Fieldwork in the Contemporary World*, ed. V. Amit, pp. 71–95 (London: Routledge, 2000). See p. 73.

12. Kirsten Hastrup and Peter Hervik, "Introduction," in *Social Experience and Anthropological Knowledge*, ed. Kirsten Hastrup and Peter Hervik, pp. 1–27 (London: Routledge, 1994). See p. 3. See also Judith Okely, "Anthropology and Autobiography: Participatory Experience and Embodied Knowledge," in *Anthropology and Autobiography*, ed. Judith Okely and Helen Callaway, pp. 1–28 (London: Routledge, 1992). See p. 8.

13. Benedict Anderson, *Imagined Communities: Reflections on the Origin and Spread of Nationalism* (London: Verso, 1983). See p. 15.

14. Christine Hine, *Virtual Ethnography* (London: Sage Publications, 2000). See p. 17.

15. Ziauddin Sardar, "alt.civilisations.faq: Cyberspace as the darker side of the west," in *Cyberfutures: Culture and Politics on the Information Highway*, ed. Ziauddin Sardar and Jerome Ravetz, pp. 33–57 (London: Pluto Press, 1996).

16. Margaret McLaughlin, Kerry Osborne, and Christine Smith, "Standards of Conduct on Usenet," in *Cybersociety: Computer-mediated Communication and Community*, ed. Steven Jones, pp. 90–111 (London: Sage Publications, 1995).

17. Steven Jones, "Information, Internet, and Community: Notes toward an Understanding of Community in the Information Age," in *CyberSociety 2.0: Revisiting Computer-mediated Communication and Community*, ed. Steven Jones, pp. 1–34 (London: Sage Publications, 1998). See p. 4.

18. Steven Jones, "Understanding Community in the Information Age," in *Cybersociety: Computer-mediated Communication and Community*, ed. Steven Jones, pp. 10–35 (London: Sage Publications, 1995).

19. Sherry Turkle, *Life on the Screen: Identity in the Age of the Internet* (New York: Touchstone, 1995).

20. Beth Kolko, Lisa Nakamura, and Gilbert Rodman, "Race in Cyberspace: An Introduction," in *Race in Cyberspace*, ed. Beth Kolko, Lisa Nakamura, and Gilbert Rodman, pp. 1–14 (London: Routledge, 2000).

21. Anthony Giddens, *The Consequences of Modernity* (Cambridge: Polity Press, 1990); Manuel Castells, *The Rise of the Network Society* (Oxford: Blackwell Publishers, 2000).

22. Nicholas Fox and Christopher Roberts, "GPs in Cyberspace: The Sociology of a 'Virtual Community,'" *Sociological Review* 47, no. 4 (November 1999): 643–671.

23. Clifford, "Spatial Practices," p. 188.

24. George Marcus, "Ethnography in/of the World System: The Emergence of Multi-Sited Ethnography," *Annual Review of Anthropology* 24 (1995): 95–117.

25. Clifford, "Spatial Practices," p. 190; see also Hine, *Virtual Ethnography*, p. 64.

26. Anthony Cohen, "Post-Fieldwork Fieldwork," *Journal of Anthropological Research* 48, no. 4 (Winter 1992): 339–354.

27. David Hakken, *Cyborgs@cyberspace?: An Ethnographer Looks at the Future* (London: Routledge, 1999). See p. 68.

PART III

EMERGING ELECTRONIC TRIBAL CULTURES

CHAPTER 9

"Like a neighborhood of sisters":
Can Culture Be Formed Electronically?

DEBORAH CLARK VANCE

The Internet opens portals into interpersonal and intercultural relations on an unprecedented scale. Interpersonal interactions are multiplying in cyberspace, where disembodied minds meet to discuss shared interests and seek information. When such individuals interact for prolonged periods, do they begin to organize themselves socially?

The processes have been widely studied by which individuals come to see themselves as sharing an identity as they join together according to race, class, age, interests, ethnicity, religion, or ability, to name a few.[1] When an assemblage of individuals meets nowhere but on a few electronic pages, however, some may doubt that they form a group, much less a tribe or culture. Yet, looking at such a phenomenon may provide insights into the essence of culture, especially if one accepts the notion that culture is primarily a mental construct.[2]

Looking at a Web site for middle-aged women, this chapter examines how participants socially construct their experience, define themselves, and describe their communication, and seeks to determine whether such interactants can be said to comprise a culture. Interpersonal and intercultural theory about identity formation, group cohesion, and communication rules inform the study.

Literature Review

Tonnies distinguishes between society (public life) and community (intimate, private, and exclusive), which he further classifies as kinship, locality, and mind.[3] Community is often used to describe people's sense of sharing, oneness, and commonality.[4] Communication theorists commonly use the term culture to describe shared practices and identities within groups.[5] Like Tonnies's community of mind, cultures emerge among groups of individuals who share something—a sociological category (African American culture, gay culture), workplace (organizational culture), or hobby (surfer culture). This chapter prefers the term culture—"a negotiated set of shared symbolic systems that guide individuals' behaviors and incline them to function as a group."[6]

Individuals become accustomed to cultural communication patterns and try to predict others' behavior to ensure their physical and psychological safety. When strangers first interact, they focus on demographic information, then explore mutual attitudes and opinions as they work to reduce uncertainty.[7] In cyberspace the personality is fluid.[8] In this space, where physical safety is not threatened and demographic information may be lacking, does uncertainty reduction take the same form as in interpersonal encounters?

Just as group culture should be regarded as constructed rather than given, the same holds for individual identity.[9] Identification begins with imitation and derives from developing an emotional tie with someone.[10] If an individual perceives an influential person as trustworthy and of good judgment (like a parent or minister), he accepts her beliefs and integrates them into his own value system; the power source embodied in the influential person garners compliance by effecting reward and punishment.[11] Identification with such a figure begins to define belonging, as individuals adopt the beliefs and values of the group to which the influential person belongs.

Forming identity involves twin processes—perceived similarity and association.[12] Individuals seek similarity in beliefs, values, education, and social status, communicating more with others they perceive to be similar.[13] Finding that the other shares a similar attitude also leads to expectations of positive appraisals.[14]

Identification based on a common reaction to or bond with a leader or an ideology provides group stability. Outsiders can identify with group attributes if they share similar attributes, but not with other group members unless they bond with the group's leader or central tenets.[15]

Cultures interpret situations and behaviors idiosyncratically.[16] In-group meaning exchange develops into a shared epistemology: Social reality thus constructed comprises an expression of a group's, as well as each individual member's, identity. Normative rules appear necessary to group functioning: Group membership derives in part from shared symbol use, meanings, norms, prescriptions, and worldview.[17] This cognitive common ground leads to patterned behaviors which acquire values that become reinforced, resulting in some patterns being accepted and others considered deviant.[18] By identifying all tacit and explicit rules of a group, one could reconstruct its culture.[19]

Developing customs and a collective awareness of its nature helps a group stabilize and perpetuate itself. Sharing a worldview creates a feeling among members of belonging to the group as distinct from being affiliated with those outside the group, a distinction that guides social relationships.[20] Making comparisons with outgroups creates external pressure to help group members cohere. Similarly, individuals have a need to belong, which creates a symbiosis between them and their group.[21] Because group members perceive their group by its own terms, they generally tend to evaluate it as insiders rather than objectively.[22] Groups also maintain themselves using internal pressures, such as a demand for conformity. Members deviating from rules, traditions, and values may elicit scolding, punishment, or ostracism.[23] Moreover, the desire to be right is a strong motivator which can induce an individual to internalize a particular belief.[24] Because rightness would be judged in terms prescribed by one's culture, being right might equate with belonging.

Settling upon a dominant ideology occurs in a fluid give-and-take process.[25] Elites create intellectual and moral leadership by shaping reality, and their worldview comes to seem like common sense. The system of assumptions, meanings, and values that constrains society—its ideology—is impressed on cultural members by an elite, without force, by becoming produced and reproduced in group practices. In a constant struggle to shape and interpret reality, ideas, values, and beliefs are negotiated, not imposed.[26]

Researchers previously believed that identities could be set aside on the Internet, whereas now it seems that Web surfers seek to reassert themselves and their identities.[27] Still, because of the anonymity afforded by technology, Web surfers have freedom in deciding what to disclose. They may not truthfully represent their physical attributes: Without a physical presence, they may not take responsibility for their words, which some theorists fear will lead to chaos.[28] When physical reality becomes uncertain, however, individuals rely on social reality.[29]

Group behavior communicates expectations, and nonverbal language can communicate attitudes.[30] In face-to-face encounters, individuals visually absorb such information, noting facial expression, clothing, body posture, physical stature, sex, and coloring of those they encounter: Cultural values attach significance to such information. Still, many Web users represent themselves openly, since Web pages are often used to self-promote and meet others with whom to establish serious relationships. In these cases, one is interested in selling oneself and has no need to hide his or her identity.[31]

The Internet has not provided an escape from gender issues and may not be as gender-free as originally predicted.[32] Social change will probably need to occur in order for the salience of gender to disappear on the Internet.[33] However, the Internet does provide some freedom: Women on the Web can tackle issues where they have felt excluded, such as those that focus on male experience or where men dominate women's discussions.[34] Yet, some Internet sites for women are intended for marketing purposes, engineering participants' behaviors and actually limiting them despite the site's empowerment rhetoric. Such sites cannot be seen as solely for women's use nor be fully successful as communities of interest.[35] For example, Oprah Winfrey's Web site's commercial nature overpowers its community building.[36]

The Internet expands notions of community as traditionally understood in the social sciences.[37] Studies have looked at how Internet sites reinforce the identity of already established groups (e.g., Lesbians, Straight Edge [i.e., a music subculture that abstains from drugs and alcohol and promotes antiestablishment politics], female Vietnam veterans),[38] but have not examined the creation and development of a cultural identity. Can a cultural group form if members do not physically interact? This study explores whether separate, anonymous individuals who meet on the Internet are able to create a new group culture.

Method

The Internet forum I examine, Boomer Women Speak (BWS), was founded by Dotsie Bregel in 2002 as a site for women to help each other. It was envisioned as a launching vehicle for a planned anthology of stories by women born during the post–World War II baby boom, 1946–1964—"baby-boomer" women. Bregel solicited stories from writers' and Christian groups and from friends and acquaintances. This free site contained no commercial messages for two years; as the hope of publishing eluded her, Bregel began accepting some unobtrusive advertisements, such as links to Amazon.com.

I learned about the site when it started and approached it as a participant-observer, entering into most of the categories, occasionally posting topics to focus discussion on participants' values and beliefs. In 2005, I posted a notice asking for informants to answer an open-ended questionnaire about their experiences on BWS. I received sixteen returned questionnaires, six of which I followed up in personal messages, requesting more details. I also posted questions in cyber–focus groups on themes that arose in the questionnaires and received responses both on the forum and in personal messages.

Grounded theory is particularly suited to studying Internet groups:[39] I used it to locate and describe relationship patterns. In this interpretive research method, the researcher interacts with data, from which a theory emerges. The researcher incorporates into her own conceptualizations the perspectives of respondents, who perceive and interpret their and others' behaviors.[40]

Another data-gathering strategy was interactive informant ethnography. I solicited responses from five key women who have participated on the site since its inception, four of whom provided their thoughts via e-mail correspondence. I assured respondents anonymity.

Language used by members is an important indicator as to how they organize their central meanings. Using a constant comparison method of analysis, I compiled and coded data from observations, archived posts, interviews, and follow-up questions, looking for patterns and grouping responses, then soliciting more information to help hone what I had so far observed. I rhetorically analyzed archived posts, scrutinizing discussion threads that reveal participants' beliefs and values, focusing on those that garnered either the highest number or the most emotional responses. I sorted and resorted the data into categories until arriving at areas that describe what best characterizes the mindset of BWS participants.

Findings

BWS attracts and holds particular individuals—not everyone who shows up stays. One's first encounter with the site is its homepage—pale yellow background with messages in blue lettering, saying, "The intricacies of our lives can help others live, survive and thrive," "connect, encourage, support," "a place to share from the heart," "connect with other women," and "friends heal friends."

When they enroll, participants create usernames, which identify their posts. Some also create personal profiles in a specified area.

Interaction occurs on the Forums page, which is divided into separate categories—General, Family, Health, Faith, Work, Social—under each of which are subcategories—Girlfriends, Arts and Crafts, Recipes, Marriage, Children, Divorce, Pets, Caring for Parents, and so on. There are also areas for Recipes, Jokes, and discussions about Books, Writing, Careers, Homemaking, Movies, and Current Events. Participants begin specific threads of conversation under the appropriate subcategory. As one reads a posted remark under any of the categories, she has the opportunity to respond by clicking on the thread and typing a message in the space provided. Overall, participants involve each other in stories about triumphs and tragedies in their daily lives. As stories unfold, participants post suggestions, opinions, encouragement, and prayers.

Frequent discussion topics include infidelity, mental illness, and family and social relationships, often covering intimate and sometimes fantastic details of tough situations. Topics eliciting the most emotionally revelatory descriptions concern weight, self-esteem, abuse, and marital issues. In some subcategories, such as Our Bodies, Health, Children, Divorce, and Singlehood, the female body is very much present in discussions on periods, menopause, ovaries, hormone therapy, mammograms, breasts, exercise, and weight issues. The preponderance of participants appear to be middle-aged women. After sifting through, coding, and sorting, I uncovered the categories of Friendship, Ideology, Protocols, Power, and Sense of Place, the first four of which are interdynamic.

Friendship

BWS creates an emotional world many find addicting. Help, friendship, and caring provide primary reasons women participate. Members feel an acceptance and warmth at BWS not found at other sites or maybe anywhere else in their lives.

The site pitches itself as a venue for emotional support and connection. Consistent with findings of other researchers, many respondents profess that in the nonvirtual world they refer to BWS women as "friends."[41] One says she has made six good BWS friends to whom she

speaks on the phone; she even sent money to one who needed it. Participants occasionally meet in person and report back to the group about
it. Plans are currently under way by a few participants for a trip to New
York to be in the audience of the *Early Show*.

However, BWS friendships are not open to all comers. As Lana says,
"I . . . do not respond when a dialogue is in progress amongst people
who are friends, because I don't think my response would be welcomed."
Some see this mutual supportiveness as strategic: Lorraine believes that
friends post to each other and that "the most sympathetic ladies who
extend themselves to others get a tremendous response. In other words,
'you reap what you sow.' "

There is a strong sense of in-group identity. Gina advises, "Don't
pick on a Boomer Sistah—you will incur the wrath of many." Participants perceive others in BWS to be like themselves, particularly in values and worldview.

Ideology

The category Faith/Religion contains subcategories Favorite Bible
Verse, Prayer Request, and Blessings/Joys, indicating a religious bent
to the site. Bregel states that God led her to begin this site; others share
her vision. Language on BWS includes phrases with religious overtones:
"praying for you," "what God has in store," "what God wants me to do"
appear frequently. Still, many respondents say they avoid posting on religious and political topics because of the rancor they can arouse.

The overwhelming political stance expressed is support for the current Republican administration and its policies, and chastisement of
all who disagree. Political discussions often mutate into tales of being
mother to soldiers, with participants expressing pride in each other's
children for their service in Iraq, and sharing prayers for their safety.
Political discussions tend to lump together the other as "them." Participants express a strong desire to hunt down terrorists, referring to
"sheet-headed, goat-eating women abusers" as the enemy. Two women
who pled for tolerance have left the site.

Areas receiving the most responses in current events are personality-
based media stories: Participants disparage Michael Jackson as a guilty
pedophile, the runaway bride as angling for a book deal, and Terry
Schiavo's husband as after the insurance money. Posts on these subjects

echo each other in bashing the target of their disgust, helping to affirm BWS's moral stance and solidify its identity.

Health discussions reveal a pro–American Medical Association brand of care—getting the necessary tests and having the common surgeries—as opposed to alternatives such as chiropractics, acupuncture, or forgoing treatment. Having hysterectomies and oophorectomies prevails among this group, with many expressing their delight at having had surgery while encouraging others in doing the same.

Power

Even among regular users, a hierarchy exists—those closest to the tenets of the site's founder comprise a core group referred to as the clique. Linda says, "There is a clique on the Boards and everyone knows it whether they acknowledge it or not." Those who spend the most time, post the most messages, and are most in tune with Bregel's philosophy seem to dominate. Some say this clique sets the tone, sometimes having their own chat while ignoring anyone who intercedes and seeming to create rules to suit themselves. Betty, a disgruntled participant who decided to leave, complained, "If someone creates a post, everyone is expected to agree with it." Shannon, identified as part of the ruling clique, resists the suggestion that new communication rules become implemented, saying, "I'd rather be myself," indicating a lack of awareness of or concern about her perceived power.

Unstated ways exist to deal with dissent and minority voices. Ignoring posts considered uninteresting or unsympathetic to one's own beliefs and values sometimes leads the ignored to leave the site. Similarly, ignoring a particular post in a thread for the same reasons (talking over them), or starting a new topic, have the same effect of making the ignored feel rejected. Linda says that if one's opinions are obviously different, "you will be pegged and if not responded to now, forget the future!!" Shunning, whether intentional or not, winnows out members: The ignored take it personally and leave the group.

Protocols

Over time and occasionally through discussion, the group has developed protocols that seem to compensate for the lack of nonverbal cues in their communication. For example, it is felt that if someone starts a thread, it is hers, and others know they should start a new topic rather than usurp it. Posters seem to know when they breach group norms, and some may do so strategically, as in steering a discussion to safer ground (i.e., away from talk focusing on non-Christian beliefs).

A topic that frustrates members is unanswered posts. Some interpret this nonresponse as rejection, although stated reasons for not responding are time, fatigue, and lack of interest. These may be legitimate reasons, but the silence is perceived as rejection, snobbery, and disagreement. Some who object to nonresponsiveness figure that if they expect to receive support, they should be providing it now to others, even if only to say, "I'm praying for you." There is a tendency to support each other in particular ways. Maggie says about posting, "I always try to stay connected to certain people who have been very supportive of me and now are hurting or need support in some manner."

Respondents identify speaking respectfully as another protocol. Sharon says, "There is . . . a core group of women I feel very safe with here; but some . . . are leaving a bad taste in my mouth. Maybe that will change as they become acclimatized to the respectful nature of BWS." This show of respect has not always been the norm. In the first two years the most active members (the clique), who are politically aligned with each other, would pounce together on others with whom they disagreed. For example, when antiwar sentiments were expressed, the clique echoed each other in mocking the poster, telling her that if she did not agree with the policy of the United States, she should "leave it." Bregel intervened, asking posters to be civil.

A noticeable vocabulary, with often mutually affirming, congratulatory, praising language, imbues the posts. Newcomers are welcomed to "the best group of women on the Internet," a "neighborhood of sisters," a "great bunch of women with really big hearts," and the like. Members repeatedly tell each other, "I'm praying for you."

Members seem to expect discussions to unfold in a particular way and are sensitive when their expectations are not met. Barbara states, "I encountered no inappropriate language on the Website, only some malicious comments." Sometimes the presence of the clique serves to deter others from posting. However, Linda has decided that "I no longer consider my expression an intrusion. I figure if the thread is on a forum, it's for all to see/respond/express."

The women insist on maintaining a women-only site and asked Bregel to prohibit men. Man-spotting is a sport that one participant, whose stated profession is phone sex, is particularly adept at: She says she can spot a man's posts a mile away and is usually right. When I asked participants how they know if they are speaking with other women, they responded that it is by how a woman "puts her words together, her thoughts and feelings about certain things" and "by the type of writing they do and what their messages are in their stories i.e. pregnancy, menopause, body issues, etc."

Bregel enforces the protocols, policing the forums for breaches of behavior and language, even deleting less than cordial or overly profane posts. When a participant gets rowdy or is male, Bregel posts warnings, sends private messages and may ask the person to leave, blocking future posts, and deleting past ones. Generally, the women like the controls and the politeness of the group, which several say they prefer to a potential free-for-all. Linda says, "In polite society one doesn't always blurt out everything one thinks."

Sense of Place

Some of the most vivid images come from descriptions of mental pictures respondents hold of where BWS exists. Respondents project their interchanges onto a mythical living room or other "safe place" where they feel comfortable sharing intimate life stories. They describe where they see themselves chatting—sitting in a room full of overstuffed chairs, drinking herb tea, passing the box of Kleenex. BWS is perceived as a safe, nurturing place, a sanctuary, home, a safety net, where hugs are exchanged. Sharon says, "The women are nestled in my heart." One of the few African American participants says, "I felt like I belonged there from my very first encounter."

Discussion

Four of the identified categories interact closely: Friendships derive from interactions with others who express similar values (ideology) and behave in ways sanctioned by the group (protocols). Protocols and ideology are restated and reinforced, especially by active members (the clique) and the site owner, who are perceived as those with power. This all occurs in a place participants perceive as safe.

The tendency on the Internet may be for nomadic, marginalized individuals to experience fragmented identities.[42] BWS users, however, are looking for communion and invest effort into BWS, which transcends its being a public forum or interest group: It has a distinctive cultural identity. BWS displays particular values, which those who join strive to maintain. Over time, group members have solidified their bonds, occasionally banding together to chase off unwanted intruders and fortify in-group beliefs.

Although the dominant ideology derives originally from Bregel and her posted topics, members have negotiated it and emerged with a predominantly conservative Christian mainstream. By insisting that it be a site dominated by Christian women who share conservative social and political views, certain individuals have gained control in areas unspecified by Bregel but tolerated by her. Central tenets are set down and reinforced by Bregel, either by intervening, deleting posts, or banning the offending person from the site. Many participants reinforce the relationships formed on the site with private communication, sometimes doing so if they sense a friend is being attacked by a newcomer or a deviant.

The mainstream has attacked or ignored perceived others for disagreeing, for posting topics out of the mainstream, or otherwise not playing along with accepted rules—being polite, self-disclosing appropriately, not sending unsolicited Private Messages—chasing off or chastising intruders who do not properly introduce themselves or who are perceived to be male. Still, the site entertains some dissenting participants—non-Christians and political liberals—who have formed friendships and share the banter on BWS. Demographically BWS comprises women from different socioeconomic levels, countries, and mother tongues—not all are white Christian Republicans. Some enjoy these differences, saying that BWS focuses on commonalities rather than differences; others congratulate themselves on the qualities that set them apart.

It is worth noting that many in the clique have in past years been more aggressive, not been supportive of everyone, and used ridicule to impress their power. Although sometimes blind to their own dominance, these old-timers were the first to land, the most vociferous, and all in agreement, so were able both to bond and to perpetuate their shared ideology. New members face them eventually, and if they can accept their values, they remain. Some newcomers admire the banter that passes among them. Still, members who are not ideologically dominant focus on the love and camaraderie, which are compelling enough for them to stay.

The perceived safety and warmth of the group depend on the monitoring and gentle enforcement of the rules by Bregel, her monitors, and other participants. Sharon privately e-mailed me that she had felt safe until encountering a thread where a new member attempted to impose her brand of Christianity. Members often try to avoid areas and topics that get heated and send private messages to each other to complain about such negative experiences.

Where this study extends current theory on culture formation is in considering BWS's reliance on typed discourse for encouraging perceptions of similarity and discouraging perceptions of dissimilarity. Ability to skillfully encode and decode others' written messages—where nonverbals do not exist—presents an obstacle. The messages' two-dimensional nature threatens any feeling of safety and warmth. Problems occur because senders or receivers lack skill in encoding or decoding messages without nonverbals.

A lack of physical presence seems to provide few if any obstacles to the interactions. Instead, it may help those with intimacy issues who might otherwise remain silent. Also, it means that individuals who may gravitate toward others who physically resemble themselves—in age, race, ethnicity—cannot exercise the usual filtering.

A bonus is the site's noncommercial nature. Many of the participants are self-described writers, published or not, whose Web sites Bregel links to BWS. Still, one member who decided to leave said she believes BWS exists to promote individuals' books and merchandise.

Conclusion

New cultural rules are emerging on Internet Web sites, despite limitations imposed by the two-dimensional nature of communication and the missing nonverbal communication tools. Forming culture online presents opportunities: Because members cannot make their accustomed demographic sight-based predictions, they find themselves interacting with others who identify solely with similar central tenets (friends heal friends, Boomer women). There ends the obvious similarity with face-to-face encounters.

Feeling safe enough to self-disclose, a common issue interpersonally, presents a problem for some BWS participants. But unlike in face-to-face encounters, success on BWS depends on one's ability to encode and decode emotional states by written words alone, stretching interpersonal communication theories.

BWS exists almost entirely visually, through typed words and icons, supplemented by an occasional photograph and links to personal Web pages. Because this site is visible to anyone surfing the Internet, presumably it attracts those who identify with its culture in some way and are the ones to register. After their initial interactions, they may decide not to stay, like one woman who described herself as in a goddess religion and became displeased with the reaction this elicited.

Interfacing on Web sites depends on an ability to convey one's own thoughts and feelings via written words, as in letter writing. However, Internet postings are public letters written to a group, not to individuals, as one doesn't know who will read and reply to a post. Some on BWS say that they self-censor and may even be less sociable on the net than off. One's personal cognitions are at play here, exposing differences in perceptions of self-disclosure: Some may experience the Web page as a solitary individual, whereas others stress the Web's public nature.

In this study, individuals' solitary experience is apparent as they encounter each other and create a group culture. But all experience is solitary and internal. Human interactions and the creating of social structures all take place in the mind. Theories dealing with culture formations are challenged by the Internet, where the in-group consists of qualities that the participants cannot quite identify. Active participants on BWS say their site is open to all women, but some sense they do not belong. More research needs to be done on perceived similarity, intergroup identification, and group formation on the Internet.

Internet technology may not cause, so much as expose processes we typically undertake—realizing our affinity, deciding whether we are in or out of a particular group, noticing the limits to which we identify. This study suggests that individuals have mistaken notions about their similarities with others—those who seem similar because of surface factors like sociographic and demographic information may not be so, and those who are similar may not be known, upsetting the usual dynamics involved in stereotyping. The reasons for defending one's group boundaries may have biological or psychological roots that are not valid in a world where technological advances allow people to form alliances without regard to physical boundaries.

Notes

1. Mark Orbe, *Constructing Co-Cultural Theory: An Explication of Culture, Power and Communication* (Thousand Oaks, Calif.: Sage, 1998).

2. Peter Berger and Thomas Luckmann, *The Social Construction of Reality: A Treatise in the Sociology of Knowledge* (New York: Doubleday, 1996); George Herbert Mead, *Mind, Self and Society* (Chicago: University of Chicago Press, 1934); W. Barnett Pearce, *Communication and the Human Condition* (Carbondale: Southern Illinois University Press, 1989).

3. Frank T. Rothaermel and Stephen Sugiyama, "Virtual Internet Communities and Commercial Success: Individual and Community-Level Theory Grounded in the Atypical Case of TimeZone.com," *Journal of Management* 27, no. 3 (May 2001) 297–312.

4. Leonard J. Shadletsky and Joan E. Aitken, *Human Communication on the Internet* (Boston: Pearson Education, 2004).

5. Gareth Morgan, *Images of Organizations* (Beverly Hills, Calif.: Sage, 1986).

6. Guo-Ming Chen and William J. Starosta, *Foundations of Intercultural Communication* (Boston: Allyn and Bacon, 1998), p. 26.

7. Charles R. Berger and R. J. Calabrese, "Some Explorations in Initial Interaction and Beyond: Toward a Developmental Theory of Interpersonal Communication," *Human Communication Research* 1 (Winter 1975): 99–112.

8. Andre Lemos, "The Labyrinth of Minitel," in *Cultures of Internet: Virtual Spaces, Real Histories, Living Bodies*, ed. Rob Shields, pp. 33–48 (Thousand Oaks, Calif.: Sage, 1996).

9. Michael L. Hecht, L. K. Larkey, and J. N. Johnson, "African American and European American Perceptions of Problematic Issues in Interethnic Communication Effectiveness," *Human Communication Research* 19, no. 2 (December 1992): 209–236.

10. J. H. Wright, "Burkeian and Freudian Theories of Identification," *Communication Quarterly* 42, no. 3 (Summer 1994): 301–310.

11. Elliot Aronson, *The Social Animal* (New York: W. H. Freeman, 1995).

12. Wright, "Theories of Identification."

13. E. M. Rogers and D. K. Bhowmik, "Homophily-Heterophily: Relational Concepts for Communication Research," *Public Opinion Quarterly* 34, no. 4 (Winter 1970–1971): 523–538.

14. Michael Sunnafrank, "On Debunking the Attitude Similarity Myth," *Communication Monographs* 59, no. 2 (June 1992): 164–179.

15. Wright, "Theories of Identification."

16. Jack Blimes, "Rules and Rhetoric: Negotiating the Social Order in a Thai Village," *Journal of Anthropological Research* 32 (Spring 1976): 44–57.

17. Michael L. Hecht, Mary Jane Collier, and Sidney A. Ribeau, *African American Communication* (Newbury Park, Calif.: Sage, 1993).

18. Maryann S. Schall, "A Communication Rules Approach to Organizational Culture," *Administrative Science Quarterly* 28 (December 1983): 557–581.

19. Ibid.

20. Henri Tajfel, *Human Categories and Social Groups* (Cambridge: Cambridge University Press, 1981).

21. Isaiah Berlin, *Against the Current: Reflections on the Origins and Spread of Nationalism* (London: Verso, 1982).

22. Sheldon Stryker, "Identity Salience and Role Performance," *Journal of Marriage and the Family* 30, no. 4 (November 1968): 558–564.

23. Muzafer Sherif and Carolyn W. Sherif, *Groups in Harmony and Tension: An Integration of Studies on Intergroup Relations* (New York: Harper and Bros. Publishers, 1966).

24. Aronson, *The Social Animal.*

25. Stuart Hall, "Signification, Representation, Ideology: Althusser and the Post-Structuralist Debates," *Critical Studies in Mass Communication* 2, no. 2 (June 1985): 91–114.

26. John Fiske, *Television Culture* (New York: Routledge, 1987).

27. Mia Consalvo and Susanna Paasonen, eds., *Women and Everyday Uses of the Internet: Agency and Identity* (New York: Peter Lang, 2002).

28. Don Thu Nguyen and Jon Alexander, "The Coming of Cyberspacetime and the End of Polity," in *Cultures of Internet: Virtual Spaces, Real Histories, Living Bodies*, ed. Rob Shields, pp. 99–124 (Thousand Oaks, Calif.: Sage, 1996).

29. Leon Festinger, "A Theory of Social Comparison Processes," *Human Relations* 7 (1954): 117–140.

30. Robert G. Harper, Arthur N. Wiens, and Joseph D. Matarazzo, *Nonverbal Communication: The State of the Art* (New York: John Wiley and Sons, 1978).

31. Susanna Paasonen, "Gender, Identity and (the Limits of) Play on the Internet," in *Women and Everyday Uses of the Internet: Agency and Identity*, ed. Mia Consalvo and Susanna Paasonen, pp. 21–39 (New York: Peter Lang, 2002).

32. Jamie M. Poster, "Trouble, Pleasure and Tactics: Anonymity and Identity in a Lesbian Chat Room," in *Women and Everyday Uses of the Internet: Agency and Identity*, ed. Mia Consalvo and Susanna Paasonen, pp. 230–252 (New York: Peter Lang, 2002).

33. Kate O'Riordan, "Windows on the Web: The Female Body and the Web Camera," in *Women and Everyday Uses of the Internet: Agency and Identity*, ed. Mia Consalvo and Susanna Paasonen, pp. 44–61 (New York: Peter Lang, 2002).

34. Jennifer M. Tiernan, "Women Veterans on the Net: Using Internet Technology to Network and Reconnect," in *Women and Everyday Uses of the Internet: Agency and Identity*, ed. Mia Consalvo and Susanna Paasonen, pp. 211–227 (New York: Peter Lang, 2002).

35. Karen E. Gustafson, "Join Now, Membership Is Free: Women's Web Sites and the Coding of Community," in *Women and Everyday Uses of the Internet: Agency and Identity*, ed. Mia Consalvo and Susanna Paasonen, pp. 168–188 (New York: Peter Lang, 2002).

36. Leda Cooks, Mari Casteneda Paredes, and Erica Scharrer, "There's 'O Place' Like Home: Searching for Community on Oprah.com," in *Women and Everyday Uses of the Internet: Agency and Identity*, ed. Mia Consalvo and Susanna Paasonen, pp. 139–161 (New York: Peter Lang, 2002).

37. Lemos, "The Labyrinth of Minitel."

38. Poster, "Trouble"; Tiernan, "Women Veterans"; J. Patrick Williams and Heith Copes, "'How Edge Are You?': Constructing Authentic Identities and Subcultural Boundaries in a Straightedge Internet Forum," *Symbolic Interaction* 28, no. 1 (Winter 2005): 67–89.

39. Jan Fernback, "There Is a There There: Notes toward a Definition of Cybercommunity," in *Doing Internet Research: Critical Issues and Methods for Examining the Net*, ed. Steve Jones, pp. 203–220 (Thousand Oaks, Calif.: Sage, 1999).

40. Anselm Strauss and Juliet Corbin, "Grounded Theory Methodology: An Overview," in *Handbook of Qualitative Research*, ed. Norman K. Denzin and Yvonna S. Lincoln, pp. 262–272 (Thousand Oaks, Calif.: Sage Publications, 1994).

41. Shadletsky and Aitken, *Human Communication*.

42. Williams and Copes, "How Edge?"

CHAPTER 10

Gerald M. Phillips as Electronic Tribal Chief: Socioforming Cyberspace

ANN ROSENTHAL

It is one thing to dream about possibilities. It is something else to attempt to achieve them.
—GERALD M. PHILLIPS, E-MAIL MESSAGE, 1993

The Internet, with millions of connected computers, exists as real physical space. Yet people refer to it as cyberspace, "the notional environment in which communication over computer networks occurs,"[1] defining it by the connecting spaces rather than the nodes, its physical connection points. A network has ultimate value in its connectivity, its end points or nodes providing the reason for the network to exist. Examining the worldwide network as connected *territory* permits a different perspective on what happens when people move to inhabit it. Just as newly discovered territory has historically been populated by humans, cyberspace, too, has become populated. Individuals buy connection points in order to be part of the territory, and the social organizations they form become real social organizations, some traditional and some adapting to the new territorial topology. Newsletters by e-mail are still newsletters, but blogs bring personal lives and interpersonal communication into the public domain.

Computer-mediated communication examines a wide variety of innovations and their effects, but I am interested here in the way humans inhabit this new territory, given their sociobiological nature. *Homo sapiens sapiens* form social groups, and communication is what they use to enable the process of societization.[2]

In this chapter, I consider the socioforming, through communication, of cyberspace into habitable territory. If physical space can be terraformed, that is, turned into terrain resembling earth and thus inhabitable by humans, then cyberspace can be socioformed, turned into space where humans can form societies. I examine the relationship between communication and the process of social organization, studying an e-mail discussion list that has endured for more than a decade, existing primarily in cyberspace. The Quiet Communications list (QC-L) has left its cultural impact on some of the cyberspaces that it has occupied, and in the manner of physical space archaeologists, I present the evidence gleaned by sifting through cybershards using the network digging tools, search engines. As an occupant of QC-L territory for nine years, I bring a participant-observer perspective to the analysis of the organization's current status. Cyberspace pioneer and communication scholar Gerald M. Phillips founded this private list, and I examine Phillips's own communication to and about the list, as well as others' reflections about their participation.

Communication and Social Organization

Scholars across numerous disciplines have examined the role communication plays in the building of human social organizations. Biologist E. O. Wilson described communication as central to the ability of species to build societies and declared human communication to be the richest found in nature.[3] Communication scholar Armand Mattelart examined the historical development of communication from a network perspective.[4] Sociologist David Stark considers the "co-evolution of collaborative organization and interactive technologies."[5] The literature is replete with reflections and theories regarding the effects of communication; McLuhan, Innis, Reed, Metcalfe, Habermas, and Postman, among others, postulate possibilities across a panoply of perspectives.[6]

The introduction of worldwide, networked communication has created new possibilities, however, since electronic networks collapse time and distance, and the study of networks has spawned a plethora of perspectives as well. Reed's Law states, "Networks that support the construction of communicating groups create value that scales *exponentially* with network size."[7] While the power of the electronic network obviously enables greater and immediate connectivity among people, I believe that it may restructure the topology of human social organization as well. The nature of a widely connected communication network uniquely allows and fosters the exploration of space and formation of bands of individuals with common pursuits or interests beyond the confines of time and proximity.

In the case of QC-L, the nature of the communication medium that continues to enable it has uniquely shaped what it has become. More powerful than television, which inspired McLuhan's belief that the medium is the message, the network as communication medium is the fundamental organizational structure of human social life. Further, the *electronic* network allows the establishment of heterarchical[8] layers within the traditional hierarchical organizations based on genetics and government, establishing new social units beyond both family and national identity. These groups represent new types of organizations that deserve a more modern appellation, but, still, as primitive in their organizational development, resemble *tribes*.

Heterarchy, though not a new term, has developed a recent contextual use in information technology. The online Web Dictionary of Cybernetics and Systems defines heterarchy as "a form of organization resembling a network or fishnet."[9] The antiquated definition, government by aliens, was revised in 1945 when Warren Sturgis McCulloch considered neural topology as heterarchical.[10] Eberhard von Goldammer extended McCulloch, declaring, "The study of heterarchical process structures is essential for any modeling of living systems in general," arguing that heterarchy and hierarchy represent important divergent constructs for studying organizations.[11] Authority in a heterarchy is determined by knowledge and function. In a hierarchy, authority is determined by status or titular designation. In essence, heterarchies exist as horizontal organizational structures, whereas hierarchies are inherently vertical.

Just as early human society grew through face-to-face interaction and was necessarily defined by geography, electronically connected humans have formed functional groups that have evolved into more closely connected and complex online social organizations with complex interpersonal relationships. QC-L exemplifies one of these new, communication-network-based tribes.

Defining Tribe

"Tribe" as a word represents McGee's concept of ideograph,[12] since it carries ideological meaning based in the Western social theory tradition—meaning translated into law, for example, in the United States. In 1901, the United States Supreme Court defined tribe as part of a ruling articulated in *Montoya v. United States:* "By a 'tribe' we understand a body of Indians of the same or a similar race, united in a community under one leadership or government, and inhabiting a particular though sometimes ill-defined territory." [13]

The opinion, written by Associate Justice Henry Billings Brown, offered this rationale for the definition:

> Owing to the natural infirmities of the Indian character, their fiery tempers, impatience of restraint, their mutual jealousies and animosities, their nomadic habits, and lack of mental training, they have as a rule shown a total want of that cohesive force necessary to the making up of a nation in the ordinary sense of the word. As they had no established laws, no recognized method of choosing their sovereigns by inheritance or election, no officers with defined powers, their governments in their original state were nothing more than a temporary submission to an intellectual or physical superior, who in some cases ruled with absolute authority, and, in others, was recognized only so long as he was able to dominate the tribe by the qualities which originally enabled him to secure their leadership. [14]

The term "tribe" still carries significant ideological content, with some scholars taking exception to any use of the term for modern social groups, since it carries negative ideological content. An online publication about indigenous peoples houses a special essay on the concept of tribe, calling for a move away from the term as a negative stereotype. [15] Chris Lowe, lead essayist and listed as affiliated at the time with Boston University, says that the view of the tribe embodied in the stereotype never actually existed:

> If by tribe we mean a social group that shares a single territory, a single language, a single political unit, a shared religious tradition, a similar economic system, and common cultural practices, such a group is rarely found in the real world. These characteristics almost never correspond precisely with each other today, nor did they at any time in the past. [16]

Rhea Rogers provides a different kind of argument about the concept of tribe based on an archaeological and ethnohistoric case study of prehistoric people living in the Southeastern United States, claiming that heterarchy best characterizes the "social system of the tribes that inhabited the upper Yadkin River Valley of North Carolina (ca. A.D. 1500)." [17]

Rogers concludes that, "tribal heterarchy is dependent on the existence of diversity, including diversity at the level of the individual."[18] Considering how hierarchy arises, Rogers suggests that it "could be generated by the co-occurrence or conflation of group identity with place."[19] Tribes can develop as either hierarchies or heterarchies depending on the diversity and dispersion of their population.

Heterarchies as layers within hierarchies offers a new paradigm for understanding how social structures can come into being within established, territorially governed bodies or genetically defined families. A worldwide electronic communication network provides the perfect venue for the growth of heterarchical tribes outside of these boundaries. Electronic tribes inhabit cyberspace, build cultural artifacts, develop rituals, have conflicts, and generally reflect the same human behaviors that occur when people are connected proximally rather than virtually. Electronic tribes do not preclude membership in other hierarchical organizations, such as families or nations. They develop topologically as internalized layers and may develop their own independence from or connections to the hierarchies in which they exist.

Gerald M. Phillips in Cyberspace

While declaring his personal difficulty in learning new computer communication technology,[20] Gerald M. Phillips, Professor and then Professor Emeritus, Speech Communication, Pennsylvania State University, became a pioneer in online communication. While he may be better known for having edited *The Interpersonal Computing and Technology Journal: An Electronic Journal for the 21st Century*, he also founded an online discussion forum that remains actively and continuously engaged as a network-based community twelve years after its creation.

Phillips created QC-L as a listserv-based discussion group in 1993,[21] the same year that Howard Rheingold published *The Virtual Community*. As of 2005, a member of the original QC-L group owns the list and acts as moderator. Surviving deaths, defections, a single ejection, marriage of two members, adoptions, and a plethora of heated political and personal exchanges, the group meets face-to-face on a mostly annual schedule, with members visiting each other as trips bring them in proximity to other members.

The original members of the discussion group shared an interest in politics, but only some of the original members remain active and topics of discussion vary widely. While original members, politically, tended to be liberal, the current group also includes individuals with highly conservative political views.

Despite the divergence from its origins, QC-L , a non-geographically-defined social unit, flourishes after more than a decade. It has also persisted despite Phillips's predicting its demise not long after its creation.[22]

QC-L as Tribe

Examining the growth of the QC list community in terms of its origins, individual roles, rituals, and leadership provides evidence that the group considers itself an online community of a unique nature. The founding of the organization was documented by one of Phillips's undergraduate students, who was also a charter list member, as a senior thesis study, and Betty Lee Dowlin (now Betty Lee Rogers) continues to be a member of QC-L. Dowlin's record of the first two years of the list's existence, including details about its formation, charter membership, and early e-mail conversations, represents firsthand evidence of what both Phillips, the list's founder, and its charter members experienced and believed regarding the organization. After two years' observation, Dowlin already recognized the unique nature of this organization, concluding that it had achieved the status of "community."[23]

Establishing the Territory

Clinton@Marist (C@M), still an active political discussion list, brought the original members of QC-L together. Most had not met face-to-face, but only through the C@M online discussion group, which had a narrow and clear purpose. List reviewer Raleigh Muns makes these comments about this list:

> It's almost a year later and why would anyone want to join a discussion group on Bill Clinton's campaign for the Presidency? He won, didn't he? Though this list is misnamed and hyperactive, it is also robust, fascinating, and to the right subscribers, of incalculable value. I'd rather it were called the "Friends of Bill" discussion list. Anyway, my perverse streak likes the gentle sarcasm implied by continuing a list under

the name "Campaigning for President . . ." a year after Bill's (first) election.[24]

Muns records 484 members of the list, cautioning potential list joiners that they have to be "e-tough"[25] because of the amount of e-mail traffic, and reports the diffuse nature of discussion topics.

> Discussion takes place on a broad range of topics, many of which seemed out of scope for the list; that is, out of scope until I realized that there was no real defined scope in the first place! The state of the American education system is worth debating, but I had a problem with understanding why such a vigorous discussion was happening on this list.
>
> The arguments are cogent and lively. Contributors appear to be academics, some in the Washington, DC area, able to supply personal insights. However, the list personality that I observed was much too diffuse for my refined palate (sly wink suffixed).[26]

If an external reviewer's comments reflect caution, Phillips's disenchantment with the direction being taken on C@M proved more dramatic. Dowlin explains how Phillips became so angry at the C@M interactions that "he became ill and finally decided to go nomail on the list."[27] Phillips missed the relationships he had formed on the list, however. Dowlin explains his reaction.

> He called Gerry Santoro at The Pennsylvania State University, and asked if there was a way to set up a list that was closed. He wanted to be able to know when someone came on the list and to be able to keep it a private list. He envisioned a community where there would be norms, and everyone would know what they were. Together they set up a list that only the list owners could access to add new addresses. It was given the name QC-L . . .[28]

In one of his early messages to the QC-L community, Phillips reflects on his time at C@M, the reasons he left, and his expectations in an online affiliation:

> I think I was one of the earliest members of C@M, and found it a vital and stimulating list in which people could disagree respectfully and with good humor. I made many good friends there. I left in anger,

because I felt I was hounded off the list by a vituperative and humorless person, intolerant in act and deed. I was not looking for sympathy, merely a place where I could engage in good conversation with intelligent people.[29]

The decision to leave the C@M community and found his own organization did not happen as a result of a single event, but apparently involved a complex decisional process for Phillips. Suffering from health problems, he refers to the process in this same thoughtful post to the Clinton list:

> I have activated myself many times since, though not lately. The threat of being "monitored," raised originally by Mr. Waldman and repeated more recently by Mr. Bell have even me intimidated. Having gone through the McCarthy era, during which time I have been monitored, and having been bushwhacked by reverse racists, I decided to give my angina a break and stay away.[30]

During this disaffection with the online political community, Phillips formed a personal philosophy of what an online community should be:

> More and more, however, the notion of a refereed and enclosed list, where there is some control over participation, is appealing. You folks on C@M might give it some thought. You may be missing something important by allowing bigots to intimidate potential participants.[31]

Phillips's conceptualization of the ideal online community also includes self-analysis and an articulation of personal conversational standards:

> I am far from a shrinking violet, but I prefer my argument to be rational, respectful, and witty. We can't do much about the latter. You either have it or you don't. But the first two criteria are sine qua non.[32]

One of the charter members recalls the beginning of the group—a dozen years later—with the same clarity as Phillips's initial description:

> He sought to form a private place, where ideas could be freely exchanged without the originator of those ideas getting caught up in the mindless hysteria generated by the less cognitively sophisticated on public lists. This was the rationale for the list being private, by invitation only, and no archives being kept. Each idea, or intellectual

exchange, was to be treated as ephemera—a step on the road to maturity, with stumbles and distractions to be noted, but not preserved for posterity.[33]

In Phillips's last college lecture, he referred to his new group, describing whom he invited and the conditions for membership:

> Now my other ego is that I'm the list manager for the QC listserv. And QC-L is a private conversation list made up of all-stars taken from other lists all over the country. They have to go through a trial period. They have to share with us what they have to say, and we decide whether we'd like to meet them in person. We had our first meeting here in State College last June, and they're coming back again this June. Incredibly strong linkages have formed.[34]

According to Phillips's talk about the group, the most puzzling stage in QC-L came shortly after its creation, when he was far less optimistic about its future:

> It was probably a mistake to try QC-L and I am prepared to disband it at the will of the membership. It was a reaction to what was going on at C@M. After witnessing the departure of two key members, finding myself losing control entirely, and seeing the anchor man do the same thing I did, I decided to detach and use my training as an alleged communications specialist, to examine the situation.[35]

Dowlin explains that this post came "about one week after the first announcement of the formation of QC-L, and at that time, all of the members of Clinton@Marist who had asked to join QC-L had been added to the list." Dowlin called the situation "comparable to [that of] any organization or group of people who find that they have a shift of major proportions."[36]

In the long post, Phillips provides his own analysis, which indicates that he understands the correlation between network-connected individuals and proximity-linked communities:

> We start with the premise that institutions often outlive their usefulness and when they do, they struggle to find some reason to sustain themselves. Economic institutions do it because when the institution fails, people lose their jobs. C@M does it because without it, some of us lose identity.

> C@M was a smashing success at the outset because it gave us what Harry Stack Sullivan called "consensual validation." The participants used each other to convince themselves (ourselves) that we were not loony for supporting this upstart from Arkansas. Opponents like Bruce were useful because they solidified us. Once the campaign started, we had a sense of purpose and out of it came a social organization.[37]

He does not call C@M a discussion group or political forum. He does link it to a sense of social reality. Without their networked social organization, some individuals lacked a sense of social identity. The separate and individualistic members also assumed specific organizational roles that Phillips identifies:

> We tolerated virtuosos (or show-offs) and we let people assume identity. Bill was "anchor man" and shared resident economist duty with Mike. Mike dutifully lectured us on morality. Gail kept us honest with challenges to the prevailing wisdom. Frank contributed his well constructed philosophical analysis. Rick tvWexler gave us important demographics, Diane brought us news for the outside world, and Rick Klau and Betty Lee brought us hope for the future. There were yeomen, who contributed their share.
>
> Dan became resident story teller, joined later by Tod. Then we saw social links developing. Members got together, saw each other face to face. Cliques began to form.[38]

This narrative account, reminiscent of culture creation stories, provides significant insight regarding Phillips's understanding of what was happening, even as he participated. Concerning the group's devolution, Dowlin also, as a group member and later as essayist, reflects, "The loyalty of the people on the list was challenged. Should the loyalty be to the community as represented by Clinton@Marist, or to the people who made it a community?"[39] Phillips explains, again through narrative, what was happening:

> Then we were challenged by newcomers. After the inauguration and the glow of victory we began to become anarchic. Some regular members departed. Who remembers Buddy and Lucy from the original group? (I do. I still correspond with them on a daily basis.) But the disruptions became unpleasant. The abrasion of new ideas, particularly by people who did not comprehend the norms of the group drove several people

to extremes. Dan decided his job needed more attention. I found, after an explosive note that I got angina. Jolinda and Bill committed a similar indiscretion with Ben.[40]

Phillips rationalizes his rebellion against the C@M organization by relating it to all social organizations:

Sad. But whatever the group was it isn't. Some of us will remember it. But it is a social microcosm. Groups rise and fall, social linkages form and are split asunder (in a sense, like divorce).

I offered QC as an alternative to hold the original group together in some way, without affecting what went on, on-line.[41]

Phillips did not yet have a sense of what QC-L would become, and he predicts its demise:

C@M will be what it will be and QC, for which there is clearly no purpose will probably wither away. And we will be life without residual memories and a few good friends. I am posting this to C@M but I am not sure if you are nomail whether the net will take posts from you. I am sure someone will keep me informed if there is any reaction to this.[42]

The reaction came from QC-L members who, as Dowlin records, "realized that whatever else might be said, they wanted QC-L , they wanted this place to correspond with those they had become close to, that was safe from outside agitation."[43]

Establishing Rituals

While QC-L members lead lives within the hierarchical realms where they live in proximity to others, they also maintain daily contact with members of the online community. Checking e-mail has become a tribal ritual, and electronic mailboxes sometimes reach the limit, even with the maximum allowance by the list management software set at one hundred messages per day. This ritual did not develop immediately or smoothly. Dowlin reports that a year after the list's creation, "The Holidays came and it became quiet. . . . Discussions began to be rather bland, or short, and there were not as many posts as usual."[44]

Early QC list activities demonstrate an understanding that social organizations develop special rules and rituals internally, as sociologist Hamood Al-Oudi explains about tribalism in Yemen: "The internal relations within a tribe are regulated by a simple set of unwritten social customs and traditions, which are spontaneously formulated by the group."[45] Dowlin's history describes some of these efforts:

> After the first struggle for identity, QC-L quickly established itself. The level of humor increased and the list was involved in limerick contests, a competition to see who could write the most outrageous proctologist reference in program language, setting up a Virtual State, with everyone taking an office, and the virtual basketball team that went to the Final Four.[46]

No real governing structure exists; however, members do assume informal titles embedded with humor, such as Director of Disinformation, continuing to satisfy one of Phillips's mandates for online affiliation.

Current members routinely check and respond to e-mail, apologizing if they discover they have failed to respond to a question asked specifically of them. One particularly interesting e-mail ritual involves the posting of questions like "I have not received one message from QC-L today; is anyone else online today?"

E-mail remains the primary daily ritual for list members; however, periodic face-to-face meetings have taken place in numerous states in the United States and one province in Canada. In addition, when traveling, members routinely inquire if any QC-L member will be available for a visit at the intended location. On one occasion several group members attended a wedding of two members of the community who had met first on the list and then in person.

Other rituals, as in all tribal cultures, have meanings that remain shrouded in the mists of time. Numerous exchanges refer to a missing pair of blue pumps, for example.

Tribal Identity and Leadership

Just as the Native American tribes conceptualized by Mr. Justice Brown, QC-L does not have formally elected leadership. Gerald M. Phillips created and populated the original band, and his intellectual progeny have maintained its structural integrity. Twelve years after its creation, QC-L remains resident in the same Internet domain. Its membership has fluctuated but in general increased. Members still focus on political topics but also interact on an interpersonal level both online and in person.

The group did endure despite Phillips's early pessimism. By his sixty-sixth birthday, December 1, 1994, during the first year of its existence, QC-L had developed rituals, shared stories, and perhaps spawned mythologies. Evidence of the developing tribal identity manifested on multiple levels on this occasion. Charter QC-L member Bill Moore, an economist, wrote a ballad, which he posted to the list. He parceled out parts for individual list members to sing, virtually. Moore called Phillips his "virtual guide to the cmc way," "a Grump for all climates, a transnational Crank."[47]

Phillips's own description of his relationship to the list varied. In his last lecture he called himself the "list manager." In his postings, he used language in his signature block that suggested his view of his own relationship to the list at the moment. For example, he called himself "Dealer in magic & spells"[48] and "The retired sage gone back to the hermit cave."[49]

The group has had only one owner, selected by Phillips, since his death. Psychologist and ceramicist Gail Barnes refers to herself as List-Mom, explaining,

> I have tried to remain just another list member, unless something specifically related to the technical issues of management arose. I settled on "Attention: List Business" as a way to separate my list persona from my role as list owner. I also decided that the moniker, ListMom, was a way to communicate my authority without threat, and without heavy-handedness. I rarely think of myself as being in charge. I certainly do not think of myself as a matriarch, in spite of the ListMom handle.[50]

She also explains how Phillips invited her to assume list management:

> Several days before Gerry's death I got a phone call from him. He told me the chores of list management were taxing his waning strength and asked me to take over as titular "List Owner". He kindly said that he was sure the project would be safe in my hands. I was very grateful for this vote of confidence. I agreed to his request, and contacted Penn State to advise them that Gerry was planning on transferring management to me. He had already told . . . the folks at Penn State in charge of

the hardware end of things, of his plan, and within 24 hours I became the owner of QC-L.[51]

Asked about her relationship to the QC-L community, she explains that she has been a member since "day one":

> My relationship is a unique one, I suspect. I had joined several other lists in the early days of bitnet [*sic*], and had an opportunity to fully examine how the personality of the list owner could inhibit or encourage participation, set the tone for members' involvement, and stamp a given list with their own dynamic. I did not want to stamp my personal quirks on QC-L, so I spent a great deal of time actively thinking about how I could "herd cats" without becoming the battered old Tom.[52]

Like all tribes, this one has been challenged territorially, and one former member publicly admits to having been removed from the community, and thereafter even creating a QC-L Web site. The leadership, however, has remained constant. The culture of reasoned exchanges laced with humor also remains the social norm, just as Phillips dictated in the beginning. As Mr. Justice Brown explains about tribes, leadership happens as a result of "temporary submission" to an individual whom the members continue to accept for his intellectual or physical superiority.

Not all list members view their community in exactly the same way; however, many consider their relationship to the group an important one. A recent post by list member Perry Stevens illustrates just how important:

> We've spent a lot of time on-list during the past decade or so talking about our relationships to one another. While many of us have met face-to-face, the most important interactions have happened right here, in written words, not through spoken ones. We know that our relationships to one another are very real, even though people who don't have virtual communities can't fully understand how or why.[53]

A Tribe by Any Other Name

No laws dictate what each type of network-based organization will be called. Popular culture and marketing have provided numerous neologisms to describe emerging net relationships. QC-L , however, seems to have stretched the boundaries of traditional e-mail lists, if something as recent as these can be said to have traditions.

Phillips knew that he had created something unique and special in this list community even though he did not live long after establishing QC-L. His disclaimer in one post indicates that he might have sensed that QC-L could become tribal. "I do not think we are quite tribal. But we do have a shared mythology."[54]

By any standard, Gerald M. Phillips ranks as an outstanding communication scholar of the late twentieth century. He published numerous books, articles in scholarly journals, and erudite essays. He also ranked at the top of his profession. He mentored countless students and directed scores of graduate research projects. As evidenced by his own testimony to what was happening as he created the new territorial entity of Quiet Communications, he also counts as a pioneer, a communication scholar-activist who socioformed cyberspace for human habitation.

Notes

1. Compact Oxford English Dictionary, http://www.askoxford.com/concise_oed/cyberspace?view=uk (accessed October 25, 2005).

2. E. O. Wilson, *Sociobiology: A New Synthesis* (Cambridge, Mass.: Harvard University Press, 1971).

3. Ibid. Wilson's controversial work on the biological basis of behaviors explains how human communication functions. In a conversation with him in April 2001 at Auburn University, I learned that he did not know his work was being used by communication scholars. I told him that communication scholars study the rhetorical impact of his work.

4. Armand Mattelart, *Networking the World: 1794–2000* (Minneapolis: University of Minnesota Press, 2000).

5. David Stark's credentials may be viewed online at http://www.columbia.edu/cu/sipa/RESEARCH/bios/dcs36.html.

6. Among media scholars' works, these represent some interesting approaches to some of the issues I discuss in this chapter: Marshall McLuhan, "Cultures in the Electronic World: Can the Bottom Line Hold Quebec?" *Perception* 1, no. 2 (November–December 1977): 66–69; Neil Postman, *Amusing Ourselves to Death* (London: Methuen, 1986); Ian Angus and Brian Shoesmith, "Dependency/Space/Policy: An Introduction to a Dialogue with Harold Innis," *Continuum: The Australian Journal of Media & Culture* 7, no. 1 (1993), http://wwwmcc.murdoch.edu.au/ReadingRoom/7.1/Angus&S.html. Bob Metcalfe invented Ethernet and wrote a law that describes the growth of networks as scaled. Reed's Law relates more to my own perception of networks and is explained in text. I also suggest adding Jürgen Habermas, *Between Facts and Norms* (Cam-

bridge, Mass.: MIT Press, 1996), or Habermas Online (http://www.csudh.edu/dearhabermas/habermas.htm).

7. David P. Reed, "That Sneaky Exponential—Beyond Metcalfe's Law to the Power of Community Building," *Context*, Winter 2002–2003, http://www.contextmag.com/archives/199903/DigitalStrategyReedsLaw.asp.

8. Heterarchy as a research construct has largely been ignored by scholars; however, as I explain the concept in text, it seems a logical way to talk about networks.

9. See note 1. I have tried to standardize on the Oxford Compact Dictionary as much as possible when definitions were necessary. If you want to see if a word carries a standard definition across numerous sources, I recommend http://www.onelook.com, which has links to numerous online dictionaries. I also refer to the Web Dictionary of Cybernetics and Systems, http://pespmc1.vub.ac.be/ASC/HETERARCHY.html.

10. Warren S. McCulloch, "A Heterarchy of Values by the Topology of Nervous Nets," http://www.vordenker.de/ggphilosophy/mcculloch_heterarchy.pdf.

11. Eberhard von Goldammer, "Heterarchy and Hierarchy: Two Complementary Categories of Description" http://www.vordenker.de/heterarchy/het_intro_en.htm.

12. Michael C. McGee, "The 'Ideograph': A Link between Rhetoric and Ideology," *Quarterly Journal of Speech* 66, no. 1 (1980): 1–16.

13. *Montoya v. United States*, 180 U.S. 266–267 (1901).

14. Ibid. This judicial opinion, which carries the weight of law, contains several important points. Tribes have leaders rather than elected officials, and the leaders remain in charge only so long as their ability to lead continues. Tribes are also considered a more primitive form of society.

15. Chris Lowe, "Talking about 'Tribe': Moving from Stereotypes to Analysis" (November 1997), http://www.africaaction.org/bp/ethall.htm (accessed October 12, 2005).

16. Ibid.

17. Rhea J. Rogers, "Tribes as Heterarchy," in *Heterarchy and the Analysis of Complex Societies*, ed. Robert M. Ehrenreich, Carole L. Crumley, and Janet E. Levy, pp. 2–16 (Washington, D.C.: American Anthropological Association, 1995). K. S. Singh, in "Concept of a Tribe: A Note," *Eastern Anthropologist* 56, no. 2 (April 2003): 195–200, points out that India had no word for tribe in its ancient literature and that tribes in India have many different group names other than "tribe."

18. Rogers, "Tribes as Heterarchy," p. 15.

19. Ibid.

20. Gerald M. Phillips, "The Luddite's Lament," n.d., is an archived document labeled as "The GMP Column (An APEX-J Column)" and can be located online at http://www.uark.edu/depts/comminfo/sage/luddite.html. In it, Phillips laments the difficulties involved in using technology for education.

21. The creation of this community has been documented in an undergraduate thesis, supervised by Gerald M. Phillips. Betty Lee Dowlin (Rogers), "Electronic Discussion Groups: A New Kind of Community" (bachelor's thesis, Pennsylvania State University, May 1995).

22. I document this belief by including the entire post by Phillips later in the text, but dissected and with commentary.

23. Dowlin's thesis is grounded in the conceptualization of community.

24. List Review Service 026 'CLINTON,' ed. Raleigh C. Muns, October 8, 1993, http://www.umsl.edu/~muns/proddir/rev026.htm.

25. Ibid.

26. Ibid.

27. Dowlin, "Electronic Discussion Groups," p. 20.

28. Ibid.

29. Phillips's e-mail messages can be found in Dowlin's thesis, and I have included full text here with commentary. QC-L no longer archives messages, although Dowlin cites QC-L archives, January 1994, as her source.

30. Phillips's e-mail messages can be found in Dowlin's thesis, and I have included full text here with commentary. QC-L no longer archives messages, although Dowlin cites QC-L archives, January 1994, as her source.

31. Phillips's e-mail messages can be found in Dowlin's thesis, and I have included full text here with commentary. QC-L no longer archives messages, although Dowlin cites QC-L archives, January 1994, as her source.

32. Phillips's e-mail messages can be found in Dowlin's thesis, and I have included full text here with commentary. QC-L no longer archives messages, although Dowlin cites QC-L archives, January 1994, as her source.

33. Gail Barnes, QC-L List Owner, personal e-mail, October 12, 2005.

34. Gerald M. Phillips, "Creating a Real Group in a Virtual World," *Interpersonal Computing and Technology: An Electronic Journal for the 21st Century* 3, no. 4 (October 1995): 42–56. This was Phillips's last lecture and published after his death. It can be accessed online at http://www.helsinki.fi/science/optek/1995/n4/gmp2.txt.

35. Phillips's e-mail messages can be found in Dowlin's thesis, and I have included full text here with commentary. QC-L no longer archives messages, although Dowlin cites QC-L archives, January 1994, as her source.

36. Dowlin, "Electronic Discussion Groups," p. 24.

37. Phillips's e-mail messages can be found in Dowlin's thesis, and I have included full text here with commentary. QC-L no longer archives messages, although Dowlin cites QC-L archives, January 1994, as her source.

38. Phillips's e-mail messages can be found in Dowlin's thesis, and I have included full text here with commentary. QC-L no longer archives messages, although Dowlin cites QC-L archives, January 1994, as her source.

39. Dowlin, "Electronic Discussion Groups," p. 24.

40. Phillips's e-mail messages can be found in Dowlin's thesis, and I have included full text here with commentary. QC-L no longer archives messages, although Dowlin cites QC-L archives, January 1994, as her source.

41. Phillips's e-mail messages can be found in Dowlin's thesis, and I have included full text here with commentary. QC-L no longer archives messages, although Dowlin cites QC-L archives, January 1994, as her source.

42. Phillips's e-mail messages can be found in Dowlin's thesis, and I have included full text here with commentary. QC-L no longer archives messages, although Dowlin cites QC-L archives, January 1994, as her source.

43. Dowlin, "Electronic Discussion Groups," p. 23.

44. Ibid., p. 31.

45. Hamood Al-Oudi, "Tribalism in Yemen: Its Laws and Systems," in *Yemen Times*, 8, no. 6 (February 9–15, 1998), http://www.yementimes.com/98/iss06/focus.htm (accessed October 25, 2005).

46. Dowlin, "Electronic Discussion Groups," p. 25.

47. Bill Moore, "On Top of Old Grumpy," http://www.uark.edu/depts/comminfo/sage/66.html.

48. This e-mail message that Phillips sent to QC-L has been archived online at http://www.uark.edu/depts/comminfo/sage/founder.html.

49. Phillips's e-mail messages can be found in Dowlin's thesis, and I have included full text here with commentary. QC-L no longer archives messages, although Dowlin cites QC-L archives, January 1994, as her source.

50. Gail Barnes, QC-L List Owner, personal e-mail, October 12, 2005.

51. Ibid.

52. Ibid.

53. Perry Stevens, QC-L Member, personal e-mail, October 12, 2005.

54. See note 47.

Digital Dreamtime, Sonic Talismans: Music Downloading and the Tribal Landscape

MICHAEL C. ZALOT

This chapter suggests that the Internet environment offers parallels to the Australian Aboriginal cosmology of Dreamtime, and within the digital Dreamtime can be found songs that bring benefit to the downloader in terms of social relations. Portable media players can be understood as talismanic, like the Aboriginal *churinga*. They do not ward off evil or bring good luck, but they can increase knowledge that enhances social status among peers. Music impacts listeners' identities, and in some cases enables subcultural identities that can be read as tribal, or pan-tribal, as they cut across groups. Our content-based "tribes," however, are contingent and transient, and they hold no ties to kinship, mortality, or the land.[1] Although there are many parallels, we have a different relationship to our virtual geography than the Aboriginal people have to their physical land, and ultimately our physical environment is marginalized through representation in a mythic virtual landscape.

The starting point of the analysis is the changes to acquiring music that have occurred over the past decade through the introduction of the Internet and related technologies. Whereas listeners previously acquired music through obtaining or creating a physical copy, digital distribution formats, peer-to-peer file-sharing software, and high-speed bandwidth have created disembodied songs that can travel across media, between computers, CDs, and portable players. No longer do listeners have to purchase an album as a package of songs; they are free to select only the tracks they like. The original Napster may have frightened and angered the recording industry through its utter disregard for copyright, but it set the stage for the corporate assimilation of downloading music by Apple, Sony, and others. Peer-to-peer software such as Gnutella,

LimeWire, and BitTorrent still proliferates, and many song files are still illicitly copied without compensating the copyright holder, though the legal landscape may be changing with the recent Supreme Court decision holding Grokster—a file-sharing software provider—liable for contributory copyright infringement.

In any case, music now exists out in the network—waiting to be retrieved, either through properly licensed channels or not. In a sense the Internet functions in part as a giant database of songs, and for many listeners, the days of rummaging through CD bins in malls might be numbered, or at least numbered fewer. After all, the music has to be "ripped" from a CD to fit in an iPod or other portable player, so why not just get it that way in the first place? Here begins the present inquiry: listening closely for the echoes of earlier, tribal knowledge in these new music technology developments.

Clearly, there is something immediate and connectionist about music. It can bring listeners closer to themselves, to their peer groups, or to their personal history through nostalgia. For many, music touches identity and emotion in ways that other, more visual, art forms simply don't. It is obviously aural, but also retains something oral, as well, as in notions of "oral culture." Often popular songs feature repetitive chants and repetitive rhythms replete with sonorous tribal drums. Marshall McLuhan would characterize these components as typical of an oral culture, where perpetuating information is tied to repeating it,[2] distinct from visual culture's isolationist and analytic modality.

Although it retains these features of oral culture, popular music underwent a transformation similar to that in speech and writing following the ascendancy of the printing press. That is to say, music was externalized and made into an object (a record) in the same way that words were given a reality outside of the presence of the speaker by writing and print. In the predownload age, records "fragmented" listeners from mass groups by allowing them to have individual relationships with particular albums and songs. For Evan Eisenberg, recordings took music, an inherently social event with components of public ritual, and turned it into a private experience revolving around an object. Eisenberg's classic study *The Recording Angel* notes that records made music a thing, a commodity to be owned.[3]

Records also, in conjunction with radio and marketing, made music a "thang."[4] That is, records enabled music to create social connections, albeit in a more transient way. Eisenberg suggests that publicly played music can momentarily tribalize situations, for example temporarily creating a content-based alliance among diverse individuals on a public bus ride. Eisenberg's primary analysis was based on vinyl records; he later addresses the object-nature of CDs and finds that they have a reduced physical presence when compared to vinyl: less bulk, smaller cover art, and so on. He does not analytically address the impact of downloading, but it is quite clear that the networked digital file "object" has even less "thingness" than a CD—no album cover or physical form other than patterns of electrical charges. John Alderman likens a digital music file to a "soul" that has been "liberated" from its body, the CD.[5] A digital song can traverse the wired world in minutes or seconds, migrating between servers, desktop machines, and portable players. It returns, in McLuhan's sense, to something more akin to oral culture, more like transient speech than a book. Streamed digital music, which involves no file transfer at all, is even more of a return to orality. On-demand thingless bitstreams leave no trace when finished and generally aren't transferable to portable players the way that downloaded files are.

The Digital Path of the Rainbow Snake

There is something tribal about the Internet. In many ways, it fulfills McLuhan's notion of an oral culture as a "magical integral world punctuated by myth, and ritual."[6] Certainly, it integrates computers, networks, and information in ways previously unexplored. As far as ritual, stories abound in any office regarding compulsive e-mail–checkers, or those on college campuses who cannot live without their online chat rooms or immersive video games. Pseudomythic archetypes, too, are there for the taking: eBay as the Universal Auction, Amazon as the Great Bookseller, Google as the Mighty Oracle, and—in either of its incarnations—Napster as the Fountain of Music. These Web-only businesses have succeeded precisely because of their geography-free appeal. Other businesses, however, use the Web to supplement real world brick-and-mortar presences. That is to say, such businesses exist simultaneously in the physical world and in the online "mythic" realm.

Physical copresence matters less in the Information Age, and so does physical presence in general. Analysts have long noted that bodies seem to matter less in cyberspace, where chat room participants can pretend to ages, races, status, and a gender that they do not possess.[7] In the words of an infamous *New Yorker* cartoon, "On the Internet, no one knows you're a dog." Of course, the actual guts of the Internet are made of wires, routers, servers, and modems, and it does take hands, eyes, and a brain to manipulate mice and keyboards in order to navigate the online world. But these physical things are quickly subsumed and made transparent to the experience. There is, in essence, something very nonphysical about using Internet space.[8]

That the Internet is largely a mental realm is an easy argument, but its modality can also be read as mythic or spiritual, particularly in the case of the World Wide Web. Starbucks and Wendy's possess something akin to a corporate personality, and that essence or spirit is largely what their Web sites represent. If the Web were a purely analytic mental realm, there would be no need for presentational graphics that convey character and mood; pure text and discursive data would suffice. Internet chat rooms can be understood as fairly mental, but Web surfing takes one out of the realm of the analytic and into the spiritual. FAQs notwithstanding, it seems that the character, the idea, and perhaps even the *soul* of Home Depot are what you see on its Web site.

Thus there are two worlds—one physical, one mythic or spiritual—that overlap each other, and resonate back and forth. If a particular retail location goes out of business, its Web site will follow it into oblivion. If Macy's changes its logo, the graphics on its Web site will have to be updated. Songs initially released as digital downloads make their way into the physical world on CDs, and vice versa. As Vincent Mosco puts it, "physical geography and cyberspace are mutually constitutive."[9] This structure of two overlapping realities parallels certain tribal beliefs—in particular the notion of Dreamtime as understood by Aboriginal Australians, a tribal people who possess what is generally regarded as the oldest continual culture in the world.

For the Aborigines, the world was created during Alcheringa, or the time of the Dreaming. Its features were made by the Sky Heroes, chief of whom is Jarapiri, or the Rainbow Snake, who created rivers, waterholes, and rain. Dreamtime is more than a creation myth—the process happens in the present, and it always is happening.[10] Consider this: although the Internet was already created, it is still continually being created. Routers and modem banks continually send packets across wires; thus they are constantly creating the network. Historically speaking, the initial connections between remote computers were set up between research institutions in the 1960s, and thereby was created the Internet. But are any of those original machines still online, or have they (and every other original component) gradually been replaced or upgraded?

People are still creating the Internet, in a sense, every time they make a connection, update a Web page, or replace a device.

The experience of using the Internet alters subjective notions of time as well. Lance Strate suggests that as well as considering cyberspace, we should examine the impact of "cybertime" as well. For Strate, cybertime causes the past and future to collapse into the present, "contributing to the almost mystical sense of timelessness associated with cyberspace."[11] Although e-mail messages and bulletin board postings were composed sometime in the past, he notes, when we read them they have an immediacy to them that causes them to speak from the present. Strate even notes that cybertime can in this way be understood as "sacred time, a mythic time or dreamtime,"[12] but he defines "dreamtime" simply as a parallel to ordinary dreaming, a common comparison for video and other electronic media. He does not mean the Alcheringa of the Aboriginal Australians, and in the end, he thinks that dreaming (lower-case d) is an inadequate metaphor because of the active nature of computer use. Ultimately, the Internet is more like William Gibson's notion of a "consensual hallucination"[13] than the surreal fragments of an evening's slumber or sitcom.

The Alcheringa is the land, and each place has its own dreaming. Some places are more powerful, more sacred than others. In modern society, it has been argued, places are less important, both because of repetitive urban sprawl[14] and due to the fact that electronic media erase distances through interconnection.[15] McLuhan himself postulated that mass media bring us together in a "global village," diminishing the importance of physical geography. Where the Australian Aborigines have a rich knowledge of the land, and understand Australia to be like a massive human body,[16] we have a series of indistinguishable Levittowns connected by highways and television. Yet for each of us, our hometown still resonates with meaning, and many other places retain importance: New York, Las Vegas, the Grand Canyon—any postcard tour of America is sure to impress the fact that our cities and landmarks retain a mythic dimension. This is sustained in part by online tourism bureaus and informational Web sites, but it also exists in the stories we have and the unspoken resonances of important places. New Orleans, Paris, Chicago—the loss of mythic geography in the electronic age is overrated.[17]

Every stone, every plant in Australia has a spiritual existence in the Dreaming. The Dreaming lies over the physical world and maps to it, and the Aboriginal tribes don't distinguish between something's physical existence and its spiritual one. As Cartesian dualists, we often make that distinction, but whether someone buys a book at a brick-and-mortar Barnes & Noble store, or from Barnes & Noble's Web site, the money goes to the same place. The difference is that because the Web site exists outside of normal physical space, someone who lives far from a store can still get at its essence, which is equally available from anywhere wired. She or he enters the digital Dreamtime, finds the Web site, and makes the purchase. The book comes out of the Dreamtime via UPS or FedEx, usually within two or three days.

We differ from the Australian Aboriginals in how we conceive the relations between our souls and the land—at least for now. Aboriginal tribes believe that their essence does not come from their parents; rather it comes directly from Dreamtime. Conception occurs when a spirit enters a woman to be born. After death, the Aborigine returns to the Dreamtime to once again live a spirit existence. All of life's accumulated baggage is cast off as a separate spirit, or "mokuy," which goes to a spot in the land that tribesmen shy away from. We frequently hear from the dead in the form of recordings,[18] though—the occasional posthumous paternity suit notwithstanding—we do not literally expect Jimi Hendrix to impregnate a woman with his own soul from beyond the grave.

The future holds, so we are told, the promise of uploading our consciousness into the network in the illusion of eternal life.[19] Techno-mavens like Ray Kurzweil will seek to convince us to put disembodied digital spirits into the virtual land, much like the Dixie Flatline info-morph in William Gibson's science fiction novel *Neuromancer*. Shortly thereafter, someone else will try to convince us to download these constructs into new bodies, whether biological, mechanical, or hybrid, thus imitating the Ancestors of Dreamtime. If we fall prey to these illusions, it is perhaps because they resonate with earlier ways of understanding existence—tribal ways.

A *Churinga* Full of Rap and Metal

Fetishes and talismans are mystic objects that many tribal cultures use. A fetish,[20] in the anthropological sense, is a natural object such as hair or blood that is imbued with the magical power to ward off evil spirits. Talismans are similar, except that they might be more complex creations—sometimes involving metalwork—and they can feature more abstract symbolism, such as a pentacle or other symbols or drawings.

Talismans may protect the wearer, but they also bring good luck; and although they are typically worn as amulets, in some cases they might even be nonphysical words or phrases.[21]

Eisenberg notes that people used to carry around poems as talismans and leaves open the possibility that music might serve a similar function.[22] He wrote at a time when portable headphones and Walkmen were popular, yet he did not explore the connection, as he was largely concerned with vinyl. Vinyl records, of course, are too cumbersome to wear (though certain rap artists in the 1990s did wear CDs). Audiocassettes present similar limitations: more than a few burdens the carrier, hence, the popularity of "mix" tapes.

But with the coming of the iPod and other portable digital music players, thousands of songs fit into a device even smaller than a cassette Walkman. The player itself might be talismanic in the traditional sense, or perhaps the playlist, or the actual songs. But to focus on luck or protection from evil spirits in modern Western culture is to miss the point. Modern Western culture may still flirt with luck, but few still carry around objects to ward off evil spirits. A more general understanding is that talismans are objects "used to attract a certain type of energy or a particular type of person."[23] Music, and knowledge about music and musicians, certainly do bring social benefits to the knower, including acquiring acquaintances and occasionally facilitating the attraction of members of the opposite sex.

Simon Frith describes knowledge about popular music as a kind of cultural capital.[24] For Frith, those who commit themselves to become "fans" of particular genres gain a position of authority from which to speak. Even those who choose not to obtain deep knowledge about, say, Christian death metal find knowledge of music to be an important social tool. Certain musicians are so famous as to become public figures, and knowledge of them becomes assumed. This is often only noticed when it goes awry; try telling someone you've never heard of the Beatles, Bruce Springsteen, or Britney Spears, and it becomes immediately apparent. At the level of genre and more especially in subgenres, the knowledge thereof is far less useful in ordinary social situations. But this deeper knowledge about more obscure songs and artists can create deeper bonds among fewer,[25] and thus has a tribal resonance to it.

The talisman of the Aborigines is known as a *churinga*.[26] It is an oblong piece of wood, decorated with symbols relating to a tribesman's sacred animal or plant, called a totem.[27] The *churinga* (sometimes spelled "tjuringa") is used in sacred ceremonies, as it ties the Aborigine directly to his ancestors in Dreamtime. When not carried, the *churinga* is kept in a hut or cave. *Churingas* can be personal items, or they can be collective; they can also be inherited. But they tie the owner to the totem, to the Dreamtime, and to the earth, as do the songs of the tribe.[28] Each tribe also has a communal stone *churinga* that represents one of the Sky Heroes.

Our personal sonic talismans are plastic, largely, with some silicon or gallium arsenide integrated circuits.[29] Apple's marketing slogans certainly equate them with identity—"Which iPod are you?" asks the Web site, and newer models can be engraved with a name or personal message. These pseudo-*churingas* are filled with songs to carry us through the day, or at least through the workout. We keep them on our dressers when not in use, and not in caves or special huts. We put songs inside them from our digital Dreamtime. Some hold the voices of the deceased, some the voices of the living. A 20GB iPod holds five thousand songs; the high-end 60GB model can hold fifteen thousand. Our communal *churingas* sit on desktops at home next to their monitors, wired up directly to the Dreamtime through broadband or DSL for our families. Songs retrieved can be a source of knowledge, reassurance, and in some cases, social power in the form of cultural or subcultural capital.

Yet there is one vital difference between our sonic talismans and those of the native Australians: the character of the identity formed through use. For the Aboriginal people, the *churinga* has strong ties to someone's totem animal or plant, and it reflects a permanent, inviolable personal identity. David Mowaljarlai, an elder of the Ngarinyin tribe, put it thus: "I know who I am. I have my identity. I'm a Ngarinyin man. My Dreaming is Hibiscus. That's my symbol, a beautiful pink flower."[30] The essence of the totem comes from Dreamtime, from the land. Musical tastes—however unshakable they may seem in adolescence—are ultimately more transient and malleable. One may love jazz forever, but flirt between swing and hard bop at different stages of life. When the Aboriginal *churinga* is acquired, blood is spilled into the land to mark the occasion of the initiate at last becoming a full adult member of the tribe. One purchases a portable music player with a sense of exciting possibilities, but with the same sense of sacred ritual accorded buying a vacuum cleaner.

Western culture is awash in transient rules and connections, as Jean-François Lyotard noted in *The Postmodern Condition*. Our castles, so to speak, are inherently built on the sand of the "temporary contract." We may experiment with identity and group membership, and change affiliations over time, but in the end, we often deny our own mortality by dashing headlong into the media(e)scape. To this end, many media products like songs offer identities for us to use, borrow, and ultimately throw away. The tribalisms of rock and hip-hop are not spiritual modalities that sustain us, though they can, of course, alter or sustain moods, create motivation, form peer groups, and so on. They can, on a personal level, become something profound, particularly in adolescence. But whatever various style of contemporary music one prefers, the artists will fade, the public will grow weary, and eventually, after a long absence, it will be remarketed as nostalgia.

Music tells many listeners who they are. To the degree that those assumptions are based on quicksand, audiences find their subjectivity called into question. Grunge? It's over. New wave? Old news. But while a style lasts, the group affiliations built around it can feel intense and authentic. They can echo tribal modes, forming boundaries of inclusion and exclusion, causing schisms like the violent feuds between East Coast and West Coast rap artists in the mid-1990s. Genres may sound tribal, like the contrived discourse of chanting slogans of togetherness-in-alienation that was prevalent in 1980s arena rock songs.[31] They may even look tribal, such as the abstract bandings of the tattoos (identified with rock music fans) that became popular in the 1990s, and can now be seen occasionally in television documentaries about tattoo-removal. Such popular culture "tribalisms" may shape lives and inform identities, but in the end, they remain a matter of preference.

Genres that deal with mortality, like gangsta rap and death metal, do exist, but whether they fully resolve the cosmological issues of existence in ways that emphasize humanity's interdependence with the land is doubtful. Even where popular songs do discuss mortality, their status as commodities of repeatable spectacle diminishes their impact.[32] Most popular songs do not broach the topic, rather they deal with more mundane subjects such as relationships. Pop culture tribalism is like an Iron Maiden T-shirt—it identifies the wearer to both those inside and outside the genre discourse of heavy metal, possibly even granting authority as an expert with subcultural capital, but it can be quickly discarded for a button-down as needed.

We have the freedom to be more than one thing. We are not born into the tribe of country music any more than we are born into the tribe of *Star Trek* fandom. It is possible to like both, or neither. Music more typically offers opportunities for identity investment than other media, and these identities may be multiple and conflicting. We are all, in a sense, permanent pan-tribalists. Some things remain, others change, and we offer varying degrees of commitment to them. The Internet accentuates this modality, enabling networked interest communities to build around transient media content, like temporary pockets of networked logic. We become, in Joshua Meyrowitz's terms, "hunters and gatherers" in the Information Age.[33] The Internet offers musical artists' Web sites and the songs themselves, which, due to their smaller file size, download far faster than television episodes and movies. Music is quick, music is vital, and music informs identity and social relationships. Yet the freedom we have in filling our *churingas* with such music obviates the possibility of stable content affiliations in the media(e)scape. There is too much to explore, and it is always changing. Information glut is the death of cohesive identity,[34] even as it constantly constructs shifting identities against the reality of mortality.

"Just a Few Words from You, Mr. Savage"

Media studies as a discipline has a blind spot for the natural environment, concerned as it is with artificial mediated ones. The land itself is ignored. The Internet has laid a mythic, representational landscape over the physical one—a digital Dreamtime—and made environmental problems into problems of representation. We are so distanced from our natural habitat that we do not see the irony in every landfill having its own Web site. It's not so much that we have "no sense of place," as Joshua Meyrowitz argues. We still have notions of where we are, who we are, and what that means to us—those are built into our subjectivity. But we lack the sense that there is something vital about ourselves that can only be understood in the land. The Internet, with its promise of networked permanence, fosters myth, narrative, and notions of continuance for individuals. Its artifices fly in the face of reconciling our biological mortality with our natural environment. Through representation, the Internet marginalizes the biological underpinnings of life just as it marginalizes the environmental impact of its own detritus—millions of discarded AOL discs, obsolete computers, modems, and 5¼" floppy discs, writable CDs filled with outdated data, and the odd unrecycled printer cartridge.

In Aldous Huxley's novel *Brave New World*, the character of John is a literate intellectual, "typographic" by McLuhan's standards. But he lives in a world of new tribalism wrought by social engineering and genetics.

The Alphas, Betas, Gammas, and so on are strongly clannish, and tied to their (secondary) oral culture through songs and chants. They also have excessive dependencies on a sedative drug called "soma." As Neil Postman notes, it's possible to see television and other media as soma—and moreover, frivolous wastes of time that might otherwise be put toward rational use for the good of society.[35] Postman's analogy is undercut to some degree by the notion that media content—here, music—enhances social relations and informs identities for certain listeners (Frith's fans and their social capital) like soma does for Lenina. Even given its non-rational nature, small doses of pop music are probably harmless, regardless of what Postman, Plato, or Theodor Adorno thought. To the degree that we need five thousand or fifteen thousand songs in our iPods to feel satisfied, however, music can render our subjectivity as contingent along the shifting lines of the popular, battered about by corporate hegemony and the whims of marketing, or subsumed in the encyclopedic glut of everything available.

At the end of *Brave New World*, John, ironically called "Savage" for his untribal ways, wants to escape to the beauty of the natural environment. To this end, he sets up a residence at a lighthouse overlooking the sea. But he cannot rest, as he is constantly beleaguered by reporters who want to portray him in the media. In the end, he hangs himself. Denied exile, he had no way out of the society or its system of representation. All he wanted to do was live (perhaps "deliberately," in Thoreau's sense) in harmony with his environment, but media coverage of him doing so prevented it.

"Just a few words from you, Mr. Savage," asks a reporter before John soundly beats him in the coccyx. One might append nowadays ". . . for the podcast," or for the blog, or the television—it really doesn't matter. We have not understood in the least the most important lesson in virtual reality by the oldest culture that still practices it. We are the land, we come from the land, and we will return to the land. In between, we are still beholden to it, no matter how long ago Burlington, New Jersey's Web site was last updated. Ours is not a "false consciousness," as Marx would have it, and we are not "inauthentic," merely different from older cultures. Yet we can hear resonances of ourselves in those cultures, particularly in the Alcheringa. Viewing our transient content-based tribalizations in the context of the Dreamtime allows us to see themes that are perhaps essentially human in our brave new virtual world, but it lays bare our limits.[36]

Notes

1. This chapter brackets all forms of authentic religious experience enabled by the Internet, as well as noncontingent influences on identity such as race and gender; this management of scope is mandated to adequately address the areas under exploration in the space allocated.

2. Marshall McLuhan saw "tribalism" as characterized by oral culture, not social organization. A media determinist, he argued that the alphabet and printing created abstract modes of thought and consciousness apart from tribal closeness, but that mass media were "retribalizing" humanity and reducing the impact of printing. See Marshall McLuhan, "Playboy Interview: Marshall McLuhan—A Candid Conversation with the High Priest of Popcult and the Metaphysician of Media," *Playboy Magazine*, March 1969, reprinted in *Essential McLuhan*, ed. Eric McLuhan and Frank Zingrone, pp. 233–269 (New York: Basic Books, 1975). This is perhaps the best distillation of his thoughts on tribalism and retribalization. Earlier, McLuhan had associated tribalism with "panic terrors" due to the closeness of tribal life (*The Guttenberg Galaxy* [Toronto: University of Toronto Press, 1962], p. 32), but such a society would not long cohere; nor do "panic terrors" adequately describe existing tribal societies such as the Australian Aborigines. See also Walter J. Ong, *Orality and Literacy: The Technologizing of the Word* (New York: Routledge, 1982), p. 136, for Ong's description of "secondary orality," which "has striking resemblances to the old in its participatory mystique, its fostering of a communal sense, its concentration on the present moment, and even its use of formulas." Even though Ong does not use the word "tribal," his analysis of secondary orality seems to both refine and extend McLuhan's work on tribalism without the necessity of panic.

3. Evan Eisenberg, *The Recording Angel: Explorations in Phonography* (New Haven, Conn.: Yale University Press, 1987).

4. Ibid., p. 69. Instead of tribal uniformity, there is diversity in the "thang"; in this, Eisenberg is in accord with McLuhan and Ong's notions of a blending of tribal and literate modalities in the modern age.

5. John Alderman, *Sonic Boom: Napster, MP3, and the New Pioneers of Music* (Cambridge, Mass.: Perseus, 2001), p. 4.

6. McLuhan, "Playboy Interview," p. 240.

7. Sherry Turkle, *Life on the Screen: Identity in the Age of the Internet* (New York: Simon & Schuster, 1997).

8. The prototype here is the character of Case in William Gibson's *Neuromancer* (New York: Ace, 2005), who disdains his own physical body and refers to it as "meat."

9. Vincent Mosco, "Webs of Myth and Power: Connectivity and the New Computer Technopolis," in *The World Wide Web and Contemporary Cultural Theory*, ed. Andrew Herman and Thomas Swiss, pp. 37–60 (New York: Routledge, 2000). See p. 41.

10. Harvey Arden, *Dreamkeepers: A Spirit-Journey into Aboriginal Australia* (New York: HarperCollins, 1994), p. 108. An Aboriginal informant named Reg Birch tells the author: "We never looked back at it. The Dreamtime, I mean. It's now, you know? It's not some other time. It's here and now going on all

around us! The Dreamtime never stopped." Thanks to my colleague Tewodros Amdeberhan for suggesting this reference. I would also like to thank Greg Chiaramonti for our discussions of Aboriginal culture, and our creative musical endeavors implicating networked tribalism, consciousness "uploading," and other things.

11. Lance Strate, "Cybertime," in *Communication and Cyberspace: Social Interaction in an Electronic Environment*, ed. Lance Strate, Ron Jacobson, and Stephanie B. Gibson, pp. 351–377 (Creskill, N.J.: Hampton, 1996). See p. 369. Strate feels that the Internet allows for different conceptions of time, and thus cybertime is a kind of "metatime" that can mimic other temporal structures.

12. Strate, "Cybertime," p. 371.

13. Gibson, *Neuromancer.*

14. James Howard Kunstler, *The Geography of Nowhere: The Rise and Decline of America's Man-Made Landscape* (New York: Touchstone, 1993), p. 131. "The road is now like television," Kunstler writes, "violent and tawdry. The landscape it runs through is littered with cartoon buildings and commercial messages. There is little sense of having arrived anywhere, because every place looks like noplace in particular."

15. Joshua Meyrowitz, *No Sense of Place: The Impact of Electronic Media on Social Behavior* (New York: Oxford University Press, 1985), p. 328. Meyrowitz, though he is largely concerned with television, nevertheless asserts that networks of computers undermine the relationships between "social space and physical place."

16. I am told anecdotally that some residents of Michigan point to their right hands as a useful analog for the state when describing locations. The geography of Cape Cod is also described in terms of an arm. But as is befitting contemporary culture, these are loose signifiers not contextualized as part of a living body.

17. To mourn the 2005 tragedy in the wake of Hurricane Katrina, New York City held a New Orleans–style Halloween funeral procession in Greenwich Village, in which a figure of a phoenix (the classic mythic symbol of rebirth) was carried, as it was in the NYC Halloween parade after the destruction of the World Trade Center in 2001.

18. Eisenberg, *Recording Angel*, p. 47. In Eisenberg's estimation, record playing is a kind of necromancy in which listeners control dead and disembodied spirits, auditory ghosts with no visible form.

19. Ray Kurzweil, *The Age of Spiritual Machines: When Computers Exceed Human Intelligence* (New York: Penguin, 2000). Kurzweil notes that "uploaded" consciousness would not result in a transfer of awareness, but suggests that people would just have to "get over" that. A useful example of the kind of problem this presents is the infomorph hologram Arnold Rimmer on the BBC sci-fi sitcom *Red Dwarf*; Rimmer is acutely aware that he is not the entity whose memories he possesses, but rather only a simulation of a deceased Second Technician with the same thought patterns.

20. Fetishes, in the Marxist sense, are objects that substitute themselves for social relations. In the case of records, Eisenberg notes, the record stands in for relationships with musicians. See Eisenberg, *Recording Angel*, p. 20.

21. "Amulets and Talismans," Wikipedia, http://en.wikipedia.org/wiki/Amulet (accessed October 1, 2005).

22. Eisenberg, *Recording Angel*, p. 10.

23. "Alternative Healing Dictionary T–Z" (Reiki.Nu), http://www.reiki.nu/treatment/healing/dictionary5/dictionary5.html (accessed October 1, 2005).

24. Simon Frith, *Performing Rites: On the Value of Popular Music* (Cambridge, Mass.: Harvard University Press, 1996), p. 9. Fans of popular cultural forms possess "superior knowledge, experience, and commitment," and therefore their judgments are given "weight." Popular music has social value in that it enables discussion and the process of making musical judgments.

25. Sarah Thornton, "The Social Logic of Subcultural Capital," in *The Subcultures Reader*, ed. K. Gelder and Sarah Thornton, pp. 200–209 (New York: Routledge, 1997). Thornton refers to such knowledge as providing "subcultural capital."

26. James Cowan, *Aborigine Dreaming: An Introduction to the Wisdom and Thought of the Aboriginal Traditions of Australia* (London: Thorsons, 2002), p. 104.

27. Although we may speak of cat "people" and dog "people," distinguishing preference among domesticated pets is not the same as totemism. Perhaps the closest we come are the eagles and wolves on airbrushed T-shirts one finds in the same mall stores that sell incense, Bruce Lee posters, and quartz crystal necklaces.

28. Cowan, *Aborigine Dreaming*, p. 112.

29. Portable USB "flash" drives (also known as "thumbdrives") serve a function similar to portable music players in that they are capable of storing any kind of data, though they do not allow for music playback directly. They come equipped with a lanyard and are worn on college campuses; it would certainly be a worthwhile essay topic of its own to unpack the implications of these cultural artifacts.

30. Arden, *Dreamkeepers*, p. 198.

31. E.g., Twisted Sister's "We're Not Gonna Take It," Skid Row's "Youth Gone Wild," Quiet Riot's "Metal Health," Icon's "On Your Feet," and many, many others.

32. Jacques Attali, *Noise: The Political Economy of Music* (Minneapolis: University of Minnesota Press, 1985).

33. Meyrowitz, *No Sense of Place*, p. 328.

34. Kenneth Gergen, *The Saturated Self: Dilemmas of Identity in Contemporary Life* (New York: Basic, 2000).

35. Neil Postman, *Amusing Ourselves to Death: Public Discourse in the Age of Show Business* (New York: Penguin, 1985).

36. Cowan notes that the Aboriginal way of life is marginalized and threatened in modern Australia, and his book is filled with a plea to accord these people the autonomy that they deserve. Cowan feels that understanding the Aboriginal closeness to the land might help their cause, and teach us a few things as well: it might enable us to better relate to the Earth and prevent ecological disaster.

CHAPTER 12

Magic, Myth, and Mayhem:
Tribalization in the Digital Age

LEONIE NAUGHTON

You have to play the game to find out why you're playing.
—JENNIFER JASON LEIGH, E*XISTENZ* (DAVID CRONENBERG, 1999)

Drawing more than 25 million participants across the world,[1] online role-playing games are a burgeoning branch of the entertainment industry. "Pause life and play" has proven a persuasive slogan for multimedia giant Sony, whose virtual universe, Everquest, attracts more than a hundred thousand paying players in any hour, every day of the year.

"Magic, Myth, and Mayhem" focuses on immensely popular online role-playing games like the opulent and increasingly lucrative 3D virtual worlds of Everquest, Second Life, Ultima Online, and Project Entropia. Paradoxically, these elaborate, simulated communities are seen to draw on, and revive, elements of folklore. That this should be effected through the "new media" is not without irony; facets of preindustrial culture being recirculated and celebrated in a postindustrial age.

Many virtual worlds draw on mythology and preindustrial motifs by incorporating elements and characteristics of two related areas of folklore: *Maerchen* (folktales) and shamanism. Massive multiplayer online role-playing games (MMORPGs) and various virtual communities are viewed as inviting visitors to indulge in retribalization, and this impulse finds its expression in even broader popular cultural forms such as movies, techno music, rave dance parties, and contemporary fashion.

In the realm of contemporary fashion, for instance, "boho" and "gypsy" have been defined as *the* styles for the start of the new millennium, with different fashion designers continuing to favor Peruvian/Incan/Tibetan patterns and designs. "Eclectic ethnic will not lie down."[2]

The popularity of body art, such as piercing and tattoos, is viewed as a further manifestation of the tribalization of popular culture. In many tribal cultures, tattoos are ascribed a religious or magical meaning. Traditionally, warriors and sailors were tattooed with their tribal symbols.[3] More recently, tattoos have become fashion statements for contemporary youth, romanticizing ancient, mystical cults and tribal civilizations (Celtic, Native American, Peruvian).

Such body art can be read in part as a rejection of the ethos of materialism and the culture of corporate capitalism, with tattoos serving to favor the ethnic, the heroic, and the spiritual merits of archaic ages and traditions. They have come to symbolize a yearning for the sort of social integration, spiritual integrity, and valor attributed to tribal civilizations in the popular imaginary. Rave culture embraces comparable romantic sentiments.

Trance dancing, collective drumming, and mesmerizing displays of fire twirling at rave/techno festivals and carnivals are further indexes of non-European, tribal ritual in contemporary youth culture. Rave started off as a pantheistic cult involving a hedonistic celebration of technology through extreme sensory stimulus—intensely amplified electronic music, kaleidoscopic light shows and visual effects, adrenaline surging, synthetic drugs, and incessant dancing.

Animistic, Third World cultures are seen to influence rave dancing styles at these events. Traditional Balinese dancing and Tai Chi moves are thought to inspire arm movements of dancers at rave parties, and repetitive foot stamping, reminiscent of an energetic "hamster on a wheel," evokes the dancing of various indigenous cultures.[4]

Paradoxically, the rave milieu sees tribal impulses and tradition augmented by displays of digital multimedia. Techno (or electronic music) is indispensable to the rave milieu. Usually this music is digitally sequenced and produced by DJs who mix and sample from recorded tracks, using synthesizers, drum machines, and computers. Techno is characterized by repetitive rhythms and noises that invite association with automated mass production lines. Techno subcategories include the pagan-sounding variants of trance and jungle.

The all-night mass revelry of the rave, with its ecstatic dancing and its collective euphoria, harks back to tribal ritual, reviving shamanistic tradition. They share an emphasis on transcendence and heightened awareness, a collective and quasi-spiritual liminality. It's perhaps less than surprising that public access to the World Wide Web gained popularity at around the same time rave culture became a conspicuous and marketable global phenomenon—in the first half of the 1990s.[5]

In essence, rave culture and virtual worlds collapse what may once have been viewed as binary opposites: pantheism and the digital technology of the electronic age. To the initiated, rave culture's central creed is technoshamanism—an apt neologism that reflects the cult's dual valorization of digital culture and transcendental ritual. Some devotees consider that rave party DJs are technoshamen because they can "work miracles,"[6] moving revelers to ecstatic rapture through the use of technology.

It is widely acknowledged that an inordinately high percentage of computer programmers and those involved in the IT industry subscribe to and practice technoshamanism. For them, the "essential core of the universe is Algorithm."[7] As Dave Green elaborates:

> Technoshamanic culture has … substituted the dances of the Whirling Dervishes with raves; and, swapped ritual bonfires with the 'magically' transformative gazes of the strobe, and internet images and computer-generated fractals which are projected onto the walls of the venue. These allow access not to the lower, middle and upper realms of traditional shamanism but to the latent realities of Gaia, also termed Cyberia.[8]

For those who subscribe to technoshamanism, technology is their goddess,[9] and their tribal network thrives online.

Raves may have become increasingly commercialized over the last decade. Still, the liminality of the rave milieu remains, and it can be traced back to traditions of folklore, traditions that are also commemorated in various quest-based virtual worlds.

Slash and Bash: Virtual Worlds and Folktales

The liminal place is everywhere and nowhere. This is the mythic time known in every nursery as 'Once upon a time', or the Arabic equivalent, 'It was and was not so'. The not-quite-physical are mythic places of myth and folklore such as the Irish Tir na Oige or the judaeo-christian paradise America. . . . Folklore is full of perceived liminality.
—BOB TRUBSHAW, "THE METAPHORS AND RITUALS OF SPACE: AN INTRODUCTION TO LIMINALITY. OR WHY CHRISTOPHER ROBIN WOULDN'T STEP ON THE CRACKS"

Folktales, or fairy tales, were part of an oral tradition of storytelling practiced by every known civilization and culture in the world. Among the best-known tales are those that the Brothers Grimm transcribed and published in the 1820s. Today such tales tend to be dismissed, mistakenly, as a trivial and inferior form of narration. Yet rarely were they infantile or regressive.

Jack Zipes reminds us that, although fairy tales may include magical and fantastic elements, over the ages they were a medium through which individuals could make sense of the social order. "No matter what has become of the fairy tale, its main impulse was at first revolutionary and progressive, not escapist, as has too often been suggested. The realm of the fairy tale contains a symbolic reflection of real socio-political issues and conflicts."[10] Folktales were a widespread form of entertainment, enjoyed by adults—not just children, as the Anglicized and demeaning term "fairy tales" suggests.

Folktales leave their indelible mark on a broad range of computer games and MMORPGs. The dramatis personae of the folktale find extremely heavy representation in virtual worlds. Visitors to these worlds assume the identities of figures from folklore and folktales such as wizards, knights, shamen, elves, ogres, druids, beast masters, warriors, enchanters, bards, magicians, trolls, and halflings, categories that are referred to as classes.

Each participant must learn particular skills to ensure survival within these communities; their quests are the very stuff of folklore and folktales. Visitors to quest-based worlds are required to familiarize themselves with arcane crafts and occult practices that vary depending on the class of character. As I later elaborate, these tasks relate to the supernatural powers of the shaman. They may include casting spells to heal and revive other players, dabbling in alchemy, enchanting, learning to levitate, flying, and practicing divination. Artisans who can master ancient crafts and pastimes such as archery, fletching, fencing, blacksmithing, and making jewelry and armor prosper in various 3D worlds.

In aesthetic terms, many virtual worlds are redolent of fairy tales in their setting, graphic design, iconography, and costuming. The programmed antagonists in Everquest, Entropia (http://www.entropia .com), and Utopia (http://games.swirve.com/utopia), for instance, are also mythical creatures drawn from myth and fairy tales. Unpredictable programming sees ogres, giants, menacing ghouls, dragons, unicorns, animated trees, and sadistic fairies wandering through fantastical stretches of wilderness and woodlands assaulting hapless players. Entering into virtual worlds like Ultima Online and Everquest, one immediately recognizes walled cities with their moats, the fortresses, caves, and ruins that feature in illustrated fairy tale books from childhood. Most characters in quest-based worlds further the illusion by sporting medieval armor, tunics, and weaponry.

Further links between folktales and virtual worlds emerge when one considers the precedence given to speech and utterance in each domain. Folktales initially depended upon word of mouth—communication in virtual worlds being referred to as chat. Text to voice software is now becoming a more widespread feature in many online role-playing games.

Chat is a distinctive form of expression with its own slang: a heavy reliance on acronyms accelerates communication. Spelling and punctuation—if the latter is used at all—are often creatively improvised. The use of onomatopoeic expletives, phonetic spelling, and incomplete sentences enhances the impression of spontaneity. In this sense, online communication is considerably closer to oral speech than conventional writing.[11] At least one prominent "new media" analyst notes that the ancient tradition of oral narration "still manifestly holds sway on the Web."[12]

The feats endurance players face in quest-based worlds are perhaps the clearest evocation of folktales and traditions of folklore. Characters follow the same basic course of action. Vladimir Propp reminds us that the impetus for many folktales involves a protagonist embarking on a journey to a distant land. Fortitude, strength, and adroitness are tested. Obstacles have to be overcome in order to complete the quest, the ultimate reward being the acquisition of precious objects and/or special magical powers.[13] Game players, like protagonists in many folktales, are also required to complete tasks of supply and manufacture in order to ensure their subsistence.

MMORPGs engage with folklore in other ways. They succeed in recreating what is classified as the "essential tone" of the fairy tale—"a slightly sinister atmosphere, . . . [an] authentic recipe of frivolity, dreaminess, blitheness and sadism."[14] In her comprehensive analysis of the fairy tale from the seventeenth century until today, Marina Warner explains that the central narrative aim of these tales is to contest fear. Fairy tales display a preoccupation with "the phantasm of the … Other." They serve to "recognize it, either by rendering it transparent and safe, the self reflected as good"—or alternatively by destroying and banishing it. She observes, "At a fundamental level, 'Beauty and the Beast' in numerous variations forms a group of tales which work out this basic plot, moving from the terrifying encounter with Otherness, to its acceptance, or, in some versions of the story, its annihilation. In either case, the menace of the Other has been met, dealt with and exorcized by the end of the fairy tale. . . . The terror has been faced and chased." [15]

Virtual worlds such as Everquest depend on a comparable dynamic: as part of their quests, players confront life-threatening monsters that become increasingly menacing over time. Participants constantly confront fear of death as they enter into grisly combat with hordes of ogres, beasts of prey, and ghouls. Initially these encounters prove fatal. Players' characters may be "killed" by an array of antagonists, only to be resurrected then killed over and over again—or at least until they learn to slaughter monsters.

Through this invitation many virtual worlds entice visitors to contest and conquer various primordial fears. Like the fairy tale, quest-based role-playing games offer the lure of triumph over the horrific and the macabre. More specifically, these worlds, like the fairy tale, deal with "limits often set by fear." Each form deals with "a protagonist who sets out to discover the unknown and overcomes its terrors." [16]

As I have suggested, the advent of the digital age has seen the revival of tribalization, folklore, and related traditions of shamanism in popular culture. Here I wish to consider aspects of those phenomena in relation to the film industry, in particular focusing on recent blockbusters and cult films. Gaming and film are viewed as interconnected and mutually dependent markets: first, because of their reliance on digital technology and second, because their markets are horizontally integrated. Modes of delivering popular culture are clearly shifting, with consumers relying more frequently on the World Wide Web for access to movies, music, pornography, telecommunications, and information about current affairs.

Virtual communities are part of the diversifying entertainment industry that once had Hollywood at its epicenter. In relation to Hollywood, what was once regarded as the "back end"—the secondary means of making profits, such as product placement, movie paraphernalia, music soundtracks, and suchlike—has become the "front end." Now film has become an advertisement for what backers have really invested in: a computer game, a television and video program, a soundtrack, music video clips, a continuous loop of home entertainment, a theme park ride. [17] Cross-fertilization of product has intensified, at least over the last ten years, with the theme park ride, the computer game, and the online role-playing game being conceptualized simultaneously—a strategy Steven Spielberg used when marketing *Jurassic Park* in 1993. [18]

The runaway success of the raw, no-budget pseudodocumentary *The Blair Witch Project* (Eduardo Sanchez et al. 1999) is a more recent and extreme manifestation of horizontal integration involving a profitable affiliation among film, television, gaming, and the World Wide Web. Apart from following the postmodern teen pic/horror template, *Blair Witch* clearly celebrates paganism and the tribal culture associated with it through an audacious fabrication of a myth about the occult and witchcraft that supposedly led to the disappearance of three college students. *Blair Witch*, which was shot as a film school project, generated $108 million during the first five weeks of its theatrical release. Marketing involved a six-month unrelenting campaign of online hype and intrigue at www.blairwitch.com.[19] The film, in turn, inspired the release of three "volumes" of Blair Witch computer games and a television series that ran for two seasons. Described as causing a "cultural tsunami,"[20] *Blair Witch Project* was one of the biggest-grossing independent films of all time. Pagan iconography and the occult are seen to feature heavily here and elsewhere. Shamanism, transmogrification, and wizardry are also popularized in blockbusters like the *Harry Potter* films.

The cult film *Run Lola Run* (*Lola rent*, Tom Tykwer, 1998) was, like most recently released features, heavily promoted online with myriad Web sites. One included an interactive game that challenged players to solve a puzzle and meet a deadline to save film characters from being assassinated by gangsters.[21]

No doubt, the film's online promotion and packaging contributed to making *Run Lola Run* one of the most successful German films of the decade at the Australian and North American box office. *Run Lola Run* served other purposes online as well: it was used as an international teaching aid. Language exercises were made available for teachers of German based on student viewing of the film.[22]

This film exemplifies the entertainment industry's dependence on cross-fertilization of product in other, more striking ways. At a textual level, narrative agency and plot mirror the strategies participants use in virtual worlds. It may not be coincidental that Sony, the owners of the MMORPG Everquest, also produced this film.

In *Run Lola Run*, the eponymous hero races the clock, obsessively experimenting with causality and the contingencies of plot. Stylized like an avatar, Lola's compulsion is to perfectly master her mission, much as a player strives to advance to the next platform in a video game or a virtual world. Each location change is punctuated by Lola impatiently waiting at a portal (the entry to the bank, the doorway that leads from her mother's apartment to the garden, the gate that separates the garden from the chaos of the city), like a role-player waiting for a 3D world to load. Charging through the streets of Berlin with her flame-red hair, Lola even *looks* like an avatar in a role-playing game. Early in the film she is actually depicted as an avatar in an animated sequence. In various montage sequences, which show Lola deliberating over which course of action to take, the editing replicates her changing points of view, familiar to a game player striving to safely navigate through a maze or a hazardous virtual terrain. On occasion Lola even moves through space like an avatar, "beaming" herself from one location to the next. And she dies in various scenes, Manni her partner is killed in others, only to be resurrected in the next episode of the film. Although tribal motifs, the occult, and pagan iconography surface in this low-budget film, they were to become even more conspicuous in a spate of recent Hollywood blockbusters—in particular, the "sword and sandal" epic.

This old Hollywood film genre, which has been box-office poison, at least since the 1960s,[23] has returned to the screen in the new millennium and is enjoying mass appeal more than forty years later. *Gladiator* (Ridley Scott, 2000) heralded the resuscitation of the genre with its sensational displays of brutality and valor on the battlefields of ancient history.

Hollywood's revival of the epic genre is viewed as a further symptom of retribalization. The Greek and Roman empires appear to have captured the imaginations of a number of directors and stars. Brad Pitt and Eric Branner donned full armor to restage antiquity—Hollywood-style—in Wolfgang Peterson's extravaganza *Troy* (2004). Baz Luhrmann started shooting a $150 million epic about Alexander the Great starring Nicole Kidman and Leonardo Di Caprio in 2004. In the same year, Oliver Stone released a director's cut of *Alexander the Great* starring Colin Farrell, Anthony Hopkins, Val Kilmer, and Angelina Jolie. (Jolie played the lead role in the film-of-the-video-game *Laura Croft—Tomb Raider* (Simon West, 2001). With their reliance on digital technology, these films act as a portal through which audiences can be transported back to ancient history and classical mythology as action spectacle.

Retribalization and related traditions of shamanism have been most recently popularized in other movie blockbusters, such as *The Lord of the Rings* trilogy. Each of these films sees Frodo set out on an episodic quest to face death and repeated resurrection—his is a cycle of "res" and "regroup," like an intrepid participant in a MMORPG. The digital rendering of spectacular battles with armies of orcs and other monstrous hordes attacking fortressed cities; the animated trees that roam the woods; the elves and halflings are all familiar to participants in fantasy virtual worlds.

Everquest draws heavily and self-consciously on the cult that surrounds the Tolkien books and the screen adaptations. That world includes the same "races" featured in the Tolkien stories, and many avid game players assume names of the characters from those books. Watching the films is akin to being a participant in a massive scale online role-playing game.

The Lord of the Rings trilogy revels in folklore traditions and mysticism, particularly with its spectacular displays of shamanistic power. Gandolf is identified as supreme shaman, with the ability to travel to other worlds, retrieve souls, and summon the spirits of nature. These are also the supernatural powers that participants in a variety of MMORPGs can summon and wield in their virtual quests. This leads me to further substantiate my initial assertion: that branches of popular culture indulge in rituals of retribalization and shamanism.

Tribalization and Shamanism

Role-playing and computer games are often denigrated as violent and ritualistic. Yet new media analysts have attributed a greater and more significant function to these pastimes. "Like the religious ceremonies of passage by which we mark birth, coming of age, marriage and death, games are ritual actions allowing us to symbolically enact the patterns that give meaning to our lives. Games can also be read as texts that offer interpretations of experience."[24]

Indeed, the majority of online role-playing games revolve around rituals of death and resurrection. They encourage tribal pastimes such as hunting in packs, looting, and engaging in battle. The structure of fantasy worlds means that participants are perpetually "looking for group," the objective being to maximize personal safety and spoils from raids.

In inviting players to indulge in rituals of retribalization, many MMORPGs draw on or allude to traditions of shamanism. (Perhaps the Web's most overt invocation of tribalism comes with the brand labeling of one of the world's largest online retail outlets—Amazon.com. Tribalism is also invoked by Zuibi, an online travel service.) Everquest and

Ultima Online involve a self-conscious celebration of the supernatural powers attributed to the shaman. They invite the correlation of shamanism and the cyberenthusiast's experience of virtual reality.

From a present-day perspective, shamans are most immediately viewed as spiritual sages, male or female. They provide solace: often they possess special healing powers and the psychic ability to connect with the afterlife. Anthropologists and historians of religion approach shamanism as an archaic magico-religious phenomenon. Quintessentially a liminal figure, the shaman lives an isolated existence at the margins of society and has knowledge of rituals that can alter states of consciousness, so bringing individuals in contact with spirits of nature and the supernatural. "The distinguishing feature of shamanism is its focus on an ecstatic trance state in which the soul of the shaman is believed to leave the body and ascend to the sky (heavens), or descend into the earth (underworld)."[25] The shaman's "ability to consciously move beyond the physical body," to undertake "journeys to hidden worlds," can also be applied to the cybercitizen's experience of various virtual worlds.

When individuals role-play in worlds like Everquest, Ultima Online, Utopia, or Cybertown, they are given the sensory impression of visiting a parallel universe—they are simultaneously embodied in one world and disembodied in another. Viewing one's own virtual representation moving through simulated cities and landscapes of cyberspace is the visual equivalent of the shaman's out-of-body experience.

Visitors to virtual worlds can scarcely avoid harrowing, near-death experiences. The corpses of players are scattered everywhere, and one constantly hears players pleading for "res," to be brought back from the dead by sages and shamen who have mastered the art of resurrection.

Project Entropia's designers make ironic comment on virtual worlds' morbid proclivities by including a "Death and Resurrection" kiosk in the world's central portal. The kiosk is rendered much like a hawker's stall—the sort that sells novelties at a fair or festival—a seemingly ironic comment on virtual worlds' capitalizing on rituals of death.

Players adjust quickly to accepting virtual death, especially when granted the possibility of returning to the living and reclaiming all earthly goods amassed in the last life. These fixations are conspicuous in social communities with contemporary settings, like The Sims Online, as much as in quest-based medieval worlds like Everquest. The Sims designers explain:

Although there is no player-killing in the game, you can indeed die. Starvation will be the most common way, but you can also electrocute or drown yourself, among other tragic means. Once you're dead, you stay dead [*sic*], wandering around the game as a ghost, until you can convince another player to resurrect you, which will require a special skill or job object. You can die on purpose, if being a ghost appeals to you.

The game's founder, Will Wright, further enthuses, "I like the idea of [The Sims Online] death parties . . . where the first thing you do when you walk into a house is die." [26]

Even though shamanism and rituals of death may feature in socially based virtual worlds, they are nevertheless more prevalent in quest-based role-playing games. For the shaman has a spiritual affinity with the dead, the dying, and lost souls. Shamans are thought to assist the dead and dying by journeying with them, guiding "them to a place where they will be content and not have them stay here adrift in the Middle World." [27] They are believed to aid individuals who have suffered life-threatening traumas, and as a result "may have lost some of their soul . . . The techniques for healing soul loss are soul retrieval techniques, and one of the classic shamanic methods is to go searching for that lost portion of the soul and restore it." [28]

These forms of shamanic healing feature prominently in Everquest, where fatalities are especially high and gruesome. Characters can die not only by drowning or in battle, but also by starving, falling from great heights, and being burned or poisoned.

In the early stages of play, resurrection is automatic, yet, with experience, players are expected to navigate back to the scene of their demise and retrieve their own corpse. If they neglect to relocate their corpse, they risk having their bodies looted. Then, they are subject to demotion and must relinquish all previously acquired game status.

Virtual death is usually very humiliating, prompting the introduction of the novel variant of shamanic healing and soul retrieval, outlined above. The Everquest manual refers to this task as "corpse dragging." Players who have been slaughtered in perilous locations can give other, more resilient players "permission to drag [their] corpse" to a safer place. [29] This is akin to shamanistic soul retrieval, providing players with the option of reintegration and resurrection.

Other shamanistic elements are incorporated into virtual worlds. Quite a few character types are granted the power to heal and cast spells. They can then use their magical powers to restore other injured players to health and to strengthen their resistance to dangerous elements such as poison and fire. Some have the power to immobilize monsters in battle. Others have mystical affinities with various spirits of nature they can conjure up in times of duress. Advanced magicians and wizards can make themselves levitate or disappear to avoid danger. Shamanistic journeys to "hidden worlds otherwise mainly known through myth, dream and near death experiences"[30] form the very basis of involvement in virtual worlds like Everquest. In effect, and by design, these games constitute a virtual shaman initiation.

Notes

1. http://www.campus-technology.com/news_article.asp?id=11309& typeid=155 (accessed August 6, 2005).

2. Pauline Weston Thomas, "Fashion Trends 2005–2006," http://www.fashion-era.com/Trends_2006/1_fashion_trends_2006_looks_autumn_05_winter.htm#Transitions_to_New_Fashion_Trends_Autumn_2005_Winter_2006 (accessed September 21, 2005).

3. Over most of the last century, in the West at least, tattoos customarily adorned the bodies of mostly working-class and lower-middle-class men. Then, tattoos were frequently associated with temerity, allegiances to groups, and rituals of initiation into manhood. They carried with them particular connotations of class or machismo. This form of body art has gained broader favor and popularity over the last decade, notably among young women. Celtic tattoos are especially popular with "generation X."

4. http://www.hyperreal.org/raves/spirit/technoshamanism/Technoshaman-Definitions.html (accessed September 12, 2005).

5. The Netscape browser was marketed in late 1994, the same time that the Criminal Justice and Public Order Act was introduced in the UK in an attempt to control unruly raves.

6. http://www.hyperreal.org/raves/spirit/technoshamanism/Technoshaman-Definitions.html (accessed September 30, 2005).

7. Ibid.

8. Dave Green, "Technoshamanism: Cyber-sorcery and Schizophrenia," http://www.cesnur.org/2001/london2001/green.htm (accessed April 14, 2005).

9. See "The Technopagan Prayer," http://www.hyperreal.org/raves/spirit/technoshamanism/Technopagan_RavePrayer.html (accessed April 7, 2005).

10. Jack Zipes, *Breaking the Magic Spell: Radical Theories of Folk and Fairy Tales* (New York: Routledge, 1992), p. 36.

11. Sherry Turkle, *Life on the Screen: Identity in the Age of the Internet* (New York: Free Press, 1997), p. 183.

12. Sean Cubitt, "Shit Happens," in *The World Wide Web and Contemporary Cultural Theory*, ed. Andrew Herman and Thomas Swiss (London: Routledge, 2000), p. 134.

13. See Vladimir Propp, *The Morphology of the Folktale* (Austin: University of Texas Press, 1968), for a detailed account of recurrent narrative structures.

14. Marina Warner, *From the Beast to the Blonde: On Fairy Tales and Their Tellers* (London: Vintage, 1995), p. 288.

15. Ibid., pp. 276–277.

16. Ibid., p. 276.

17. James Schamus, "To the Rear of the Back End," in *Contemporary Hollywood Cinema*, ed. S. Neale and M. Smith (London: Routledge, 1998), p. 94.

18. Thomas Schatz, "So, Medium—Message? What's the Plot?" (paper presented at the 2000 Film and Television Trade Forum, Vancouver International Film Festival, September 2000).

19. Accessed October 6, 2005.

20. "Movies: Curse of the Blair Witch," *Newsweek Entertainment*, January 26, 2004, http://msnbc.msn.com/id/3988556/ (accessed September 10, 2005).

21. Viewers were also able to conduct a whole variety of virtual tours related to the film, including visiting shooting locations online. http://german.tqn.com/library/bllolafotos.html (accessed March 10, 2004).

22. http://german.tqn.com/library/bllolaex.html (accessed March 10, 2004).

23. *Cleopatra* was an expensive flop after it was released in 1963, and a year later *The Fall of the Roman Empire* had a similar fate.

24. Janet Murray, *Hamlet on the Holodeck: The Future of Narrative in Cyberspace* (Cambridge, Mass.: MIT Press, 1998), p. 143.

25. "FAQ. Shamanism General—Overview," http://www.deoxy.org/shaover.htm (accessed February 10, 2002).

26. Geoff Green, "The Sims Online: Indulge Your Inner Weirdo," http://www.gamers.com/game1016135/previews (accessed January 10, 2004).

27. Michael Harner quoted in http://www.shamanism.org/articles/857415539.htm#0 (accessed February 2, 2002).

28. Ibid.

29. http://eqlive.station.sony.com/manual/manual.jsp?id=46807.

30. Michael Harner quoted in http://www.shamanism.org/articles/8574155 39.htm#0 (accessed February 2, 2002).

PART IV

CYBERCRIME AND COUNTERCULTURE AMONG ELECTRONIC TRIBES

CHAPTER 13

Mundanes at the Gate ... and Perverts Within: Managing Internal and External Threats to Community Online

STEVE ABRAMS AND SMARAGD GRÜN

One of the first things Mary Sue Slasher does every morning is to check her friends list on LiveJournal.com to see what's going on with her friends and fandoms. Community happens fast online ... if she doesn't keep up, she'll never catch up. She also checks her e-mail to see whether there are any responses to posts and comments she'd made the previous evening. Because the slash community is so big, it's impossible to read everything, even in a smaller fandom. However, she has several LJ filters set up to help her manage the constant challenge of filtering through the sheer volume of slash stories and discussion to find the pieces she wants.

At work, Mary Sue immerses herself in her work, waiting until her lunch hour to check her LiveJournal. She knows she won't be able to really catch up until she gets home, but she needs to keep in touch. She finds posts with links to new stories, art, and news articles on fannish topics, and she reads some reviews of current slashy shows and movies. She's excited to see one of her favorite authors, a "thought leader" in fandom, weighing in on an extended metadiscussion, and she makes a mental note to read it through when she gets home. There are personal posts, keeping her up to date on a recent fannish kerfuffle, as well as mundane (nonfan) events in her friends' lives. Though she reads her friends' posts daily, she has no idea where many of them actually live. Still, they are some of the most important people in her life.

Introduction

Mary Sue's imaginary day reflects anecdotes from multiple members of the slash fan fiction community recounting their routine, slash-related practices and the extent to which they have adopted, and adapted, computer and Internet technologies since the dawn of the public Internet in the early 1990s. It presents an evolving view of slash, compared to the one described by Henry Jenkins in *Textual Poachers: Television Fans & Participatory Culture*[1] (which generally covers the pre-Internet era of slash between the early 1970s[2] and the early 1990s). Jenkins characterizes slash as "a genre of fan stories positing homoerotic affairs between [television] series protagonists,"[3] focusing his analysis on the content of the slash fiction, relative to a series' canon (source material), and what it has to say about gender and sexual identity in modern society. He claims that slash "may be fandom's most original contribution to the field of popular literature."[4] He did not, however, report many details of the community of fans—almost entirely female—that developed in this pre-Internet era of paper-based "zines" (fan magazines containing fiction, commentary, or both) and annual "cons" (conventions), but he concluded his analysis by observing that "the meaning of slash resides as much in the social ties created by the exchange of narratives, the sharing of gossip, and the play with identity as it does with the words on the page."[5]

In early 2004, we began a study into the nature of these social ties by interviewing fifteen committed "slashfen" (fans of slash) at one of several slash conventions, referred to here as "CON,"[6] held annually in the United States. The study was focused on the construction of identity and community by slashfen using the blogging service LiveJournal. com. Though by no means comprehensive, and certainly biased toward online activities, the reports of these slashfen indicated aggregate totals of 156 years of slash-related activity and 144 years of Internet use, with five respondents reporting their entries to the world of slash as occurring up to a decade before the advent of the public Internet. The interviews, totaling 16.2 hours in duration, were semistructured, and the results were analyzed under a Grounded Theory approach. Interviewees were thirteen females and two males, all of whom were experienced users of the Internet. Only one interviewee did not regularly use Live-Journal, though she reported having "tried it out" [E].[7] All were native English speakers; thirteen were U.S. citizens. These interviews afford an interesting peek into this online community, its adoption of Internet technologies, and the contributions these technologies make to the long-term survival and growth of this community. In addition to those of interviewees, some comments from the second author of this chapter, based on her diverse experiences as a slash fan/author and occurring in the context of discussion of interview results, are included in appropriate areas and attributed to "Smaragd."

The advent of the Internet, and its ensuing array of technologies of interaction, had a tremendous impact on the slash community. Rhiannon Bury claims that "the data available indicates that publishing and accessing of slash is now primarily done online,"[8] in contrast to Jenkins's depiction of the pre-Internet slash world as wholly print-based. However, some things haven't been changed by the move online, and these core features—the "fic,"[9] the individual fan, and the mundane (nonfan) world in which they are embedded—serve as a good starting point for our exploration of that which *has* changed.

The Fan and the Fic

It is difficult to discuss the fan or the fic separately, so closely are they identified with each other in the minds of many slashfen. Though it may be a simple hobby to some, it is a way of life to our interviewees and is intimately linked to their own identities:

> [G]: "I am two persons . . . one of them is me and one is my original character."
> [N]: "The 'thing' that is slash in us is so integral that *we* wouldn't exist, wouldn't be the same person without slash."

This strong identification with slash is also reflected in how slashfen felt when they first discovered slashfic:

> [J]: "I felt like I'd fallen down the 'rabbit hole.' . . . I'd always done slash in my head but, now, there it is in print."
> [A]: "I felt like I was home . . . seriously, I felt like I was home."
> [C]: "I thought 'YES!' . . . that's exactly what's going on [in the TV show]. I knew it! I knew it! I knew it!"

Slash versus Mundane/Fannish Worlds

Jenkins observed that "slash was originally met with considerable resistance from fans who felt such writing was an improper use of program materials and violated the original characterizations" and that "some cons [are] still refusing to allow the public distribution of homoerotic publications for fear of offending actor guests and many fans violently offended by the very idea of slash."[10] Our interviewees had similar perceptions of how slash is viewed by the nonslash, fannish world:

[D]: "Slash is the thing other fans make fun of."
[J]: "Slash is a 'ghetto' part of fandom, very pejorative; nonslashers were extraordinarily self-righteous and contemptuous about slash; one didn't always admit to slashing . . . sort of an 'in the closet' aspect to it."

Beyond fandom, in the mundane world, slashfen perceive an even bleaker environment. Even as the visibility of gay rights and culture has grown in recent decades, religious extremists and political opportunists around the world have adopted strongly antihomosexual stances, and their followers could perceive slash as a celebration of homosexuality:

[G]: "I lost a job because I was considered a security risk since I wrote my slashfic under my real name. This led me to create [my online persona]."
[Smaragd]: "Many slashers fear exposure to their family, their neighbors, their coworkers, especially in the religious and socially conservative middle America."

Fan fiction itself inherently involves the reuse of another's intellectual property, without explicit permission and potentially exposing slashfen to penalties for violation of copyright law:

[N]: "We really try to keep this secret from the mundanes, because it's wholly unacceptable to most . . . [that] it's copyright violation, that it's illegal. Then, too, it's geeky [to be a fan] and embarrassing, AND we write explicit sex . . . it's a perfect triangle of things you don't tell mundanes."
[A]: "In the minds of outsiders, I'm sure they think we're stealing."

Fandom is often viewed as beneficial to copyright owners because it sustains a loyal fan base for their product. Genfic and hetfic typically extend the source material along lines consistent with the producers' intentions, albeit sometimes more explicitly than the broadcast market would allow. Slashfic, on the other hand, not only re-uses another's property, but takes it in directions that are potentially offensive to its producers and consumers. Slashfic intentionally *perverts* the source material, in the sense of an enjoyment in subverting mundane norms one doesn't respect, along homosexual and homosocial[11] themes. Slashfen delight in that perversion: "Everyone here is a pervert [by mundane standards] ... and we like it like that" [H].

Jenkins similarly observes that slashfen "romanticize the 'shocking' and 'scandalous' quality of their underground activities."[12] Even so, slashfen know the threat that flaunting their perversity poses, to themselves and to slash; many of the normative practices described in the rest of this chapter are couched in terms of politeness and consideration for nonslashers, yet clearly contain a subtext of self-protection.

"Just Like Me"

If there is a common basis for a slash community, before and after the advent of the Internet, it's the recognition of others who share a strong identification with slashfic. The joy of finding others "just like me" is the most repeated sentiment heard during this study, reflecting not only homophilous interests in particular fandoms and particular character pairings, but the extent to which they are made to feel different by mundanes and nonslash fans who are hostile to the very premise of slash.

> [E]: "I knew about slash but I couldn't find anyone. Then I [found] a slash mentor and other people just like me."
> [L]: "I live in a world that doesn't really 'get' me. Going to cons and being online with people who 'get' me, who understand where I'm coming from and are coming from the same place . . . it's nice to have that."
> [N]: "Hanging around with other slashers is incredibly enjoyable and freeing because you finally found other people with whom you can talk about these things you've hidden your entire life."

The Practice of Slash

Many fans produce slash content, which has grown beyond textual stories to include art, recommendation lists, icons, and music videos. While authoring slash is fundamentally a solitary activity, some authors have long sought other slashfen to "beta-read" (critique) their fic before it's made publicly available. For most fans, however, the "practice of slash" can be broadly characterized as a continual iteration between absorbing source material, viewing slash content, and discussing both with others … which often leads back to new source material and content. Fandoms wax and wane with the availability of source material, leading some fans to seek additional sources. For example, since Jenkins wrote *Textual Poachers*, an emergent subgenre has been "real person slash" (RPS), in which source material derives, not from the canon of a TV series or movie, but from the public personae that celebrities (e.g., actors, sports figures, politicians, musicians) present to the world in the course of their interviews and public activities.[13]

The greatest changes in the practice of slash, however, occurred with the community's adaptation of their practices to the services afforded by the Internet. In the rest of this chapter, we will explore these changes, and their consequences, in the development of a model of electronic tribalism, which we argue could only exist with online interaction and which affords some explanatory power for the long-term survival of the slash community in a hostile world.

Slash Community before the Internet

[J]: "I discovered a [slash] zine, mildly erotic by today's standards, at a [Star] Trek con in 1982. It had Kirk and Spock on the cover, but the dealer had it hidden under a sheet, in the back, so as not to offend potential customers."
[C]: "At the con, I found zines and, with zines, I found flyers. One of the flyers said it was for explicit male-male homoerotica . . . it was all slash [for me] from then on; this was mid-1980s, when zines were the only outlet."
[Smaragd]: "Before the Internet, you had to 'know someone who knew someone who knew someone' to get slash."

In the pre-Internet era, these experiences were typical in the way slashfic could be found. By [J]'s account, slashfen "got on [an editor's] mailing list for their zine" in order to learn about new slashfic. Editors would "make a circuit of the cons," hawking their zines as dealers. "You met pseudonyms [authors] at cons. Pseudonyms were winked at. The secret way you got to know the real identity of a pseudonym was to ask a dealer, who'd then nod towards someone." A zine editor, at that time, was "the alpha female," coordinating her own "stable of authors," to produce fic for a "group of hangers-on" to read and discuss.

Comments were mailed to editors for publication in subsequent zines, where slashers were able to get a sense of others "just like her," even if direct interaction was limited. Though "zine stories were published under pseudonyms, comments were printed with real names" [J] and, sometimes, with pseudonyms [Smaragd]. Editors also brokered relationships by passing on mail to authors referenced in the letters by their pseudonyms. If the author so wished, she could then contact the letter writer directly. In some cases, this resulted in face-to-face gatherings of slashfen around an author, or just among themselves, between cons. "Zine-based community was small, [but] we knew who the editors were, knew who the authors were, knew who wrote [high] quality, who wrote dreck [low quality]" [J].

Slash Community on the Internet

The Internet opened to the general public in March 1991,[14] providing a new starting point for many slashfen to find fic via Usenet alt.* newsgroups:

> [J]: "My earliest Internet activity was to go to Usenet to get slash."
> [B]: "I came across alt.sex.fetish.startrek. One of the women there sold me a zine. I knew about slash, as a genre, but didn't get into this people part of it until the end of 1994."

Although individual slashers used e-mail among themselves, community-oriented e-mail lists also sprang up during this early period:

> [C]: "The Internet burst upon the slash community circa 1991, at [CON 2]. People . . . had started an e-mail list that was not specific to a fandom. I was about the 30th person at the con to subscribe to it. Once I got on, I started forming relationships with others there."
> [L]: "When I first started in fandom, it was all done on mailing lists."

The first multimedia Web browser appeared in 1993,[15] and the slash community soon followed with slash authors creating their own Web pages, with links to their fic:

[D]: "Once I found authors' Web pages, linked from Usenet postings, I didn't go to Usenet groups anymore."
[M]: "I found recommendation pages for fic on the Web, which linked to author's pages . . . a lot of this early slash activity online was oriented around [specific] authors."

Following these individual Web sites, multiple-author Web archives of slashfic became a new entry point for new slashfen in the mid- to late 1990s:

[A]: "I went on the Web to find slash for a new TV show and, from there, I found slash for other fandoms, all archived online. The minute I found slash, I read very little genfic anymore."
[K]: "I found out about slash when I found a Web archive. I felt like I'd stumbled on a gold mine . . . 3,000 stories, oh my! I read through them all . . . alphabetically."

In mid-1996, the Internet saw a rapid increase in the number of women using the World Wide Web,[16] which resulted in "a veritable slash explosion."[17] This benefited the community not only by increasing the supply of slashfic, but by increasing the opportunities for social interaction—both online and offline—on which the community's survival depended. This explosion was enabled not only by the presence of more women online, but the availability of new online tools that enabled slashfen to take greater control over the resources available to them. However, some technical expertise was necessary for anyone to administer a Web server or a mailing list server:

[N]: "The first mailing lists were the Majordomo-type lists and you had to have your own server and special software. Only a few people could [technically manage] such lists. There were only a handful, [maybe] one per fandom."
[L]: "You had to know something about computers to run the mailing list."
[D]: "I managed Web servers, in my job, so it was natural [for me] to run my own site on my own server."

Because of the expertise required, there were few slash mailing lists, but they tended to attract large numbers of slashfen because of the opportunity to interact with others "just like me" they afforded. However, such mailing lists had problems of their own:

[A]: "[List owners] were very strict . . . in keeping discussion 'on-topic' [oriented to the specific focus of a list]. You could get kicked off for going off-topic."

[N]: "You had to stick to the fandom for the list, there was no discussion of personal life, or anything like that. Everybody was like 'take that offline.'"

[L]: "Back before LiveJournal . . . mailing lists would tend to degenerate into back-and-forth arguments all the time. You know, one person pisses another person off, then everyone else has to take sides. And it just got to be too much back-biting and sniping."

In 1997, the functionalities of mailing lists and Web sites merged with the creation of OneList[18] and its successor "Web-group" services: eGroups.com[19] and Yahoo! Groups.[20] These Web-groups were basically Web-based systems for creating and managing e-mail lists. Suddenly, the control of mailing lists shifted from a few technically adept people to many less-expert Web users. Previous e-mail lists were constrained by their adept administrators, but they attracted many members of a fandom. Web-groups were less constrained, but that freedom resulted in ever more finely divided groups within the community as slashfen could avoid conflict by starting their own Web-group:

[N]: "This thing called OneList came out, which was Web-based. Anybody could create a [mailing] list. Everyone was creating lists, right and left, for every tiny aspect of every fandom. It was exponential growth."

[P]: "Before eGroups took over the universe, slash interaction was mostly on mailing lists, spread over many servers."

[L]: "[The Web-groups] started to splinter into smaller and smaller, more specific discussion groups."

Slash Community on LiveJournal.com

Circa 2001, the slash community began migrating to the blogging service at LiveJournal.com:

[A]: "In 2001, the idea was passed around to 'check out this thing called LiveJournal' and a raftload of us jumped over there [from our Web-group]."

[J]: "People have flocked to this [LiveJournal] like it's the holy damned grail."

[N]: "LiveJournal hit and, in the three years since, LiveJournal has grown, pretty much, to take over almost every part of slash fandom."

LiveJournal[21] is an Open Source blogging system.[22] One feature that distinguishes it from the other technological media mentioned above is an easy-to-use, automated aggregator called a "friends list" (or "flist").[23] Each LiveJournal user designates other LiveJournal users as posting blog entries she wants to read, in a process called "friending" them. The LiveJournal software then aggregates the blog postings of one's friends into a navigable "friends page" (an "LJ"). LiveJournal users can then read the aggregated postings in their LJ and comment on them. While the postings are a unidirectional broadcast of individual interests, events in daily life, and slash content, comments on each posting are visible to other readers (which may then evoke their own comments), and, thus, they form the basis for intersubjective interaction and consequent social relationships.

LiveJournal was broadly embraced by the slash community, resulting in a migration from previous Internet services:

[K]: "LiveJournal for me has been wonderful, it's freed me from the confines of mailing lists. . . . I've got a place where I can put stuff that's off-the-wall."
[G]: "We were trying to set something up for our [slash subgenre] group, but we didn't want to go through all the rigamarole of setting up a Yahoo! group. So, we chose LiveJournal. It was free. One could start a community there."
[L]: "I think [Web-groups] kind of tore fandom apart a little. For a while, I was really very much on the periphery of fandom. I went to cons, I talked to the friends I'd always talked to, and I kept up with them personally. Then LiveJournal brought me back into fandom in a more participatory way."

Part of LiveJournal's attractiveness is due to the capacity it affords to control access to one's postings through "friends-locking" (or "flock"-ing). In some cases, this feature isn't used, and the postings are accessible by the public and Internet search engines: "I don't friends-lock [my posts] . . . what you see is what you get" [M]. When it *is* used, it's generally used for very personal reasons or to hide the postings from the mundane world:

[P]: "I write RPS, but I wouldn't do it without LiveJournal, where I can flock it so they [the actors] can't find it."

[G]: "If it's my fic or details about my personal life, I'll friends-lock it."

[F]: "I flock my LJ when I make nasty comments about a story."

[B]: "I rarely put very personal information in my LJ and, when I do, I friends-lock it. Mostly 'get it off my chest' kinds of things."

When understood as a metaphor for aggregating blog postings, Live-Journal's use of the term "friend" for this technology system is un-problematic. In reality, as *every* interviewee pointed out, LiveJournal "friends" are not *friends* in the popular sense of those involved in positive social relationships:[24]

[A]: "LiveJournal friends are not necessarily *real* friends."

[N]: "There are some people on my flist I don't particularly like, as people, but I enjoy their writing."

[H]: "My flist is just those people I like to read."

This seemingly trivial semantic issue can lead to very real social problems when people are "de-friended," or removed, from one's flist. Such culling is necessary because people's interests can diverge over time. In addition, it's easy to accumulate LJ friends to the point where it's impossible to keep up with reading all their LJ entries. At the time of these interviews, the fourteen LiveJournal-using slashfen interviewed reported an average of ninety-seven LJ friends in their flists:

[P]: "I feel guilty if I'm not at least skimming my friends' entries. I'm also afraid I might be missing something in the scene."

[C]: "There's not enough time . . . reading and commenting take up all my time."

[Smaragd]: "[T]hings happen so fast. You have 100 people friended, and if they all happen to post in one 3-hour period, you'll be so far behind in your reading, it's hell to catch up. And if a kerfuffle breaks out and you miss the initial posts, you'll really never be able to understand how it unfolded."

De-friending can be a contentious social issue because of the visibility of friending and the shift to invisibility as a result of de-friending:

[A]: "De-friending can be sticky . . . you get hurt feelings."
[P]: "There's a 'politics of friending' that arises because 'if you un-friend me, I'm going to be upset because you don't like me anymore.' I think it has a greater impact in the slash community [than other LiveJournal communities] because we're mostly women and women interact differently than men. There's a greater emotional loading to the term 'friend.'"

However, LiveJournal offers a filtering feature, called "friends groups," that enables LiveJournal users to define subsets of their flists, which they can then use both to filter people out of their aggregated blog stream and to limit access to their postings to only close friends and intimates. With such filters, LiveJournal users can leave people visibly on their flists, but effectively remove them from communication:

[L]: "I'll be talking about my feelings and I don't want that available to anyone with a Web browser [so I filter them]. I want to know who's reading those posts."
[H]: "Yes, I've got some filters set up, mostly for close friends and what I want to tell them that I don't want the whole world to know."

In addition to this granularity of access control, LiveJournal affords each user a considerable degree of creative control over how their own LJ is presented, through embedded HTML-like codes: colors, layouts, graphical icons, and standardized fields to indicate such things as the user's mood and the music being listened to at the time of the entry. Icon use is particularly expressive:

[A]: "Some of my icons are mood-specific, like 'I'm in a bitchy mood right now, so you may not want to read this.' I have a [specific] icon to say 'I'm here for you.' Some are holiday cards, some flowers."
[G]: "I use a different set of icons for my [subgenre of] slash, so people will know I'm speaking from a different voice than usual."

LiveJournal users can be quite territorial about their own LJs, and the creative effort they expend, leading to the emergence of social norms specific to LiveJournal (in addition to existing slash community norms[25]):

[A]: "It's *my* journal. If other people read it and don't like it, tough. I'm doing it for myself."
[N]: "Nothing is off-topic within [one's own] LJ."

There are several kinds of activities that encourage interaction among slashfen on LJ beyond that of posting and reading. These include commenting, icon sharing, challenges,[26] surveys, and, perhaps most importantly for social cohesion, referrals. Referrals are typically pointers to authors or sources of slash content/source material that one slasher thinks another slasher might like, reflecting a degree of mutual understanding.

> [K]: "Commenting is half the fun of it, I mean you really get a chance to know people."
> [A]: "I stopped subscribing to mailing lists because my flist keeps me informed about what's going on in my fandoms."
> [K]: "Within my circle of friends, we're constantly telling each other to go here or there to check out a story we think others will like."

Interaction among slashfen on LiveJournal is generally characterized as being nice and polite, particularly in contrast to the previously mentioned problems with mailing lists and Web-groups:

> [G]: "When I entered this community, I didn't realize I was among the most polite, well-mannered communities in fandom. They're all adults, no screaming 14-year-olds."
> [M]: "Relative to the whole wide world of mundanes, the slash world is much smaller and I think this makes us better-behaved . . . we keep each other in line."

However, all but two interviewees referred to "kerfuffles" of which they'd been aware. A kerfuffle is a conflict arising within a fannish community and which, generally, gets blown out of proportion when many weigh in with their opinions. Kerfuffles generally can be traced to some violation of a social norm or rule within the community and are one means by which such norms are perpetuated. Although the social norm may involve slash content itself, the root cause of the kerfuffle is the violation of a norm and not the content. The sources of conflict are not found in the practices of slash (i.e., sharing content, creation of additional LJ personae, or criticism); instead, sources of conflict are norm violations of plagiarizing another's work, misrepresenting identity, and criticizing in someone else's LJ space. Social practices and LiveJournal's features (including the filters mentioned above) provide ways of reducing opportunities for conflict:

[L]: "Every fandom has its crazy people and LiveJournal makes it much easier to avoid them. You know, with mailing lists and [Web-groups], you can't really avoid the drama."

[N]: "Someone will start a kerfuffle and, to get out of it, she'll make a sockpuppet (another LJ account) and kill off the (offending) account. The thing is that everybody knows it's the same person . . . and this is accepted practice!"

[P]: "Some people put their policies about friending and de-friending in their bio. For example, 'if someone fails to cut-tag²⁷ a long post or a spoiler, I will de-friend you.' This heads off potential offense and applies a bit of pressure towards conformity."

Today, social relationships are often initiated via the slashfic itself, and, once a connection is made online, it can extend to intermittent face-to-face meetings at cons and local gatherings. The combination of on-line and offline interaction synergistically sustains relationships:

[J]: "It's a little odd but, in this community, you get to know someone's kinks before you get to know them. You read their fic, you e-mail them about it, and sometimes that can evolve into a really strong friendship."

[A]: "The people I've met face-to-face are the ones I tend to read their LiveJournal more, comment more, get to know them more closely, etc."

During interviews, it became clear that there exist some special groups of slashfen that appear to share a stronger bond extending beyond that which relates to simply accessing/discussing slashfic:

[P]: "LiveJournal is more personal than other fannish spaces. We know more about each other." "There are a lot of inter-friended cliques that defend each other against criticism in comments to their LJs."

[G]: "I write my fic for my close circle of friends."

[A]: "Some [icons] are secret messages to a special few . . . most won't know the story behind them."

[C]: "I met some people through LiveJournal, then took things offline for more personal interaction and bonding."

[L]: "I filter my posts. . . . I have one for my really close friends, the people I actually know, the people I see more than once a year, people I talk to on the phone sometimes. Those kinds of filters I will use for more personal content, so that only my really close friends see it."

Discussion

While it's tempting to draw parallels between the slash fan community's wanderings between various Internet-based services and the popular image of a nomadic, desert tribe wandering from oasis to oasis, we believe the tribal nature of the slash community online is more complex than that. This presents some challenges, however, because there is no rigorous definition of "tribe" from which to build. To develop an understanding of this tribal nature, then, we start by considering the slash community as a secret society.

The clandestine nature of the slash community, relative to the mundane world, has been explicit from its earliest self-awareness. Georg Simmel was the first to write extensively on the nature of such "secret societies," observing that they were constituted by trust between members [28] and that they were always a secondary phenomenon occurring within existing, complex societies.[29] Bonnie Erickson further distinguished between secret societies that are fraternal in nature (i.e., "safe") and those operating under external threat from the larger society in which they are embedded: "For societies under risk, the crucial motive is a desire to maximize security."[30] Drawing from social network theory, she argues that, when the focus of the secrecy involves severe threats,[31] should the secret be exposed, the secret society organizes itself in a hierarchical fashion. When the focus of the secrecy is a (perhaps) less-severe perversion of external norms,[32] the organization is more fluid and diffuse: "As a hierarchy, this [structure] is unrecognizable, but as a friendship network it is typical."[33] Erickson attributes this range of structures—from strict hierarchy to diffuse cloud—for secret societies under risk to the degree to which the recruitment of new members is centrally controlled.

This explains, to some extent, the very different characters of the slash community, before the Internet and after. Before the Internet, slashers sought social relationships with others "just like me" to maximize their potential access to slash fiction. This community was hierarchical in nature, with zine editors at the apex, mediating the "legitimate peripheral participation"[34] of novices into the community and brokering access to authors to protect their identities. After the slash community moved online, slashfen could find slashfic without knowing a single member of the slash community and could choose to form social relationships primarily on the basis of common interest in the content. Slash stories became the equivalent of an online search engine, enabling slashfen to find each other through their writing. The Internet subverted centralized control over access to fic, and, hence, there were no controls on recruitment into the "secret society" of slash, resulting in a very diffuse community. Without such controls, the "explosion" of the slash community online is understandable. However, with such growth, the potential for exposure increases with each new, self-recruited member. In a mundane society increasingly protective of such things, slash-fen continue to flout mundane norms and to ignore their violation of intellectual property laws. Knowledge of slashfen, and what they do, is trivially found on the Internet. How, then, do they manage to continue without mundane penalties? How does this secret society sustain its strong feelings of kinship with a very large and growing community? How do members maintain strong social bonds when their interests diverge?

We propose that the answer to these questions lies in the *tribal* nature of their online community. Though tribalism is often associated with notions of primitivism, the historical use of the term "tribe" has been malleable enough to accommodate a wide variety of defining criteria: as breeding populations, linguistic groupings, economic systems, political groups, and cultural units.[35] At its most fundamental level, tribal social structures emerge from conflict (real or perceived): "The *raison d'être* of a tribe is conflict, basically for scarce resources. Tribalism extends the peace group."[36] Elaborating the conflict thesis, and reprising Simmel's argument about secret societies, M. H. Fried argues that tribalism is a "secondary" phenomenon resulting from conflict, both real and perceived, "seen as a reaction to the presence of one or more complex political structures . . . in its direct or indirect environment."[37] In this way, the slash community's way of organizing itself into tribal forms can be considered as a reaction to the threats perceived to emanate from the more complexly-organized mundane society in which it is embedded.

To better understand the interaction between secretive slash tribalism and a dominant, mundane civilization, we turn to fourteenth-century Arab sociologist ibn Khaldûn, whose treatise *The Muqaddimah: An Introduction to History*[38] explores the relationships between Berber tribes and the dominant Arab civilization. Ibn Khaldûn developed a model of their relationships based on *"asabiya,"* which is translated as "group feeling." A more contemporary rendering of the term would be a combination of "social identity" and "social cohesion." The model, briefly, begins with tribes whose members, because they must cooperate in their contention with the rigors of desert existence, naturally develop high levels of *asabiya*. Should a tribe find an oasis of sufficient fecundity and establish a sedentary lifestyle, it forms the seed from which a "civilized" (i.e., nontribal) society can grow from village to a town to a city and on to empire. Civilized life leads to the development of the arts, sciences, and commercial enterprises. However, civilization also provides for the introduction of luxuries into formerly austere lives, and, with luxuries, *asabiya* declines. People become focused on their individual needs and desires, at the expense of the collective ones. Soon, *asabiya* declines to the point where conflict arises, the civilized society eventually collapses, and people return to a tribal existence (where *asabiya* can increase again).

Slashfen feel a strong kinship with each other, due to their common interests and the threats perceived from the mundane "desert" in which they exist, so a high level of *asabiya* is understandable. The Internet has offered a fecund "oasis" of slashfic and opportunities for interaction well beyond what could have been imagined, had slash remained print-based. Following ibn Khaldûn's model further, we've seen that conflicts arose in some online media, motivating slashfen to migrate to new services as they appeared. The slash community seems relatively content, however, with LiveJournal as their current technological medium of interaction. LiveJournal appears to meet their most important needs, unlike previous Internet services.

We identified three key features as important to the slashfen we interviewed: ease-of-use, support for creative expression, and control-of-visibility.[39] We assessed each of the technologies mentioned in interviews, at approximately the time their use was dominant within the slash community, relative to these three features, and present the results in Table 13.1.

Creative expression appears to have generally increased over time, from the perspective of our interviewees, but there appears to have been a continual trade-off between ease-of-use and control-of-visibility until the most recent migration to LiveJournal. Creative expression is the core of the slash community, both online and offline, and ease-of-use broadens the scope of potential members of that community. However, it is the control-of-visibility afforded by Internet services that enacts a tribal structure on the community in its maintenance of its *asabiya*.

When control-of-visibility was centralized to systems administrators, individual users saw conflicts (e.g., with e-mail list services and Web-groups) they could do nothing about, except to try to ignore them. When control was localized to the individuals themselves, they could unsubscribe, un-join, de-friend, or filter out miscreants who brought

Table 13.1. Technologies used by the slash community online, presented in approximate chronological order according to their primacy within the slash community as a means of interaction. Technologies are assessed from summarized interview data (in *italics*) according to the three criteria shown.

Technologies of Interaction	Ease-of-use	Creative expression	Control-of-visibility
Usenet	High	Low	Low
	No effort needed to gather postings	*Text-based; low tolerance for extensive text graphics*	*Everyone receives all postings*
Personal e-mail lists	Moderate	Low	High
	Hard to keep addresses current	*Text-based; graphics via attachment*	*Total control over who receives mail*
E-mail list services	High	Low	Low
	No effort for recipients to maintain	*Constrained by list owners (e.g., stay on-topic)*	*Controlled by list owners*
Web-groups	Moderate	Moderate	Low
	Tedious to create and maintain via Web	*Can include graphics, but tedious to do so*	*Controlled by group owners*
LiveJournal	High	High	High
	Intuitive interface for managing own LJ and Friends List	*Extensive control over look and feel, e.g., icons/graphics, formatting*	*Total control over who has access to individual LJ entries*

conflict to their online slash experience. With conflict thus removed, *asabiya* can be maintained and strong bonds of trust and affection can develop among the remaining interactants, bonds that persist over changes in time and interests. It is these groups, employing the features of technologies of interaction to sustain their collective *asabiya* in real time, that we consider to be "electronic tribes" in the fullest sense. Whether an ego-centered network ("innermost circle") of close friends or a mutually supportive set of "interfriended cliques," these tribes survive online by interacting and avoiding conflict in ways not always possible in the "real" world.

B. A. Nardi describes such relationships as existing on a "field of connection" "comprised of feelings of affinity, commitment, and attention," which "must be kept in a state of sufficient excitation or activation to promote effective communication."[40] Slashfen on LiveJournal establish affinity through sharing their experience and their practice of slash in a common space online, as well as via "informal conversations" about their personal lives, frustrations, and needs beyond the world of slash. They establish the commitment of "simply being there" and gain the attention of other slashfen through their fic, by posting entries to their LJs, by commenting in others' LJs, and by participating in LJ communities, thereby defining their "scope for ongoing communication for projects of mutual interest."[41]

Not all online groups of friends can sustain their fields of connection in the face of internal and external conflicts. As with ibn Khaldûn's model, *asabiya* can wax and wane over time, sometimes collapsing completely as former intimates drift apart into different interests and activities. Similarly, Nardi observes that a field of connection is a "labile state of readiness that degrades over time" if insufficiently activated through interaction.[42] As with the tribes above, slashfen can use technological affordances to structure their interactions, but their focus is more ephemerally oriented toward their shared activities—such as commenting on a particular story, taking sides in a kerfuffle, or planning to attend a con—than on each other. Something occurs that "activates" their field of connection, increasing their interaction and *asabiya*. Over time, interests and passions cool and *asabiya* declines. We consider these less-enduring groups as "semitribes" along the lines of A. L. Kroeber's notion of "tribelets" as "groups of small size, definitely owning a restricted territory [or focus of activity] . . . speaking usually a dialect [fannish interest] identical with that of several of their neighbors, but wholly autonomous."[43] Groups oriented to activities within particular fandoms, as well as some activities that can cut across fandoms (e.g., RPS, fem-fem, chan, incest), are, thus, semitribal in their nature.

Given a basis-in-affect for tribes and a basis-in-activity for semitribes, it's clear that these categories need not be mutually exclusive. Nor do "tribes" and "semitribes" completely characterize the slash community; slashfen refer to "feral" slashers, who are unaware of the community, and "lurkers," who are aware of the community but don't actively participate. "Tribe" and "semitribe" characterize two social structures, which emerge in the slash community from their collective sustenance of *asabiya* through a combination of community norms (fundamentally oriented to protect the continued availability of slashfic) and the individual structuring of interaction, afforded by technologies of interaction, to reduce opportunities for conflict with the mundane world as well as with each other. In this way, the slash community has managed its transition from an offline activity to an online community, protected itself from external and internal threats to its collective *asabiya*, and accommodated extreme growth online without coming apart at the seams.

Notes

1. Henry Jenkins, *Textual Poachers: Television Fans & Participatory Culture* (New York: Routledge, 1992).

2. Jenkins, *Textual Poachers*, p. 187. See also http://en.wikipedia.org/wiki/Slash_fiction#Slash_Timeline (accessed November 28, 2005), which reports 1974 as the date of the earliest known published slash story.

3. Jenkins, *Textual Poachers*, p. 186.

4. Ibid., p. 189.

5. Ibid., p. 222.

6. CON is not the actual name of the convention and is used to ensure the conditions of anonymity under which the interviews were conducted.

7. Although all of our interview subjects were identified only by their slash pseudonyms, the extent to which individuals are tied to these identities required they be further aliased by unique letters.

8. Rhiannon Bury, *Cyberspaces of Their Own: Female Fandoms Online*, vol. 25 of *Digital Formations*, ed. Steve Jones (New York: Peter Lang, 2005).

9. "Fic" refers to "fiction," or created content, including nontextual variants such as music videos ("vids"), art/graphics, and filk music. "Genfic" refers to nonsexual fan fiction and "hetfic" refers to heterosexual fan fiction.

10. Jenkins, *Textual Poachers*, p. 187.

11. Ibid., p. 202.

12. Ibid., p. 201.

13. See http://en.wikipedia.org/wiki/Slash_fiction#Real_People_Slash; see also http://en.wikipedia.org/wiki/Real_person_fiction (accessed November 26, 2005).

14. Hobbes' Internet Timeline, http://www.zakon.org/robert/internet/timeline/.

15. See http://www.news.uiuc.edu/ii/03/0417/mosaic.html.

16. See demographics for 1994–2004 in GVU's WWW User Surveys results at http://www.cc.gatech.edu/gvu/user_surveys/ (accessed November 26, 2005).

17. Bury, *Cyberspaces of Their Own*, p. 74.

18. See http://wingedpig.com/ol/index.html.

19. See http://en.wikipedia.org/wiki/EGroups (accessed November 26, 2005).

20. Now at http://groups.yahoo.com/; see also http://en.wikipedia.org/wiki/Yahoo%21_Groups (accessed November 26, 2005).

21. For our purposes here, "LiveJournal" will refer to the network blogging

service, and its associated technologies; "LJ" will be used in reference to an individual's set of aggregated journal entries, comments, memories, profile, etc.

22. Ravi Kumar, Jasmine Novak, Prabhakar Raghavan, and Andrew Tomkins, "Structure and Evolution of Blogspace," *Communications of the ACM* 47, no. 12 (December 2004): 35–39.

23. "Friends list" refers to a list of LiveJournal usernames.

24. This misnomer extends beyond LiveJournal users. For example, Kumar et al., in "Structure and Evolution of Blogspace," clearly consider the LiveJournal "friend" relationship to be identical with the popular understanding of "friend" and misanalyze it as a variable independent from shared interests: e.g., " . . . eliciting some striking correlations in the friendships among bloggers and their interests" (which is not surprising, given that they reflect the same thing).

25. These norms include: don't show slash to actors/producers, don't leave "chan" (slash fic involving minors) or RPS where mundanes can easily find it, use a spell-checker, don't quote real-life comments with identifiable names, and so on.

26. A "challenge" is typically a call for people to write fic with a particular theme, time constraint, or length.

27. A LiveJournal "cut-tag" hides some content of a posting behind a URL to require an explicit reader action to view.

28. Georg Simmel, "The Sociology of Secrecy and of Secret Societies," *American Journal of Sociology* 11, no. 4 (January 1906): 470.

29. Ibid., p. 483.

30. Bonnie H. Erickson, "Secret Societies and Social Structure," *Social Forces* 60, no. 1 (September 1981): 188.

31. Erickson's examples of such hierarchical organization include prisoners at Auschwitz during World War II and the White Lotus rebels in imperial China in the early nineteenth century.

32. Erickson's example of diffuse organization under risk is an extended network of English marijuana users.

33. Erickson, "Secret Societies and Social Structure," p. 193.

34. Jean Lave and Etienne Wenger, *Situated Learning: Legitimate Peripheral Participation, Learning in Doing* (Cambridge, England; New York: Cambridge University Press, 1991), p. 29.

35. M. H. Fried, *The Notion of Tribe* (Menlo Park, Calif.: Cummings, 1975).

36. M. H. Fried, "On the Concepts of 'Tribe' and 'Tribal Society,' " in *Essays on the Problem of Tribe*, ed. J. Helm et al. (Seattle: American Ethnological Society, distributed by the University of Washington Press, 1968), p. 11.

37. Fried, *The Notion of Tribe*, p. 100.

38. Ibn Khaldûn, *The Muqaddimah: An Introduction to History*, trans. Franz Rosenthal (Princeton, N.J.: Princeton University Press, 1958).

39. Control-of-visibility refers not only to the granularity of controlling access to one's contributions, in whatever medium, but also the extent to which individuals know the type of person who will be privy to their contributions.

40. B. A. Nardi, "Beyond Bandwidth: Dimensions of Connection in Interpersonal Communication," *Computer Supported Cooperative Work (CSCW)* 14, no. 2 (April 2005): 92.

41. Ibid., p. 112.

42. Ibid., p. 98.

43. A. L. Kroeber, *The Patwin and Their Neighbors*, University of California Publications in American Archaeology and Ethnology 29 (1932): 258. Quoted in Fried, *The Notion of Tribe*, p. 57.

CHAPTER 14

Brotherhood of Blood:
Aryan Tribalism and Skinhead Cybercrews

JODY M. ROY

In 2005, law enforcement agencies reported the presence of 21,500 youth gangs in the United States; more than 730,000 teenagers and young adults now hold official status as gang members.[1] Overwhelmingly, American youth gangs are classified as "delinquent" because their purpose, and their members' bond, centers around for-profit criminal enterprise.[2] MS-13, Gangster Disciples, Crips, Vice Lords, Latin Kings, and a host of other gangs control much of America's illicit economy, trafficking drugs and prostitutes, and coordinating complex, new-age criminal schemes like identity-theft rings. Violence, of course, pervades gang life. With multimillion-dollar black markets at stake, today's gangs fight turf wars with automatic weapons. New members are violently "jumped in" to prove their mettle as soldiers. Rivals are "taken out" with deadly force. For members of delinquent gangs, violence is the bloody price of doing business.

But for the small minority of American youth gangs classified as "ideological," violence is a political statement.[3] United by their "whiteness" and motivated by the aims of the larger, adult white supremacy movement, racist skinhead gangs, or "crews," are perhaps the most notorious ideological gangs on the contemporary American scene.[4] In 2004, forty-eight distinct racist skinhead gangs, many with splinter crews in several regions, were active in the United States. Because most crews operate semicovertly, exact membership numbers cannot be known; however, monitoring agencies estimate that gangs like Hammerskin Nation and National Socialist Skinhead Front now count at least several thousand young people as official members.[5] Even more white youth hover near the crews, sharing their "white pride" philosophy, if not yet the right to wear the colors of the brotherhood of blood, a right usually earned by committing acts of violence against racial minorities.[6]

In this chapter, I explore how virtual communication is changing the actual behavior of skinhead gangs and the racist youth who identify with those gangs. Following a survey of the formation and function of skinhead gangs within the American white supremacy movement, I describe the vast electronic community of radical racists that has evolved since 1995, and how "cyberhate" generally has strengthened and, in some ways, unified the movement. I then offer specific analysis of samples of electronic communication among members of two of the movement's dominant, but discordant camps: Christian Identity and Creativity. I isolate distinguishing traits of Aryan tribalism revealed within their rhetorical battles. Finally, I assess an ominous phenomenon enabled by cyberhate: the skinhead "cybercrew," youth indoctrinated into profound levels of hatred by virtual tribal mentors, but operating outside the control of actual gang leaders.

The American Hate Scene

By the 1960s, the American white supremacy movement was defined by two distinct brands of organized racism: the domestic, neo-Confederate lineage of groups like the Ku Klux Klan and the European, neo-Nazi lineage imported by George Lincoln Rockwell's National Socialist White People's Party.[7] Both impulses offered full-service hate groups for adult racists, and even adult role models for racist youth, but failed to offer teenagers a clearly defined organizational role within the movement. However, a trend unfolding within British youth culture was about to collide with American racism: the skinhead gang phenomenon would be born of the collision.

As the "mod" subculture swept across Britain in the 1960s, some working-class youth took offense at both the drug use and the androgynous hairstyles and fashions flaunted by mod-mavens like Rolling Stones front man Mick Jagger. In protest, "hard mods" shaved their heads and uniformed themselves in classic workers' attire: Ben Sherman shirts, Levi's jeans, Doctor Marten steel-toed boots, Alpha MA-1 flight jackets, and thin braces, or suspenders. They zealously opposed the popular recreational drug use of the era, preferring to socialize as their fathers had, over beers in the pubs and in the stands during local soccer matches. Within just a few years of the onset of the hard-mod trend, most larger

British cities were home to several hard-mod "crews," bands of young men from the same lower-income neighborhoods who rallied around particular soccer teams. Rival hard-mod crews brawled often, cementing their notoriety as some of Britain's toughest, most violent youth.

When the punk rock craze took over the London club scene in the late 1970s, the aggressive hard-mods were among the first fans to flock into the mosh pits. The raw and edgy music of bands like the Sex Pistols and the Clash seemed an apt soundtrack for the hard-mod movement. But the reality of hard-mod violence clashed with the violent posturing preferred by most punks; major venues began banning hard-mod crews from admission to concerts.[8] Some hard-mods determined to create an alternative music scene, forming their own bands that fused punk with heavy metal and even ska influences. The most famous of the early hard-mod bands, Skrewdriver, sang antielite anthems of the working class; they also sang about "white pride."[9] When Skrewdriver's lead singer, Ian Stewart, publicly affiliated with the neo-Nazi National Front, many of his hard-mod fans, by then nicknamed "skinheads," followed. Rather than simply brawl with each other, the new breed of skinhead crews aimed much of their violence at minority immigrants; they enacted Stewart's lyrics, described by one skinhead observer as "music to riot by."[10]

Although individual hard-mod skinheads occasionally surfaced in New York City's punk clubs in the late 1970s, America's first racist skinhead crew formed in Chicago in 1984. Named "Romantic Violence," the crew adopted the swastika as its tag, coordinated white-power leafleting, and physically assaulted minorities.[11] Today, Romantic Violence is one of forty-eight racist skinhead gangs known to operate in the United States; a few, such as the Northern Hammerskins, control dozens of local crews.[12]

While each crew is unique, some rites of passage and symbols are universal within skinhead culture. In contrast to the "jump in" initiation rites of most delinquent gangs, wherein the initiate must endure a physical assault of predetermined length by the gang itself, prospective skinheads normally are asked to prove their loyalty to both the gang and the white race by committing an act of violence against a member of a targeted minority group; put bluntly, to become a skinhead gang member is to commit at least one violent hate crime. Skinhead gang initiates' heads are shaved, often ritually by crew leaders, both as a symbolic rebirth into the skinhead clan and as a public declaration of "white pride." The traditions of their hard-mod forefathers are maintained in skinhead fashion and social practices. Yet, while some skinheads stay true to the hard-mod look for years, many now grow their hair back in after their probationary period as a "freshcut" to avoid arousing the attention of law enforcement. For the same reason, many skinheads wear their full uniform attire only during rallies and place tattoos strategically on easily concealed areas of the body: the elbows, the chest below the collarbones, the lower back, inside the lower lip, and the scalp. Tattoos common across all skinhead gangs include Nazi symbols, ancient Norse and Celtic symbols, spider webs, slogans like "White Pride" and "Rahowa," and codes such as "88" and "14 Words."[13]

Regardless of their particular crew affiliation, American racist skinheads share an unwavering belief in the "ZOG" conspiracy theory touted by adult white supremacy groups for decades. The theory holds that ZOG, or the Zionist Occupational Government, a vast and ancient international Jewish cabal, has infiltrated Western governments, media, and major corporations. Only the "superior" Aryan race stands between ZOG and its goal, world domination. The "inferior" races (neither Aryan nor Jewish) are pawns in ZOG's most devious scheme: destroying the Aryan bloodline via race mixing. Believers in the ZOG conspiracy view protecting the "pure" Aryan bloodline as the paramount challenge of contemporary life, a matter of survival.[14]

Were it not for the shrewd outreach of adult white supremacy groups, the skinhead crew phenomenon might never have taken hold in America. But adult hate group leaders almost immediately recognized the value of skinhead crews: the crews could be a fertile recruiting ground for the next generation of adult white supremacists without requiring the adult groups actually to admit teenagers into their ranks. Additionally, teenagers often will do things adults will not or cannot do, and, if caught, often will not be punished as severely as an adult would be for committing the same crime.[15] As a result, skinheads are the ideal foot soldiers in the adult movement's war against ZOG. By the late 1980s, leading white supremacy groups were actively cultivating relationships with skinhead crews. Christian Identity strongholds like Aryan Nations and many Klan factions shared their literature with crews, and even showcased white-power bands at rallies to encourage skinhead attendance.[16] Matt Hale's World Church of the Creator and Creativity-sympathetic White Aryan Resistance followed suit, and even enlisted skinheads within their ranks.[17]

But in the early 1990s, skinheads learned their own support infrastructure was taking shape. Founded by a business-savvy twenty-year-old skinhead, Resistance Records quickly emerged as the leading distributor of white-power music in the world and then rapidly expanded its array of services for racist youth. Unlike the hand-me-down racist literature adult groups usually offered crews, Resistance gave skinheads their own "skin-zine," *Resistance*, written for and by skinheads. Resistance sponsored rave-style white-power concerts in major cities, linked skinheads to suppliers of white-power clothing and paraphernalia, and, through the edgy music of their large stable of European and American recording artists, provided racist youth with lyrical lectures about skinhead ideology, history, and culture.[18]

Significantly, the young staff of Resistance Records used professional database and direct-mail technologies to build the first large skinhead mailing list; all subscribers to *Resistance*, as well as all customers who ever had purchased white-power music, clothing, or literature from the Resistance catalogue or its affiliated suppliers, were entered into computerized files.[19] The Resistance Records mailing list enabled a nearly universal reach of communication into skinhead gang membership and prospective recruit rosters throughout North America and Europe. Skinhead gang membership and activity exploded under the guidance of Resistance Records.

Then, in 1997, United States and Canadian authorities circled in to silence Resistance Records. On the grounds of a delinquent sales tax payment, federal and state agents raided the company's Detroit, Michigan, headquarters, seizing all property, including the hard drives that housed the mailing list containing the names and addresses of thousands of skinhead crew members and prospective recruits. Across the river in Windsor, Ontario, Canadian officials hit key Resistance staffers with a far more serious charge: conspiracy to advocate genocide. Movement supporters of all ages rallied around Resistance, donating money to "fight the costly legal battle" to free the corporation.[20] After much maneuvering, Resistance Records ultimately was purchased by William Pierce's National Alliance, then the largest white supremacy organization in the United States, the direct descendant of Rockwell's National Socialist White People's Party.[21]

While the Canadian government later dropped the "conspiracy to advocate genocide" charges originally filed against the skinheads at the helm of Resistance Records, many other skinheads are prosecuted eventually for committing acts of vandalism, intimidation, arson, assault, and even murder in the name of "white power." Of course, in the twenty-first century, crimes committed by known skinhead gang members almost always qualify for the federal hate-crime sentencing enhancers phased into law in the late 1990s. Thus, the most violent skinhead juvenile offenders now often are waived into the adult criminal system. Behind bars, skinheads are welcomed immediately into white supremacist prison gangs like the Nazi Low Riders or the Aryan Brotherhood, one of the most powerful and violent gangs in the entire American prison system.[22] The hardened criminals who lead such prison gangs offer their young skinhead charges not only protection, but also an advanced education in the tactics of racially motivated violence.

Upon their release from prison, some skinheads return to their original crews more violent and more racist than when they left. Other skinheads, whether incarcerated for a time or not, at least appear to move away from the white supremacy movement as they get older. Of course, because of the covert nature of the movement, no one really knows what happens to most skinheads when they grow up. Shortly after an Oregon jury held him liable for facilitating the East Side White Pride crew's murder of an Ethiopian immigrant, the leader of White Aryan Resistance, Tom Metzger, spoke ominously to this issue: "The movement will not be stopped in the puny town of Portland. We're too deep. We're imbedded now. Don't you understand? We're in your colleges, we're in your armies, we're in your police forces, we're in your technical areas, we're in your banks. Where do you think a lot of these skinheads disappeared to?"[23]

The Era of Cyberhate

Although virtually all American youth gangs "are becoming more sophisticated in their use of computers and technology," in particular using the Internet "to communicate, facilitate criminal activity, and avoid detection by law enforcement,"[24] skinhead gangs were among the first to mine the potential of cyberspace. Since "hate sites" began appearing in 1995, the white supremacy movement has established a significant online presence. By 2004, Web surfers could access 468 actively maintained, U.S.-based hate sites, including 26 "skinhead" sites, 79 "neo-Nazi" sites, 38 "neo-Confederate" sites, and more than 100 other sites dedicated specifically to "white pride" and racial and religious bigotry.[25] Now ten years old, Stormfront.com is the most extensive hate site, providing a variety of open-access "relatively non-sectarian" racist resources, linking users to hundreds of other hate sites, and serving more than 52,000 subscribers inside its vast network of thematic and "sectarian" chat rooms.[26]

Hate sites have created an electronic community of white supremacists, and, in turn, that electronic community has changed and continues to change how the white supremacy movement operates. In this section, I discuss four ways in which the electronic community seems to be uniting and strengthening the white supremacy movement, in general, and skinhead gangs, in particular. I detail how Web sites build bridges between once-segregated contingents of the movement, invite prospective recruits into membership, enable expansion of skinhead gangs, and securely connect geographically dispersed crews.

First, the Internet provides an open channel of communication between established, adult white supremacy organizations and skinhead crews. The new technology has eradicated most of the barriers that once segregated the Aryan old guard from racist youth. At the most basic level, the electronic community provides groups like Aryan Nations and the National Alliance with a cost-effective way to share their vast libraries of racist literature with skinhead youth; from free "pdf" downloads of neo-Nazi treatises to online interpretations of the daily news, hate sites give even "freshcuts" twenty-four-hour-a-day access to the teachings of the movement's reigning elite.[27] Of course, distance has no meaning in cyberspace; San Diego–based White Aryan Resistance now can post teen-friendly racist cartoons, jokes, and song lyrics online for the "entertainment," and, of course, indoctrination, of skinhead gang members around the nation.[28] More subtly, the Internet nullifies the ageism inherent in most American racist organizations since the nineteenth century; age is invisible online, leaving ideological adherence as the sole standard against which a Web site or an individual user is judged. The electronic community of white supremacy promotes an interconnectedness among racists from all regions and of all ages that is unprecedented in the history of American hatred.

Second, cyberspace provides an accessible point of entry into what is, in reality, a tightly closed organizational system. Most contemporary white supremacy groups, including most skinhead gangs, operate at least semicovertly. Few members' real names are made public. Mailing addresses are post office box numbers. Telephone numbers connect callers to prerecorded hotline messages. The groups' belief in the ZOG conspiracy—and the fact that many of the groups actually are under close surveillance by government agencies—make them suspicious of all outside inquiries, including those submitted by people hoping to join the movement.[29] Before the era of cyberhate, white supremacist organizations often sacrificed their ability to reach prospective recruits in service of their overriding concerns, real and imagined, about security. As a result, obtaining authentic information about movement ideology and organizations, let alone about specific activities and meetings, was virtually impossible unless a person already was inside the movement. Now, the movement publicizes its creed online, not only hooking some Web users as prospective recruits, but, more generally, providing even casual observers with an education in advanced theories like ZOG, once discussed only in the privacy of closed meetings.

For youth, the wall around the movement was not just impenetrable but, at times, dangerous before the birth of the electronic community. Adult groups, of course, were not especially interested in recruiting teenagers; only skinhead gangs were. Yet, due to one of the great ironies in the history of contemporary street gangs, skinhead crews were at least as likely to attack a self-declared skinhead who approached without invitation as they were to socialize with him.

Racist skinheads reserve their most profound hatred and much of their most brutal violence for members of "SHARP" gangs; "Skinheads Against Racial Prejudice" are viewed by racist skinheads to be "race traitors," white youth corrupted by, and working for, the ZOG conspiracy. Nevertheless, racist and SHARP crews share a history: the two warring factions both trace their origins to the British hard-mods, and both maintain allegiance to the style traditions of their hard-mod forefathers. Before the Internet era, only the gang members themselves and those who spent years studying them could reliably discern the subtle differences that distinguish a racist skinhead's public uniform from that worn by a SHARP. Self-declared racist skinheads who threaded the wrong color laces through their boots risked being mistaken for SHARPs. In similar fashion, youth who inadvertently donned colors reserved for high-ranking racist crew members also risked the wrath of the gangs.

Today, self-declared skinheads can study symbol codes posted on the Web. By taking care to avoid both SHARP signs and the insignia earned by rank within racist crews, youth now can safely groom themselves to attract the attention of skinhead gang recruiters. As a result, the electronic community of white supremacy makes it possible for youth to initiate their own recruitment by a racist skinhead crew, a maneuver that might have proved fatal ten years ago.

A third significant impact of the electronic community for skinheads involves expanding the gang network. A decade ago, skinhead crews had to move members physically into strategic positions to drum up membership for crew expansions into new regions of the country; indoctrination of new crews required a long-term commitment of gang resources to on-site training in the new town. Now, the Internet facilitates distance-education of all sorts, including the education of skinhead "freshcuts" recruited for expansion crews. Although older gangs like Hammerskin Nation retain strict control over their franchises, a relatively new trend known as "_ASH" gangs offers any racist youth the template to form his own crew. "_ASH"-supportive Web sites within the electronic community instruct users in skinhead traditions and ideology, and provide tip sheets for recruiting a complement of founding members for the "(City) Area SkinHeads" crew.[30] Further, for racist youth who cannot find or form an actual crew with which to affiliate, hate sites fill the role of "cybercrew," a phenomenon that will be discussed in detail later in this chapter.

Finally, the World Wide Web has created a worldwide community of racist skinhead youth. British, French, and German neo-Nazi skinheads swap war stories with American crew members via Web sites. On sites like Hammerskin.net, America's leading skinhead gangs efficiently convey information to their geographically dispersed crews, publicizing upcoming national events like graffiti blitzes on Adolf Hitler's birthday, spreading the word about rendezvous points for white-power raves, and, ominously, sometimes sharing information about the names, physical descriptions, and whereabouts of "ZOG conspirators" and "race traitors."[31]

While the secretive underworld of white supremacy has laid out a welcome mat in cyberspace, the electronic community simultaneously functions to secure the movement's most valuable and closely kept secret: the membership rosters of its various organizations. Pseudonymous user names attached to free e-mail accounts make the racist "personas" who maintain and inhabit the electronic community difficult for authorities to trace. The great skinhead security breach of 1997, when the U.S. government seized the Resistance Records' database containing the real names and home mailing addresses of most active skinheads, is unlikely ever to happen again in the era of cyberhate.

Electronic Tribal Warfare

In recent decades, the pseudoscience of Creativity has challenged the biblical revisionism of Christian Identity for philosophical control of the American white supremacy movement.[32] While the Internet fosters many forms of collaboration and unification within the movement, it also serves as a battlefield where Identity Christians and Creators vie for position and power. In this section, I identify the protocols of Aryan tribalism that surface when Identity Christians and Creators believe a prospective recruit has entered into their online discussion forums.

Identity theology is an overtly racist Christian sect based on the "Anglo-Israelism" teachings of the Reverend Wesley Swift. Popularized in the 1970s and 1980s by the Reverend Richard Butler, head of Aryan Nations, Identity is the dominant faith of contemporary white supremacists.[33] Skinheads nurtured by Aryan Nationalists, as well as those mentored by most Klan factions and the National Alliance, have been baptized into Identity.

At its core, Identity claims that Northern European "Aryans" are the bloodline of the "true" tribes of Israel, directly descended from Adam in the image of God. In contrast, non-Aryan "mud" are the progeny of what Identity theologians contend was Eve's carnal encounter with Satan, the line of Cain, Satan's literal son. Identity adherents maintain that "mud" are soul-less, satanic creatures, allowed by God to exist solely as a test of Aryan fidelity to God's will. The apocalypse prophesied in Revelations is interpreted as a definitive global race war between the Aryan children of God and the "mud" children of Satan; ZOG is anti-Christ. Identity Christians believe they must annihilate ZOG and its "mud" pawns to prove their worth to God, and, thus, usher in the Kingdom of Heaven.[34]

In 2004, thirty-six dedicated Identity Web sites, some of them among the largest hate sites online, were actively maintained by U.S.-based sponsors.[35] Most Identity sites provide users with vast collections of tracts of information about the theology itself, from exegesis of biblical passages to contemporary missionary homiletics authored by leading Identity ministers. Additionally, groups supportive of Christian Identity embed the theology in online political polemics. Inside the sectarian chat rooms of Web sites like Stormfront, small congregations of Identity Christians interact with each other and with prospective converts, displaying key traits of Aryan tribalism as they position the faith of Identity as the ultimate grounding for contemporary white supremacy.

One such interchange was inspired by "Jeremy," who, in August 2005, posted the simple query "Im new to NS [National Socialism] and yet still hold my Christian values dearly. What does it take to be a convert to Christian identity and what does CI truly mean?"[36] Five registered forum members, with histories ranging from 39 to over 2,100 postings within Stormfront chat rooms, responded to Jeremy, and to each other, over the course of several days.

The first answer came from "Klaliff," a "friend of Stormfront" and recognized Stormfront moderator. Significantly, white supremacy movement insiders immediately would recognize Klaliff's insinuation of rank; the term "Klaliff" is "Klanese" for vice president of a Klavern. Further, Klaliff's user name is accompanied by a visual icon in the image of a torch-bearing, hooded Klansman on horseback. Klaliff began, "Welcome, Jeremy," then offered a rather lengthy summary of the key tenets of Identity, and pointed Jeremy toward "must read" books. He stressed, though, that CI is not simply a philosophy nor even a theology, but rather "a daily walk with God. It's fellowshipping with like-minded people . . . hard core Christian separatists. . . . It's a way of life." After what appeared to be welcoming rhetoric, Klaliff then dramatically changed his tone, declaring, "My honest take on reading this post is that you don't have the discipline that Christianity demands." Likewise, "Purelily" responded, "Welcome to the elite!" but also warned Jeremy, "CI is not something you 'convert' to. You either believe in the identity . . . or you don't." Such definitive shifts in tone and position offer a glimpse of the exclusionary, hierarchical nature of the Identity camp.

Other postings maintained the seemingly contradictory tension between welcoming the would-be convert and strictly controlling the virtual forum and, by extension, the actual flock of Identity Christians. "Redneck Rampage" encouraged Jeremy simply to "get a Bible and concordance and start reading," noting, "thier [Klaliff's] posts are like reading a book. LOL [laugh out loud]," before recommending a few Web sites. Klaliff reappeared an hour later, asserting his authority with the dogmatically dismissive retort, "You want to be aware that the sites posted by Redneck Rampage maintain the Dual Seedline doctrine, which is not a doctrine consistently held across all of CI." Redneck Rampage never reappeared in the chat room. "Johnereb63," also a "friend of Stormfront," ignored Jeremy altogether, instead praising the ranking elder with "very well done once again, Klaliff!" and other deferential laudations. Of course, as the only other designated "friend of Stormfront" participating in the thread, Johnereb63's commendation redoubled the influence Klaliff wielded over the rank-and-file participants as keeper of the ethos.

Three days after his initial posting, Jeremy sent the simple note, "I thank you all." After two days of silence on the thread, Klaliff attempted to reengage the prospective recruit with, "How are you doing Jeremy? Any questions?" Although Purelily and others continued to post brief statements elaborating specific theological points in Klaliff's original message, Jeremy himself never reentered the conversation.

The "Jeremy" thread reveals three significant traits of Aryan tribalism within Christian Identity. First, the tribe is exclusive by virtue of its dogmatic authoritarianism; while queries are welcome, dissension is not. Identity is portrayed as an absolute system of faith requiring total commitment. The naïvely curious, like Jeremy, are given little time to prove their fitness for the faith; the heretical, like Redneck Rampage, are silenced swiftly. Second, and not surprising within an arena heavily influenced by Nazism, hierarchy is presumed, and rank is respected. As in actual Identity strongholds like Aryan Nation, the chat room may invite open discussion, but it is not an egalitarian forum. Klaliff and Johnereb63 are acknowledged in sidebars as having special status within Stormfront. Further, Klaliff's ever-present user name and Klan icon remind all forum members that he at least claims to hold rank within the oldest white supremacy group in America; his censure of Redneck Rampage reminds all members that disrespecting superiors will bring about harsh consequences. Less obviously, a third trait of Identity Christians per se, their complete confidence in their power within the movement, is revealed by what is not discussed in the thread: the members of the dominant camp never even acknowledge the existence of Creativity.

Ben Klassen first launched the Creativity movement in the 1980s, just as the skinhead gang phenomenon was taking hold in America. His masterworks, *The White Man's Bible* (1986) and *Nature's Eternal Religion* (1992), defined the North Carolina–based Church of the Creator, where Klassen personally mentored high-ranking skinhead leaders.[37] Creativity truly became a significant force within the white supremacy movement after Klassen's 1993 suicide, when an outspoken young neo-Nazi named Matt Hale founded the World Church of the Creator and declared himself Klassen's rightful heir, the "pontifex maximus" of Creators.[38] When several prominent white-power bands followed Hale's lead in their lyrics, Creativity gained even more ground among young racists.[39]

Although Creators remain a minority within the white supremacy movement, in recent years, Hale and his "church" have garnered widespread notoriety both inside and outside the movement. In 1999, the national media tracked Ben Smith, a rogue skinhead member of Hale's organization, along his three-day murderous rampage through Indiana and Illinois.[40] More recently, the spotlight turned on Hale himself after he was charged with hiring an assassin to dispose of the United States federal court judge who ruled against him in a trademark suit over the name "World Church of the Creator." In 2003, Hale relented on the trademark issue and renamed his organization "The Creativity Movement." In the spring of 2005, he entered a level-seven "super max" federal penitentiary to serve out a forty-year sentence for his role in the unsuccessful assassination plot.[41] Although Klassen remains the central prophet of Creativity, Matt Hale now is the unrivaled martyr of the movement.

From Klassen's foundational writings to Hale's missionary diatribes, Creativity offers white supremacists a profound alternative to Christian Identity; Creativity is not simply un-Christian, it is vehemently anti-Christian. Heavily influenced by Nietzschean philosophy, Darwinian theory, eugenics, and, of course, Nazism, Creators deny "spiritual" religions outright, instead worshiping at the alter of science and reason in what they dub a "racial religion."[42] Creators view human history as the history of species warfare; non-Aryans are thought to be not simply inferior races, but actually subhuman species. While ZOG is recognized as a cunning foe in the current battle for survival, Creators maintain that the innate "superiority" of the Aryan species ensures ultimate victory so long as Aryans rally together in concerted action to protect the purity of the Aryan bloodline.[43]

It is impossible to get an exact count of the number of Creativity sites currently active on the Internet. In the aftermath of Hale's failure in the trademark suit, all sites using the phrase "World Church of the Creator" had to be dismantled. The names and locations of most original Creativity sites remain in flux. However, Creativity theory is still available within the electronic community of white supremacy on the sites of sympathetic organizations like White Aryan Resistance.[44] Creators themselves congregate within the Stormfront forums, in particular within "sectarian" Creator chat rooms, where discussions of Hale's plight and the group's future sometimes are interrupted by queries posted by racists considering a move into the Creativity camp.

Claiming to be a non-Creator intrigued by the philosophy, "Samuel Adams" unleashed an intense interaction in 2004 by asking the Creators to help him understand whether or not Creativity is a "religion."[45] Many registered Stormfront forum members, with post histories ranging from 19 to over 2,000, entered the discussion. Significantly, a couple of Identity Christians revealed themselves within the forum after several Creators took aim at the dominant camp. Analysis of the thread reveals key features of Aryan tribalism within the Creativity Movement.

After explaining, "I work with several creators and have even read Klassen," Samuel Adams expressed his frustrations in trying to comprehend the very concept of a "religion" that opposes spirituality. He wrote, "It is confusing. you dont pray to god, you dont pray to klassen, dont believe in an afterlife, when you die you get nothing from saving your race, there is no consequences for not saving your race, or any other things which make a 'religion' effective, namely belief in a higher power . . . any insight or ideas would be helpful." "Dianedeutsch" offered the first reply, calling forth the centrality of evolution within Creativity theory by politely explaining, "we enjoy life while its ours and hope it's better (because of what we've done) for the next generation . . . and the one after that . . . and the one after that" [ellipses and parentheses in original]. For movement insiders, the content of Dianedeutsch's post is echoed in her icon, a stylized graphic of "The 14 Words," movement code for the creed, "We must secure the existence of our people and a future for white children." [46]

The thread might have stopped with Dianedeutsch's answer to the original posting had Samuel Adams not reappeared with a follow-up question: "can/could a christian or odinist become a creator as it is a racial religion and they might personally need some type of spiritual religion? . . . it wouldn't make them any less of a creator or any less useful to the cause would it?" [47] "Karl14," sporting Hale's original World Church of the Creator crest as his icon, pounced on Samuel Adams. He declared, "it is our duty as Creators to work to completely overcome superstition [Identity Christianity] and replace it with reason." He warned, "You make the mistake of not taking us seriously as a religion . . . and your questions reflect that." Karl14 signed off with Klassen's legendary directive "RAHOWA! [Racial Holy War] Total racial warfare, total white victory!"

Karl14's slap at Christian Identity quickly elicited a response from "Imperial Aryan," who identified himself as an Identity Christian, but assured the forum he bore no hostility toward Creators. Imperial Aryan argued, "the most important thing in our Movement is the survival and preservation of our Race. That's all that really matters, not a specific belief or outlook." The presence of an Identity Christian inside the forum immediately changed the tone of the thread. "CreatorOre" emerged and turned on Samuel Adams, submitting a snide line-by-line critique of his original posting, and, referencing Samuel Adams's claim to "work with several creators," condescendingly asked, "What kind of work? Service, construction . . . ?" CreatorOre labeled elements of Samuel Adams's remarks "absurd" and "ridiculous" before concluding all spiritual religions, including Christian Identity, are simply "a crutch."

A second Identity Christian, "Standproud," then revealed himself to the forum, proliferating the rhetorical brawl by attacking Klassen's argument that there is no scientific or logical proof of the existence of a god. Standproud assured the forum he had experienced "personal proof" of the God of Christian Identity. Standproud mocked the Creators via rhetorical questions: "what is reason? ok lets test reason . . . we came from monkey's . . . does that sound logical to you? if it does then we should release all apes from zoo's because there ancestors may claim reparations." Standproud even scolded his fellow Identity Christian, Imperial Aryan, for displaying a lack of commitment to Identity in his conciliatory posting.

Karl14 and CreatorOre unleashed a torrent of attacks in reaction to Standproud. Karl14 began bluntly, "what the hell are you talking about?" He declared Standproud's zoo analogy "idiotic," then recommended Identity Christians like Standproud should "pick up a book other than the Bible sometime, they can be real educational." CreatorOre circled in on Standproud's claim of "personal proof" of the existence of God, taunting, "Did 'god' speak to you through some means that can't be—or wasn't—recorded?" He concluded his assault by declaring, "'God' is an imaginary thing."

Nearly two weeks after inspiring the controversial thread, Samuel Adams finally resurfaced in the forum. His collegial opening comments clearly seemed designed to calm the war raging between the two camps present inside the same chat room. But his posting shifted to an ominous tone when he responded directly to CreatorOre's suggestion that he had worked as nothing more than a construction laborer on behalf of the movement. Samuel Adams commanded CreatorOre, "email me at my non-stormfront email address, and leave your name, rank in the church, and a way to contact you." He then darkly offered, "I can tell matt hale and his family hi for you if you like. I can tell other important people in the cause hi for you if you wish too. . . . So basically, no. i am not just a construction worker for the church." In an underworld where leaders like Hale actually do conspire to have their enemies assassinated, Samuel Adams's "virtual" intimidation of CreatorOre silenced the entire forum.

The postings in the "Samuel Adams" thread reveal several important traits of Aryan tribalism among Creators. First, although the actual leadership of Creativity has been decimated, fidelity to the legacies of

Klassen and Hale remains the defining characteristic of affiliation with and rank within Creativity. Creators tolerate questions about their beliefs, but not the questioning of Klassen's "genius," echoing the dogmatism witnessed in the Identity camp. Second, Creators display respect for and, it appears, even fear of the hierarchy; the assertion of a direct link to Hale establishes a participant's status sufficiently to warn off further attacks within the electronic forum. Finally, communication among Creators demonstrates that they define themselves in relation to Identity Christians. Contrary to their insistence that Identity is little more than "superstition," the group's vehement attacks on Christian Identity indicate that Creators perceive the Identity camp to be in a position of dominance within the white supremacy movement.

While hate sites generally have fostered collaboration among white supremacists, the dynamic, interactive electronic communication that occurs inside Stormfront forums suggests that the movement remains sharply divided on the question of religion. Yet, regardless of philosophical divisions between the two camps, Identity Christians and Creators share important traits that define Aryan tribalism. Both groups are dogmatically authoritarian and strictly hierarchical. Membership in either camp requires complete submission to the teachings of recognized prophets. Although age, per se, is invisible online, subtle and overt communicative cues identify the ideological "elders" of the Aryan tribe; an elder's intimations of rank within the hierarchy of an actual movement organization immediately compel deference from, or even silence, the rank-and-file racists gathered inside the electronic meeting halls of the Aryan tribe.

Virtual Hate, Real Violence

A palpable undercurrent of threatened and actual physical coercion backs the authority of the "Alpha males" at the top of the command hierarchies of America's most notorious hate groups. The heads of neo-Confederate and neo-Nazi organizations strictly control not only their official membership rosters, but also how members behave, rarely risking their groups' long-term agendas or security to satisfy one member's fleeting desire to lash out with violence. Ironically, America probably owes a debt of gratitude to the white supremacy movement for the relative rarity of major incidents of racially motivated violence from the 1970s until the mid-1990s. As leading white supremacy organizations like the National Alliance and Aryan Nations expanded their membership in the later decades of the twentieth century, they also expanded their network of control over American racists. Likewise, as skinhead gang leaders enlisted the most virulently racist American youth in formal crew structures, the leaders established a dominance over the "freshcuts" that provided perhaps the only check on their propensity for violence.

Significantly, much of the worst violence associated with the white supremacy movement since the mid-1990s has been perpetrated not by movement insiders enacting the orders of recognized leaders, but rather by rogues like Ben Smith and Buford Furrow, expelled from hate groups for insubordination, and "wannabes" like Timothy McVeigh, never invited to join in the first place.[48] Domestic terrorism expert Brian Levin explains, "The Internet has become the principal recruitment tool, attracting the loners and the disturbed."[49] In the era of cyberhate, rogue racists and wannabe skinheads do not need to belong to an actual hate group to get or to maintain access to the ideology of hatred. The electronic community of white supremacy now provides all of the resources a person needs to declare "Rahowa! Racial Holy War!" But, unlike actual hate groups and skinhead crews, the electronic community cannot always deliver on the threats of violence Aryan tribal elders issue both to compel submission and to expel the uncooperative or undesirable. The same online anonymity that protects the identity of movement insiders also protects the identity of rogues and wannabes lurking in cyberspace. From the day the first hate site launched, the white supremacy movement sacrificed its ability to police its own borders; hate sites are an open door into the mentality of the movement for wannabes and, perhaps of even greater concern, a door that cannot be closed on racists deemed "uncontrollable" even by violent, veteran skinhead crew chiefs.

Angst-ridden and technology-savvy by virtue of their age alone, adolescents are particularly vulnerable to the seductive allure and easy availability of cyberhate. Youth who cannot find a real skinhead crew in their area, or who have been declared "unfit" by real crew leaders, now can inhabit a "cybercrew" of their own making by positioning themselves inside the amorphous webs of ideology and interaction openly available on hate sites. Any teenager with a modem can educate himself about skinhead history, outfit himself in authentic skinhead regalia, and even ally himself with Christian Identity or Creativity. Using a catchy movement moniker as his alias, he can observe the protocols of Aryan tribalism that govern communication among racists rallying in cyberspace, and then insinuate himself into the tribe by performing its culture. From the solitude of his bedroom, he can build a virtual social life through online discussion forums, where he can commune with "like-minded people," learn why he should hate "mud" and battle "ZOG," and even find the names of "race traitors" who deserve to die.

But when that young man logs off from his cybercrew of ageless, faceless fellow race warriors he knows only by pseudonymous user names, he is alone with his hatred. The "Klaliffs" he must defer to within his cybercrew cannot control him offline, for they do not even know his real name. As he laces up his Doc Marten boots and reaches for a baseball bat or a gun, there is no actual, hardened skinhead crew leader in the room to forcibly back him down from his violent impulses; no young neo-Nazi "übermensch" is present to curb the boy's aggression in the moment in service of the long-term agenda of a larger cause. There is simply an angry, armed teenager, who believes, as one former Identity skinhead voiced it, "I've got a permission slip from God to come kick your ass." [50]

Notes

1. National Alliance of Gang Investigators Associations, *2005 National Gang Threat Assessment* (Washington, D.C.: NAGIC, 2005) p. ix.

2. Professional Security Television Network, "Suburban Gangs, Part I" (March 2000); Midwest Gang Investigators Association, *Gangster Gazette* compact disc, June 2005.

3. Professional Security Television Network, "Suburban Gangs."

4. Not all skinhead gangs are racist; in fact, some are antiracist. In this chapter, unless otherwise noted, the term "skinhead" is used to refer only to racist skinheads.

5. Southern Poverty Law Center, "2004: Active Hate Groups in the United States," *Intelligence Report* 117 (Spring 2005): 55. The report explains that the statistic understates the actual number of skinhead crews, because skinheads themselves are "migratory" and, in some cases, "not affiliated with groups."

6. The term "brotherhood" is apt because females traditionally play only ancillary roles within actual white supremacy organizations. Although some females self-identity as racist skinheads, overwhelmingly such women are labeled "skinchicks" by their male counterparts. "Skinchicks" are the sisters, girlfriends, and wives of actual skinhead gang members; normally their rank within the crews is a by-product of their relationships with male skinheads, not an independent status.

7. The National Socialist White People's Party went by the name National Coalition to Free America from Jewish Control from 1954 to 1957 and the American Nazi Party from 1957 to 1967. Rockwell himself was assassi-

nated in 1967 by a rogue follower he had expelled from his organization for insubordination.

8. Nick Knight, *Skinhead* (London: Omnibus Press, 1982), p. 24.

9. Skrewdriver, "Discography" and "Lyrics," http://www.skrewdriver.com.

10. Jack Moore, *Skinheads Shaved for Battle: A Cultural History of American Skinheads* (Bowling Green, Ohio: Bowling Green State University Press, 1993), p. 47.

11. Anti-Defamation League of B'nai B'rith, *Shaved for Battle: Skinheads Target American Youth* (New York: Anti-Defamation League of B'nai B'rith, 1987).

12. Southern Poverty Law Center, "2004: Active Hate Groups," pp. 52–58.

13. "Rahowa" is an acronym for "Racial Holy War"; "88" is code for "Heil Hitler," as "H" is the eighth letter of the alphabet; "14" references "The 14 Words," the creed declaring, "We must secure the existence of our people and a future for white children."

14. Although ZOG theory can be found in many white supremacist books and on virtually all Web sites sponsored by movement organizations and their affiliates, the most comprehensive, frequently updated, publicly accessible treatises are e-published by Aryan Nations (http://www.Aryan-nations.org).

15. Since federal hate-crime sentencing enhancers were enacted into law shortly after the 1998 murder of Matthew Shepard, most violent skinhead juvenile offenders are waived into the adult criminal system.

16. Aryan Nations, "Aryan Olympics" circular (Hayden, Idaho: Church of Jesus Christ Christian, 1989). A representative example of adult-skinhead cooperation in the late 1980s and early 1990s involved the relationship between Pennsylvania Klaverns of the Invisible Empire of the Ku Klux Klan and Philadelphia's Strike Force crew. Frank Meeink (Strike Force Commander, 1988–1991), Interview by Jody M. Roy, June 20, 2004, unpublished videotape.

17. Hale specifically encouraged skinheads to sign on as his "storm troopers," the armed security force that traveled with Hale in public. World Church of the Creator, "Racial Loyalty!" http://www.wcotc.org (accessed September 19, 1999). Tom Metzger, head of White Aryan Resistance, featured skinheads in various WAR media and corresponded heavily with crew leaders. In fact, an Oregon jury held Metzger liable for facilitating, via correspondence, Portland's East Side White Pride crew's murder of Mulageta Seraw, an Ethiopian immigrant. Morris Dees and Steven Fiffer, *Hate on Trial: The Case against America's Most Dangerous Neo-Nazi* (New York: Villard Books, 1993).

18. *Resistance* (Detroit: Resistance Records, 1994–1997); George Burdi (founder of Resistance Records), Interview by Jody M. Roy, April 9, 2002, unpublished videotape.

19. George Burdi interview.

20. Resistance Records, untitled direct-mail piece (Detroit: Resistance Records, September 1997).

21. George Burdi interview. Following Pierce's death in 2002, several of his lieutenants vied for control of the National Alliance. The group splintered in the summer of 2005; now most former National Alliance units and their members answer to Kevin Strom, leader of the newly formed National Vanguard. "Clarification on the Status of National Alliance," May 2005, http://www

.adl.org/learn/extremisminamericaupdates/groups/nationalalliance (accessed July 11, 2005).

22. Arizona Department of Corrections, "Validated Security Threat Groups," http://www.adc.state.az.us/stg/stg.html.

23. Dees and Fiffer, *Hate on Trial*.

24. National Alliance of Gang Investigators Associations, *2005 National Gang Threat Assessment*, p. vi.

25. Southern Poverty Law Center, "Active Hate Websites in the United States in 2004," *Intelligence Report* 117 (Spring 2005): 59.

26. Southern Poverty Law Center, "The Forums," *Intelligence Report* 118 (Summer 2005): 55. By November 2005, Stormfront claimed on its main page to have in excess of 64,000 subscribers.

27. Virtually all major hate groups offer free materials online. Among the most extensive online resource sites are www.Aryan-nations.org and www .natall.org, the main Web site of the National Alliance.

28. The White Aryan Resistance Web site, www.resist.com, offers political commentary, baseline white supremacist theory, and an extensive collection of racist jokes, cartoons, poems, and song lyrics.

29. According to a Federal Bureau of Investigation report made public in April 2005, 22 domestic terror groups were then the subject of 338 active FBI field investigations. Both Aryan Nations and National Alliance are mentioned specifically in the report. Although no particular skinhead gang is named, the report indicates groups that sponsor white-power concerts are being monitored; skinhead gangs, of course, are the primary organizers of such events. Vic Walter, Avni Patel, and Jessica Wang, "Secret FBI Report Highlights Domestic Terror: Experts Warn of Future Timothy McVeighs" (New York: ABC News, April 18, 2005), Anti-Defamation League of B'nai B'rith, http://www .militia-watchdog.org (accessed April 18, 2005).

30. Formation of "_ASH" crews is a frequent topic of discussion on the forum www.skinhead.net, where both racist skinheads and SHARPs (Skinheads Against Racial Prejudice) post messages. "_ASH" crews may be formed by either racist or SHARP skinheads, because the system is nothing more than an organizational template in the hard-mod tradition.

31. Within hours of Matt Hale's being sentenced to forty years in prison for conspiring to hire the assassination of a federal judge, the vanguardnewsnetwork.com forum (April 6, 2005) posed the question "Do you think that the laws of the United States should be democratically and peacefully changed to make it legal or even mandatory to string up federal judges such as James T. Moody . . . for their increasingly heinous hate crimes against the indigenous White citizenry, such as 40 year sentencing of Matt Hale?" The posting included Judge Moody's office address and notes on where he normally parks his car, details elided in the excerpt quoted here.

32. A third philosophical grounding for contemporary white supremacy, "Wotanism" (aka "Odinism"), is a reinterpretation of ancient Norse mythology as a modern racial-spiritualism. Only some people who identify themselves as "Wotanist/Odinist" hold racist views; delineation of the racist version of the mythology can be found at http://www.odinic-rite.org. To the extent Wotanism

is gaining momentum within the white supremacy movement in recent years, it seems particularly popular among youth and young adults, perhaps because it is largely metaphorical and, thus, does not require adherence to particular behavioral codes. However, Wotanism remains less influential among skinhead crews than either Identity or Creativity, likely because it has no clear leadership or definitive organizational structure. Regardless of their actual philosophical affiliation, almost all skinhead crews rely heavily on Odinist symbolism for gang insignia.

33. After some positioning by another "leader," August B. Kreis III took the reins of Aryan Nations following Butler's death in 2004. In the Butler era, Aryan Nations called its ministry "The Church of Jesus Christ Christian" and normally referenced the theology as "Christian Identity." In 2005, Kreis seems to be introducing new terminology by replacing "Christian Identity" with "Aryan Identity," and publicly calling the ministry "Tabernacle of the Phinehas Priesthood." Significantly, organizational arms of Aryan Nations, such as Bob Matthews's The Order, have been known to operate completely covertly for years before the group acknowledges it is housed within the master organization. The newly public use of the term Phinehas Priesthood may be such a case. If it is, it is significant to note that Eric Rudolph claims to be a member of the Priesthood.

34. Aryan Nations, "Tabernacle of the Phinehas Priesthood—Aryan Nations—Aryan Messianic Identity: Commentary of the Bible with the New Aryan Translation," http://www.Aryan-nations.org/holyorder/commentary.

35. Southern Poverty Law Center, "2004: Active Hate Websites," p. 62.

36. "Wanting to Convert" http://www.stormfront.com/forum/showthread. php?t=224834 (August 15, 2005–August 24, 2005). All quotations from the "Wanting to Convert" (aka "Jeremy") thread reprinted in this chapter display the forum participants' original spelling, grammar, style, and emphases, even when inaccurate, to convey the tone of the thread. Because technical errors pervade the original discourse, the author of this chapter does not insert "[*sic*]" into the quotations; the convention would make reading the quotations abnormally cumbersome. However, unless explicitly noted otherwise, ellipsis points in quotations are not original to the discourse as posted on the forum.

37. Ben Klassen, *The White Man's Bible* (North Carolina: Creativity Publishing, 1986); Ben Klassen, *Nature's Eternal Religion* (North Carolina: Creativity Publishing, 1992). Among the skinheads Klassen tutored was the young leader who founded Resistance Records in 1992; he studied under Klassen in 1990. George Burdi interview.

38. World Church of the Creator, "Racial Loyalty!"; Klassen, *Nature's Eternal Religion*.

39. The most influential North American white-power band, Rahowa, fused their music to Creativity beginning in 1992; their first compact disc, released in 1992, remained one of the top-selling recordings in the Resistance Records catalogue at least until 1995. George Burdi interview; Rahowa, *Declaration of War* compact disc (Detroit: Resistance Records, 1992).

40. Indiana University Alumni Association, "University Mourns Murdered Student," *The College* 23 (Fall 1999): 17. Smith, an Indiana University

undergraduate student at the time of his murder spree, killed Won-Joon Yoon, a Korean graduate student, at Indiana University, and Ricky Byrdsong, a basketball coach, at Northwestern University. Smith injured nine other people in Indiana and Illinois.

41. Mike Robinson, "White Supremacist Sentenced to 40 Years for Trying to Have Federal Judge Killed," *Chicago Tribune*, April 6, 2005, http://www.militia-watchdog.org.

42. Klassen, *Nature's Eternal Religion*, pp. 3–7.

43. Ibid., p. 11.

44. White Aryan Resistance, http://www.resist.com.

45. "A Question About Creativity," http://www.stormfront.com/forum/showthread.php?=882044 (February 6, 2004–February 17, 2004). All quotations from the "A Question About Creativity" (aka "Samuel Adams") thread reprinted in this chapter display the forum participants' original spelling, grammar, style, and emphases, even when inaccurate, to convey the tone of the thread. Because technical errors pervade the original discourse, the author of this chapter does not insert "[*sic*]" into the quotations; the convention would make reading the quotations abnormally cumbersome. However, unless explicitly noted otherwise, ellipsis points in quotations are not original to the discourse as posted on the forum.

46. The 14 Words creed was popularized by David Lane, a high-ranking member of The Order Bruder Schweigen, the deeply covert Aryan Nations faction headed by infamous white-supremacy bank-robbery mastermind, Robert Matthews. Lane is in prison for crimes committed on behalf of The Order; he declares himself to be a "political prisoner." Although incarcerated, Lane has published extensively on The 14 Words. See David Lane, *Deceived, Damned, and Defiant* (Napa, Calif.: 14 Words Press, 1999).

47. See note 32.

48. Smith, a former World Church member, killed two and injured nine in a two-state, three-day killing spree in 1999. The same year, renegade Aryan Nationalist Buford Furrow opened fire inside a Los Angeles Jewish Community Center, killing several adults and wounding children before shooting a postal worker on the sidewalk outside. Timothy McVeigh, the infamous Oklahoma City bomber, was in possession of copies of key pages of William Pierce's *The Turner Diaries* when apprehended; *The Turner Diaries* is a "novel" about a racial-purist militia that blows up a federal office building using an ammonium nitrate truck-bomb. Patrick E. Cole, "McVeigh: Diaries Dearest," *Time* 49, no. 13 (1997): 26.

49. Walter, Patel, and Wang.

50. Frank Meeink interview.

CHAPTER 15

Radical Tribes at Warre: Primitivists on the Net

MATHIEU O'NEIL

In its broadest terms, the contrast between tribe and civilization is between war and peace. In the social condition of Warre (Hobbes), force is a resort legitimately available to all men.
—MARSHALL D. SAHLINS, *TRIBESMEN*

As for the negative consequences of eliminating industrial society—well, you can't eat your cake and have it too. To gain one thing you have to sacrifice another.
—THEODORE KACZYNSKI, *INDUSTRIAL SOCIETY AND ITS FUTURE*

W hy "tribes"? In the anthropological tradition, a tribe was a sociopolitically homogenous and autonomous group. Its members shared patterns of speech, basic cultural characteristics, and a territory. Today the term is universally used and universally undefined. Obviously, there is something in the word that appeals to the imagination: perhaps the idea that we can escape the atomized mass and reconstitute earlier, stronger ties between individuals. In order to understand the formation of online tribal identity, I use the concepts of "boundary" and "field" to analyze economic and political aspects of tribalism in anarcho-primitivist networks.

Neotribes in the Lifestyle Market

Tribalism's popular resurgence can be traced back to the 1960s counter-culture, described by Theodore Roszak as youth's reaction to a regime of technocrats and experts.[1] Gary Snyder called for groups of youths to organize tribally, to create a community of comradeship in personal relationships and responsibilities and to be at one with nature.[2] In Australia, at the Aquarius Festival held at Nimbin in 1973, the tribe was the preferred social unit and symbol of precapitalism. There was undoubtedly an amount of naïveté in this countercultural embrace, as tribalism at Aquarius was associated with liberation from the kinds of social restrictions that form an essential part of tribal societies, such as hierarchies of status, inequity between gender and age groups, and taboos and fears surrounding the natural functions of the body.[3]

Today, as ever, a key aspect of any social formation is its ability to persist by retaining members. This hinges on individual motivation (the will to contribute), but also on the feeling of belonging, of associating to what is close to one's concerns. For Michel Maffesoli, the concept of historical center has exploded into a multiplicity of "subterranean centralities" that each have their own history and that share an ethos, a way of being together.[4] These tribes may have goals, may have finality; but this is not essential; what is important is the energy expended on constituting the group *as such*. Furthermore, what matters is not so much belonging to a gang, a family, or a community as switching from one group to another. In contrast to the stability induced by classical tribalism, "neo-tribalism is characterized by fluidity, occasional gatherings and dispersal."[5] In other words, within a particular tribe, there are many members who belong to a multitude of other tribes. Others have expanded Maffesoli's thesis: for Kevin Hetherington, the deregulation of the modern forms of solidarity and identity based on class, occupation, locality, and gender has led to a recomposition into "tribal" identities and forms of sociation.[6] In Rob Shields's view, tribal identities serve to illustrate the temporal nature of collective identities in modern consumer society as individuals continually move between different sites of collective expression and "reconstruct" themselves accordingly.[7] In this sense, identity is an experimental construct where individuals select lifestyles, which are in no way indicative of a specific class background.[8]

What all these readings fail to convey is why these associations should be called "tribes." In fact, it could be argued that here "tribe" is simply a different way of saying "subculture," minus the "rigid lines of division over forms of sociation which may [be] more fleeting, and in many cases arbitrary, than the concept of subculture, with its connotations of coherency and solidarity, allows for."[9] Hence these tribes' uncritical embrace of the dominant capitalist culture, a position consonant with David

Chaney's assertion that a fully developed mass society liberates rather than oppresses individuals by offering avenues for individual expression through a range of commodities and resources that can be worked into particular lifestyle *sites* and *strategies*.[10] This selection of personas in the marketplace has been a mainstay of cultural studies orthodoxy since the 1970s—the celebration of "resistance" through consumption. Yet however artfully they have been collaged by consumer-bricoleurs, the choices have been prepackaged; and it is strange to think that the kinds of lives most consumers live, and the kinds of effects mass consumerism is having on the planet, do not feature in the equation.

The loose ties evoked so far would seem appropriate to describe on-line tribes, which appear at first to be transient gatherings of disembodied voices from around the world. I want to consider a different premise: that the tribal impulse originates with the affirmation of group boundaries, and that tribes are vehicles for radical thought. In Anthony Cohen's words, "boundaries are marked because communities interact in some way or other with entities from which they are, or wish to be, distinguished."[11] In this view, there can be no inclusion and belonging without exclusion and differentiation. An extreme case of boundary-building is found in groups that unconditionally reject everything that is not themselves: anarcho-primitivists fit that description.

Roots and Economy of the Online Primitivist Field

While anarchists have traditionally critiqued the manifestations of hierarchical thinking and authoritarian social relations, anarcho-primitivists attack the assumptions behind that thinking.[12] They reject techno-industrial development, which they equate with individual oppression and environmental destruction. On the biospheric level, primitivists paint an apocalyptic portrait of species extinction, proliferating dead zones, the pervasive poisoning of air, water, and soil. In terms of individual autonomy, anarcho-primitivists argue that we live in a world where the accumulation of technical knowledge is astonishing, and yet we are probably much more lacking in technical know-how than our ancestors: technology can only be created and repaired by *someone else*. For Theodore Kaczynski (the so-called "Unabomber") the freedoms we have are those consistent with the system's ends, such as the economic freedom to consume, or press freedom to criticize inefficiency and corruption; however, individuals or groups are devoid of the true power to control the life-and-death issues of existence—food, clothing, shelter, and defense.[13] The solution? "With disenchantment comes a growing sense that something different is urgently needed."[14] Anarcho-primitivists advocate a return to a tribal mode of living, based on small-scale sustainable communities of hunters and gatherers or permaculture-practicing farmers. The most radical primitivist author is John Zerzan, who asserts that "mounting evidence" indicates that before the Neolithic shift from a foraging or gatherer-hunter mode of existence to an agricultural lifeway, most people had ample free time, considerable gender autonomy or equality, an ethos of egalitarianism and sharing, and no organized violence.[15] Zerzan believes the root cause of the problem to be civilization, that is to say the domestication of plants, animals, and humans that led to patriarchy and the division of labor.[16]

Field theory, as defined by Pierre Bourdieu, sees society as differentiated into a number of semiautonomous fields governed by their own "game rules," yet with parallel basic oppositions and general structures.[17] Fields can be distinguished both according to the kinds of specific capital (capital is "heteronomous," external to the field, or "autonomous," unique to that field) that are valued in them, and by their degree of relative autonomy from each other and in particular from the dominant political and economic fields.[18] Anarcho-primitivism is a highly autonomous political-cultural field of restricted production (oriented toward other producers), in contrast to fields of large-scale production (produced for general audiences). As in all marginal fields, the production and exchange of cultural artifacts represent the means for primitivist actors to engage in the genuinely felt rejection of dominant norms whilst also exhibiting their underground distinction from mainstream, or "common," culture.[19] Valuable positions on the online primitivist field are attained through the establishment of freely accessible resources. The dominant tribe on the primitivist online field is made of individuals and groups who have adapted offline magazines to the Web (*Green Anarchy, Do or Die, Green Anarchist*), constituted online archives (Primitivism.com, Insurgent Desire), set up distribution hubs (Beating Hearts Press, Re-Pressed), or sites offering practical guidelines for "rewilding" (Wildroots, Earth Skills, Abotech). Members of the LiveJournal community on primitivism, because they have little to contribute in the way of digital resources beyond their blog postings, consequently possess less primitivist cultural capital.

Primitivists share a self-image and a set of symbols that cannot be understood by outsiders. These constitute the boundary lines distinguishing members of the group from the rest of the world. Anarcho-primitivism has a variety of influences. First among these is the school of anthropology, which presents so-called "primitive" peoples in a positive light. The canonical text is Marshall Sahlins's "The Original Affluent Society," which holds that primitive people did not work hard, or continuously.[20] Sahlins had previously challenged orthodox views of evolution, stating that technological advance leads to an increase in work and decrease in leisure.[21] That life before civilization was not "brutish and short" is the primitivist doxa. For Bob Black, "by their lifeways the hunter-gatherers give the lie to the Hobbesian hoax."[22]

Anarcho-primitivism also lies at the confluence of several strands of radical thought, such as the antitechnological anarchism of Detroit's *Fifth Estate* journal, in which Fredy Perlman first wrote of the "song and dance of primitive communities," and David Watson extolled the virtues of preindustrial systems and tribal religions.[23] A more mainstream type of antitechnological criticism, including Jacques Ellul, Langdon Winner, and Kirkpatrick Sale, also deserves a mention.[24] Radical environmental groups like the Animal Liberation Front and Earth First! constitute an activist current. Inspired by Edward Abbey's popular tale of eco-sabotage[25] and by the "deep ecology" of Arne Naess[26] and of Bill Devall and George Sessions,[27] Earth First! sees humanity as being "in the midst of an unprecedented, anthropogenic extinction crisis."[28] Earth First! cofounder Dave Foreman advocates "bio-regionalism": by "reinhabiting a place, by dwelling in it, we become that place. We are *of* it. Our most fundamental duty is self-defense. We are the wilderness defending itself."[29] Another strand is eco-feminism, which describes commonalities between the subordination of women, indigenous people, and nature in terms of their inferior positioning in Western thought and their common exploitation by the capitalist economy.[30] A final influence is that of the Internationale Situationniste, a radical group that played an important role in the Paris May 1968 revolt. The Situationists' antiauthoritarian council communism has a continuing appeal for radicals due to the group's striking slogans, refusal to compromise, and millenarian conviction that the I. S. had formulated the most lucid critique of "spectacular" society (of the reified commodity as image).[31] When John Zerzan writes that "the essence of language is the symbol. Always a substitution. Always a paler re-presentation of what is at hand, what presents itself directly to us,"[32] he is echoing Guy Debord's opening lines to *The Society of the Spectacle*, "everything that was directly lived has receded into a representation."[33] However, the Situationists are so well known that the distinctive profits earned by referring to them have been depreciated: primitivists must therefore refer to much more obscure "ultraleft" Europeans, such as Jacques Camatte, for example.[34]

While all these strands of thought appear in anarcho-primitivist *texts*, they are not physically present in Web sites in the form of *links* to other sites. This points to an important difference from dominant Internet practice, resulting from online primitivists' deep ambivalence about their use of the medium. On the one hand, by posting large quantities of free data, primitivists are active participants in the Internet's decentralized "free economy." (This lack of organization or centralization in the setup of production and free provision of content has been described by Richard Barbrook as proof that the Internet represents "really existing anarcho-communism."[35]) At the same time, primitivists do not participate in the Internet "link economy," the attribution by and reception of links. Instead, primitivist Web sites exchange a "review capital" closely resembling that of the "zine" (underground magazine) world, where the value of publications is defined by mutual reviews.[36]

Kung Fighting! Warre as Palimpsest

There is no easier way of reinforcing boundaries and bonds than having an enemy.[37] For James Boon, every discourse, like every culture, inclines toward what it is not: toward an implicit negativity.[38] Cohen writes that groups respond assertively to encroachment upon their boundaries because members find identities as individuals through occupancy of the group's social space: "If outsiders trespass in that space, then occupants' own sense of self is felt to be debased and defaced."[39] According to war historian Gérard Chaliand, the most violent conflicts are those against similar peoples, who occupy positions spatially close to the attackers, offering a narcissistic (though insufferably antagonistic) reflection of their own image.[40] The most radical conflict is that of the Same against the Same, being only slightly more intense than that against the Other perceived as radically Other, as its essence is perceived as Other.

In the case of anarcho-primitivists, offline conflicts are based on difference, while online conflicts are based on similarity. There are different types of offline conflictuality, starting with "going feral," a process that simultaneously indicates detachment from a state of domesticity, "the parent *culture*," and identification with the *natural* environment.[41] Another type of conflict is that which involves indigenous people, such as the Free Papua Movement (Organisasi Papua Merdeka, or OPM) in Indonesian Irian Jaya, as such groups are not only engaged in battles against the state, industrial expansionism, and corporate exploitation, but are "the only communities that have maintained a relatively harmonious relationship with the natural world." [42] The boundaries of the primitivist tribe are particularly expressed in letters of comments to magazines, which provide a narcissistic reflection of members' beliefs in the opinions of others. Special prominence is given to letters from "prisoners of warre" against the state and corporations, who represent the embodiment of the struggle. [43] A third type of offline conflict, which resembles earlier anarchist traditions of direct action in the Western world, thus involves eco-sabotage, animal liberation, and violent resistance to state authority.

If anarcho-primitivists were to engage in similar acts of resistance, sabotage, or terrorism *online*, they would be faced with the problematic notion of having to master the technological tools of "hacktivism" so as to conduct (for example) Web site defacements, or computer virus infestations, or Distributed Denial of Service attacks (whereby a targeted Web site is inundated with browser "hits," causing it to crash). They would have to become *primitivist hackers*, taking the contradiction to dizzying heights. The technophobia that makes online primitivists poor linkers also makes them poor attackers outside their tribe, because in this field conflict takes the form of textual exchanges, and online primitivists do not wish to converse with the state and corporations. This means that the erection of boundaries occurs solely within the tribe, rendering online primitivist practice the precise opposite of Sahlins's characterization of "peacemaking [as] the wisdom of tribal institutions," because "in a situation of Warre, where every man is empowered to proceed against every man, peacemaking cannot be an occasional inter-tribal event. It becomes a continuous process, going on within society itself." [44] This state of affairs is possible, of course, because the conflicts occurring on the online primitivist field are symbolic fights involving no loss of life, limb, or liberty.

In the words of Victor Turner, fields are "an ensemble of relationships between actors antagonistically oriented to the same prizes or values." [45] Since to exist in a field is to differ, a dialectic of distinction ensures the constant production of change as new actors enter and attempt to make their mark on the field. [46] Moreover, cultural fields are characterized by "more or less overt struggles over the definition of the legitimate principles of the division of the field." [47] Following a mechanism of inversion, value in the online primitivist field derives from that which is furthest from what the field, in fact, produces (words on screens). In other words, action is endowed with the greatest prestige in this virtual environment; hence, the maximum legitimacy awarded to prisoner-authors such as Kaczynski or jailed activists Rob "Los Ricos" Thaxton and Jeff "Free" Luer and their *Heartcheck* magazine. Tribes also compete to determine what the stakes of the competition are. In a sense, the players are attempting to answer the question "What is anarchism?" This struggle is a replay of the nineteenth-century opposition between a minority of "individualistic" anarchists such as Max Stirner and their "social" counterparts. The traditionally dominant variants of social anarchism such as anarcho-communism and anarcho-syndicalism are discounted by primitivists on the grounds that their reliance on organization and control renders them inherently authoritarian:

> This pamphlet is yet another pathetic attempt to dust off the same old tired crap of anarcho-syndicalism (complete with its fetishization of technology, industry, progress, organization and the working class) and once again quote a bunch of dead Euro-dudes in order to demonstrate that the only anarchism that will be tolerated is one that Bakunin or Kropotkin would approve of.[48]

Cornelius Castoriadis suggests that it was Marx who introduced into the workers' movement the centrality of technique, of production, of the economy.[49] Indeed, Engels famously wrote about the necessity of authority in industrial production, transport, and above all during a revolution, which he defined as "certainly the most authoritarian thing there is [. . .] the act whereby one part of the population imposes its will upon the other part by means of rifles, bayonets and cannons."[50] So when John Zerzan of *Green Anarchy* took part in an online debate with Michael Albert of *ZMagazine*, he did not enter into a discussion of the finer points of Albert's "participatory economics" (as Albert did of primitivism). After Albert challenged the central primitivist notion that divisions of labor or talent necessarily lead to hierarchies of power and influence, Zerzan's reply was curt: "No matter how you slice it, 'parecon' or otherwise, people won't go into the factories, mines, smelters, warehouses, etc. for unavoidably toxic, miserable toil, unless they are forced. [. . .] Your leftist blueprint cannot be realized, in my opinion, without coercion. As an anarchist, I'm not interested."[51]

The central dividing axis of the contemporary ultraleft and anarchist fields is the question of what is being opposed. Among this close-knit group of enemies, theoretical and ideological chasms hinge upon whether society is defined as "modern" (dispensing with traditions in the name of progress), "industrial" (filling an artificial world with technical objects, abolishing nature and humanity), "capitalist" (subsuming everything to the commodity), or "spectacular" (negating true life). Primitivists reject all forms of conventional progressive or radical politics because they decry them as embracing the Enlightenment-born ideology of progress and techno-scientific reason. This put them at odds with a prominent voice on the anarchist field, that of Murray Bookchin. In *Post-Scarcity Anarchism* (1971), Bookchin had argued that anarchism represented the application of ecological ideas to society, based on empowering individuals and communities, decentralizing power, and increasing diversity: "Just as the ecologist seeks to expand the range of the eco-system and promote free interplay between species, so the anarchist seeks to expand the range of social experiments and remove all fetters to its development."[52] In 1987 Bookchin published a pamphlet criticizing deep ecology's nativism, asserting that there were "barely disguised racists, survivalists, macho Daniel Boones, and outright social reactionaries" employing the term ecology to express their views.[53] He also described the deep ecologist solution of reducing the world's population as an act of "eco-brutalism" reminiscent of Hitler.[54]

A few years later, Bookchin launched an attack against what he called "lifestyle anarchists."[55] Contrasting the personalistic commitment to individual autonomy of "lifestylers" with his collectivist commitment to social freedom, Bookchin directed some of his most abrasive comments onto primitivists, describing their "edenic glorification of prehistory" as "absurd balderdash"[56] and ridiculing Zerzan's "reductionist and simplistic" notion that self-domestication through language, ritual, and art inspired the subsequent taming of plants and animals that followed.[57] This generated a flurry of angry anarcho-primitivist responses, notably from the *Fifth Estate*'s David Watson.[58] Bob Black joined the fray, in the process revealing why, in his opinion, the definition of the legitimate principles of the division of the field had assumed such importance for anarchists after the fall of the Berlin Wall: "[The] anarchists are at a turning point. For the first time in history, they are the only revolutionary current."[59] Bookchin responded to these critics with a new essay where he disparaged Watson for serving up "all the puerile rubbish about aboriginal lifeways [of the 1960s],"[60] and concluded his piece by dismissing Black's "irresponsible, juvenile bravado."[61] Bob Black shot back with a rant where he derided Bookchin's "reiteration of the bourgeois Hobbesian myth of the lives of pre-urban anarchist foragers as solitary, poor, nasty, brutish and short, in dramatic contrast to the life of Murray Bookchin: nasty, brutish, and long."[62] In addition, since Bookchin had based his criticism of the primitive affluence thesis on a book by anthropologist Edwin Wilmsen which affirmed that the !Kung Bushmen—contrary to primitivist orthodoxy—lived miserable lives,[63] Black lost no time in attempting to demolish Wilmsen's credentials in yet another essay.[64]

This polemical back-and-forth took a more concentrated form during the exchange between Ken Knabb, the main translator of Situationist texts in the United States, and John Filiss, creator of the Primitivism. com archive. Knabb's essay on revolutionary politics, *Public Secrets*, included a critique of anarcho-primitivism from an ultraleft perspective, affirming that primitivism offers no practical means of achieving its goals in a libertarian manner because a mere revolution could never be enough to satisfy the "eternal ontological rebelliousness" of primitivists.[65] This section of Knabb's text was posted by John Filiss on the "Anarchy Board" discussion list together with Filiss's point-by-point comments and refutations. Knabb then reappropriated this cut-up and added his comments to the mix, posting the result on his Bureau of Public Secrets Web site.[66] Not to be outdone, Filiss then copied this new version, added yet another layer of commentary—commenting on Knabb's reactions to his earlier comments about the original text—and posted it on his Primitivism site, under his own signature.[67] The combination of text editing and digital networking technologies thus facilitates a synchronous presentation of that most diachronic form of intellectual exchange, the literary dogfight, in which authors can seize their opponents' text, modify it by changing the font characteristics or by adding breaks, and insert their own thoughts, in a potentially never-ending conflictual palimpsest.

Weapons on the Field of Battle

When discussing their situation in the field of anarchism, anarcho-primitivists are wont to describe themselves as both an irresistible force and as victims of the extraordinary malignity of their detractors. As new entrants in the anarchist field, they adopt heretical or subversive strategies.[68] They attempt to partially revolutionize the field by claiming to be returning to the origins, the essence, the truth of the game, against the trivialization and degradation into which it has since drifted: "The main opposition [during Zerzan's speaking tour] came from anarcho-leftists [. . .] I didn't hear anything new in their protestations, except, in their defensiveness, evidence that they are losing and know it."[69] Anarcho-primitivism has itself been challenged by even more recent entrants on the anarchist field, known as "insurrectionary anarchists." The stakes in this struggle are the definition of "green anarchy," or "post-left anarchy." This aggressive debate with fellow-travelers has assumed a ritualized dimension, as when a *Green Anarchy* reviewer refers in passing to this "notable conflict [. . .] the perpetual insurrectionary/primitivist debate."[70] In one instance, the insurrectionary journal *Killing King Abacus* (KKA) published a somewhat unfavorable estimation of primitivism, in which it was asserted that the "idealization of nature [is] derived from an extreme pessimism towards the possibility of any fundamental change in our society."[71] This criticism was indirectly met by a counterattack in the pages of *Green Anarchy*, in which John Zerzan, in the course of an unfavorable review of another insurrectionary journal, *Willful Disobedience*, asserted that insurrectionary anarchism was "a trendy, but possibly hollow movement."[72] Zerzan's criticism was posted to the Anti-politics message board, where it generated the following exchange:

> Kevin Tucker [Coalition Against Civilization/*Species Traitor*]: Since the publication of KKA I have seen a lot more division among g@-ists [green anarchists] Some bullshit contention involved, a kind of camps, for lack of a better wordage. [. . .] SashaK *[Killing King Abacus]*: We marked out some diffevrences between us and pr . . . you can hardly call that an attack . . . it's pretty mild to my reading. By interpreting this as an "attack" you leave no room to discuss our differences, almost a "you're with us or against us." [. . .] Wolfi Landstreicher *[Willful Disobedience]*: To think of criticisms and the drawing of distinctions as attacks . . . creation of sects and camps . . . indicates that one's ideas are becoming rigid, a kind of doctrine to be accepted or rejected rather than ideas to be used, questioned, tested.[73]

These three accusations represent a crescendo of anarchistic negativity. First, sowing division, weakening the tribe; second, forcing others to take sides—in other words, authoritarianism; third, adopting a preconceived ideal against which the world (and one's own life) is measured—an "archetypally ideological,"[74] rather than critical, stance.

A widespread means of enforcing boundaries and of reasserting norms is to disparage an opponent's views by using a derogatory term such as "leftist," "authoritarian," or "trendy." This last term is used by antiprimitivists such as Bookchin, who reviles "today's fashionable technophobia,"[75] and Knabb, who asserts that he conducted a brief debunking of "trendy technophobia."[76] It is also leveled at the rival insurrectionary tribe by primitivist elder Zerzan ("the trendy and possibly hollow movement").[77] Accusations of "trendiness," aiming to discredit new entrants, are classic expressions of *conservation* strategies, showing that primitivists can switch between antagonistic roles on the field, depending on their positions and on that of their adversaries.

Ritualistic arguments over earlier examples of ideal social organization are also used as weapons. As previously noted, anarcho-primitivists base their claims on anthropologies of hunter-gatherers. Their "leftist" enemies hark back to examples of popular uprisings such as the organization of society by anarchists during the Spanish Civil War, "probably the single richest example of the potentials of autonomous popular creativity."[78] Yet frequent references to history and anthropology present primitivists with a problem: how to refer to "experts" without appearing to embrace a conventional system of hierarchical knowledge. In the conflict against Bookchin, Bob Black seemed to be simultaneously mocking his opponent's stuffy academicism (Bookchin, wrote Black, is a "self-important, pompous ass"[79]) and reproaching his lack of scientific rigor: "Unlike in [another book] Bookchin *this time* provides a source for his claim that . . ."[80] [. . .] "In the sequence in which Bookchin places it, the Feyerabend quotation—*unreferenced*—looks like a summons to freak out"[81] (emphasis added). This ambivalent relationship to high culture and scientific standards is typical of underground culture in general and of anarchists in particular, who want to be perceived as authoritative, without appearing authoritarian.

The Last Electronic Tribe?

Objections to primitivism are too numerous to list here. To pick an obvious example, in a world where six billion people have to be fed, there can be no viable alternatives to agriculture. This does not signify, however, that current "agribusiness" practices need be supported. At the same time, the primitivist outrage at the state of the planet brings into sharp focus the social dislocation and environmental destruction caused by industrialization. In this chapter, I have attempted to assess the usefulness of the anthropological concept of "tribe" within the context of field theory as applied to the Internet. The membership of the "neo-tribes" posited by Maffesoli et al. is nonascribed: actors adopt personas (masks) and organize themselves in space. They constitute unstable and affectual resource hubs. In contrast, members of the radical tribe examined in this chapter base their interactions on ethics rather than aesthetics, and share a common belief system rather than a common feeling. Online primitivists, though networked, are welded to a stable identity, which develops over time in a series of ritualized offerings and conflicts. In part this stems from the nature of the Internet, which favors the progressive accumulation of textual and visual traces of presence over more immediate and embodied modes of communication and interaction; but it also derives from the stated aim of these groups, which is clearly historical: to extract themselves from the social compact. Similarly, offline, if primitivists adopt visual markers of their identity, these are not necessarily the kind that can be easily purchased and rapidly discarded, as in this primitivist account of urban existence: "We were all intentionally broke & jobless, some of us even tattooing our faces to lessen the probability of future employment." [82]

I have used the term "tribe" to characterize types of Internet social aggregation that are sites for the centrifugal generation of stateless conflictuality. This is, perhaps, what defines online "tribes," as opposed to online "communities." At the same time, radical tribes are but one example of what Manuel Castells calls "project identities"—social movements aiming to transform the dominant structures of society. [83] Interestingly, when Kaczynski in his manifesto listed "rebels against the system," he wedged "radical environmentalists" between "nazis" and "militiamen." [84] In fact, the anarcho-primitivist field occupies a position structurally equivalent to that of other marginal fields, such as that of the far-right groups, who also search for a virtual community to compensate for a lack of critical mass in their own town or country. [85] As Castells notes, the network structure of the Internet reproduces exactly the autonomous, spontaneous networking of militia groups, "without boundaries, and without a definite plan, but sharing a purpose, a feeling, and most of all, an enemy." [86]

This is, of course, highly paradoxical, since if the primitivist vision were to be realized, there would be no more electronic communication and organization. This is why they are "the last electronic tribe." The irony of fierce opponents of industrialism and technology communicating via technological networks is not lost on online anarcho-primitivists.

A range of rationalizing discursive strategies have appeared, such as the following justifications for electronic communication by a group of primitivists. John Connor complained that it was "disappointing that the orthodox try to preserve their partial critique by asking the impossible of anti-tech critics, demanding they *personally* live free of technology when technological society exercises control over them by denying them the means to do so." Jonathan Slyk was less ambiguous: "The point is not to run away from society and civilization—but to destroy it." [87]

The relationship of the online primitivist field to the dominant field of economic and political power is an admittedly extreme illustration of a central question for contemporary dissenters: how has the integration of nominally radical tribes into electronic networks affected their potential for resistance? Primitivists would reply that *Das Kapital* was sold in bookstores and that Kaczynski used the post office to send his bombs and manifesto: the ends justify the means. The difference is that technological networks such as the Internet operate both as the dominant ideology of our time *as well as* popular vectors of resistance to domination. In this sense, the description of the Internet as an "anarcho-communist" utopia reinforces the notion that a cornucopia exists in the here and now—thus providing a great service to state and corporate promoters of the network society, as it is impossible to access free or pirated data without purchasing the requisite hardware and network connection. While it is unclear to what extent electronic networking affects the autonomy of the offline primitivist field, it is hard to see how establishing primitivist Web sites (despite the best efforts of members of the tribe to limit their connectivity and accumulation of link capital) can fail to reinforce existing hierarchies of information and power, which are today based on access to dominant networks. Moreover, the example of online primitivism may be worth pondering for other radicals, as the decrease in the physical and psychological costs of engaging in internecine warfare (to such an extent that warre subsumes all other intent, becoming an out-of-control force) do not necessarily augur well for the capacity of online anarchist tribes to effect change.

Notes

1. Theodore Roszak, *The Making of a Counterculture: Reflections on the Technocratic Society and Its Youthful Opposition* (Berkeley: University of California Press, 1968), p. vii.

2. Gary Snyder, "Why Tribe?" *International Times*, April 1, 1968, pp. 5–18.

3. Janice Newton, "Aborigines, Tribes and the Counterculture," *Social Analysis* 23 (1988): 53–71.

4. Michel Maffesoli, "La fin de l'idéal démocratique," *Le Monde*, January 28, 1995, p. 16.

5. Michel Maffesoli, *The Time of the Tribes: The Decline of Individualism in Mass Societies* (London; Thousand Oaks, Calif.; New Delhi: Sage, 1996), p. 76.

6. Kevin Hetherington, "Stonehenge and Its Festivals: Spaces of Consumption," in *Lifestyle Shopping: The Subject of Consumption*, ed. Rob Shields (London: Routledge, 1992), p. 93.

7. Rob Shields, "The Individual, Consumption Cultures and the Fate of Community," in *Lifestyle Shopping: The Subject of Consumption*, ed. Rob Shields, pp. 99–113 (London: Routledge, 1992).

8. Andy Bennett, "Subcultures or Neo-Tribes? Rethinking the Relationship Between Youth, Style and Musical Style," *Sociology* 33, no. 3 (1999): 599–617.

9. Ibid., p. 607.

10. David Chaney, *Lifestyles* (London: Routledge, 1996).

11. Anthony P. Cohen, *The Symbolic Construction of Community* (London and New York: Tavistock, 1985), p. 12.

12. Lawrence Jarach, "Why Primitivism (without Adjectives) Makes Me Nervous," *Anarchy: A Journal of Desire Armed* 52 (2002): 19, http://www.insurgentdesire.org.uk/nervous.htm (accessed June 21, 2007).

13. Theodore Kaczynski, "Thesis 94," *Industrial Society and Its Future* (1995), http://en.wikisource.org/wiki/Industrial_Society_and_Its_Future.

14. John Zerzan, "Why Primitivism?" *Telos* 124 (Summer 2002): 167.

15. Ibid., p. 171.

16. Ibid., p. 167.

17. Pierre Bourdieu, "The Social Space and the Genesis of Groups," *Theory and Society* 14, no. 6 (November 1985): 723–744.

18. Rodney Benson, "Field Theory in Comparative Context: A New Paradigm for Media Studies," *Theory and Society* 28, no. 3 (June 1999): 464.

19. Mathieu O'Neil, "Exclusion and Inclusion in Personal Media Networks," in *Mobile Boundaries/Rigid Worlds*, ed. Michael Fine, Nicholas Smith, and Amanda Wise (2005), http://www.crsi.mq.edu.au/mobileboundaries.htm.

20. Marshall Sahlins, "The Original Affluent Society," in *Stone Age Economics*, pp. 1–40 (Chicago: Aldine-Atherton, 1972).

21. Marshall D. Sahlins, *Tribesmen* (Englewood Cliffs, N.J.: Prentice-Hall, 1968), p. 79.

22. Bob Black, "Primitive Affluence: A Postscript to Sahlins," in *Friendly Fire* (Brooklyn, N.Y.: Autonomedia, 1992), p. 23, http://www.insurgentdesire.org.uk/primaffluence.htm.

23. Fredy Perlman, *Against His-Story, Against Leviathan* (Detroit: Black and Red, 1983); David Watson, *Against the Megamachine: Essays on Empire and Its Enemies* (Brooklyn, N.Y.: Autonomedia/Fifth Estate, 1997).

24. Langdon Winner, *The Whale and the Reactor: A Search for Limits in an*

Age of High Technology (Chicago: University of Chicago Press, 1986); Jacques Ellul, *The Technological Bluff* (Grand Rapids, Mich.: William B. Eerdmans Publishing Co., 1990); Kirkpatrick Sale, *Rebels against the Future: The Luddites and Their War on the Industrial Revolution—Lessons for the Computer Age* (New York: Addison-Wesley, 1995).

25. Edward Abbey, *The Monkey Wrench Gang* (Philadelphia: Lippincott, 1975).

26. Arne Naess, *Ecology, Community and Lifestyle: Outline of an Ecosophy* (Cambridge: Cambridge University Press, 1990).

27. William Devall and George Sessions, *Deep Ecology* (Salt Lake City: Gibbs M. Smith, Inc., 1985).

28. Bron Taylor, "Earth First! and Global Narratives of Popular Ecological Resistance," in *Ecological Resistance Movements: The Global Emergence of Radical and Popular Environmentalism*, ed. Bron Taylor (Albany: State University of New York Press, 1995), p. 16.

29. Dave Foreman in Bron Taylor, "Earth First!'s Religious Radicalism," in *Ecological Prospects: Scientific, Religious, and Aesthetic Perspectives*, ed. Christopher Chapple (Albany: State University of New York Press), p. 204.

30. Ariel Salleh and Meira Hansen, "On Production and Reproduction, Identity and Non-Identity in Ecofeminist Theory," *Organization & Environment* 12, no. 2 (June 1999): 207–218.

31. Greil Marcus, *Lipstick Traces: A Secret History of the Twentieth Century* (London: Secker and Warburg, 1989).

32. John Zerzan, "Too Marvelous for Words (Language Briefly Revisited)," *Green Anarchy* 19 (Spring 2005): 32, http://www.greenanarchy.org.

33. Guy Debord, *The Society of the Spectacle* (orig. 1967; New York: Zone Books, 1994), p. 12.

34. Jacques Camatte, *This World We Must Leave and Other Essays* (Brooklyn, N.Y.: Autonomedia, 1996).

35. Richard Barbrook, "The High-Tech Gift Economy," *First Monday* 3, no. 12 (December 1998), http://www.firstmonday.org/issues/issue3_12/barbrook/.

36. O'Neil, "Exclusion and Inclusion," p. 4.

37. Desmond Morris and Peter Marsh, *Tribes* (London: Pyramid Books, 1988), p. 130.

38. James A. Boon, *Other Tribes, Other Scribes: Symbolic Anthropology in the Comparative Study of Cultures, Histories, Religions and Texts* (Cambridge: Cambridge University Press, 1982), p. 232.

39. Cohen, *Symbolic Construction*, p. 109.

40. Gérard Chaliand, "Introduction," in *Anthologie mondiale de la stratégie* (Paris: Robert Laffont, 1990), p. xvi.

41. Graham St. John, "Alternative Cultural Heterotopia: ConFest as Australia's Marginal Centre" (Ph.D. diss., La Trobe University, Melbourne, Victoria, Australia, 2000), p. 153.

42. John Zerzan, Eric Blair, and Green Anarchy Collective, "Notes on Green Anarchy & Primitivism," *ZMagazine* (2002), http://www.zmag.org/summprim.htm *(accessed June 21, 2007)*.

43. Anonymous, "Letters," *Green Anarchy* 15 (2003): 64, http://www.greenanarchy.org/ *(accessed June 21, 2007)*.

44. Sahlins, *Tribesmen*, p. 8.

45. Victor Turner, *Dramas, Fields and Metaphors* (Ithaca, N.Y.: Cornell University Press, 1974), p. 135.

46. Pierre Bourdieu, *The Rules of Art* (Stanford, Calif.: Stanford University Press, 1995), p. 154.

47. Pierre Bourdieu, "The Social Space," p. 730.

48. Anonymous, "Review of *Anarchism vs. Primitivism* by Brian Oliver Sheppard," *Green Anarchy* 13 (Summer 2003): 26, http://www.greenanarchy.org/.

49. Cornelius Castoriadis, *La montée de l'insignifiance* (Paris: Seuil, 1996).

50. Friedrich Engels, "On Authority," in *Marx-Engels Reader* (orig. 1872; New York: W. W. Norton, 1978), p. 733.

51. John Zerzan, "Zerzan Responds 1," *ZMagazine* (2002), http://www.zmag .org/zerzanresp1.htm *(accessed June 21, 2007)*.

52. Murray Bookchin, *Post-Scarcity Anarchism* (London: Wildwood House, 1971), p. 78.

53. Murray Bookchin, "Social Ecology vs. Deep Ecology: A Challenge for the Ecology Movement," *Green Perspectives* 4–5 (1987): 4.

54. Ibid., p. 16.

55. Murray Bookchin, *Social Anarchism or Lifestyle Anarchism: An Unbridgeable Chasm* (San Francisco: AK Press, 1995).

56. Ibid., p. 37.

57. Ibid., p. 42.

58. David Watson, *Beyond Bookchin: Preface for a Future Social Ecology* (Brooklyn, N.Y.: Autonomedia, 1996).

59. Bob Black, *Anarchy after Leftism* (Berkeley, Calif.: C.A.L. Press, 1996), p. 140.

60. Murray Bookchin, "Whither Anarchism? A Reply to Recent Anarchist Critics," in *Anarchism, Marxism and the Future of the Left* (San Francisco: AK Press, 1999), p. 188.

61. Ibid., p. 244.

62. Bob Black, "Withered Anarchism: A Surrebuttal to Murray Bookchin" (1999), http://www.primitivism.com/withered-anarchism.htm (accessed June 21, 2007).

63. Edwin Wilmsen, *Land Filled with Flies: A Political Economy of the Kalahari* (Chicago: University of Chicago Press, 1989).

64. Bob Black, "Book Filled with Lies" (1999), http://www.primitivism .com/book-lies.htm *(accessed June 21, 2007)*.

65. Ken Knabb, *Public Secrets* (Berkeley: Bureau of Public Secrets, 1997); quotation on p. 31.

66. Ken Knabb, "The Poverty of Primitivism" (2001), http://www.bopsecrets .org/CF/primitivism.htm (accessed June 21, 2007).

67. John Filiss, "Intellectual Impoverishment" (2001), http://www .primitivism.com/impoverishment.htm (accessed June 21, 2007).

68. Pierre Bourdieu, *Questions de sociologie* (Paris: Les Editions de minuit, 1984), p. 116.

69. Lawrence Jarach interviews John Zerzan, "A Dialog on Primitivism," *Anarchy: A Journal of Desire Armed* 19, no. 1 (2001): 25.

70. Volonta Terraroturra, "Review of *Barbaric Thoughts: A Revolutionary Critique of Civilization* by Venomous Butterfly Publications," *Green Anarchy* 18 (Fall/Winter 2004), http://www.greenanarchy.org/.

71. Anonymous, "Notes on Alienation," *Killing King Abacus* 2 (Summer 2001), http://www.geocities.com/kk_abacus/kka/ALIEN.html (accessed June 21, 2007).

72. John Zerzan, *"Willful Disobedience:* More Radical Than Thou?" *Green Anarchy* 7 (Fall/Winter 2001): 21, http://www.greenanarchy.org/.

73. Kevin Tucker, SashaKVillon, Wolfi Landstreicher, "Zerzan's Critique of Insurrectionary Anarchism and Response," Anti-Politics Forum (2001), http://anti-politics.net/forum/viewtopic.php?t=178.

74. Jason McQuinn, "Why I Am Not a Primitivist," *Anarchy: A Journal of Desire Armed* 19, no. 1 (2001), http://www.insurgentdesire.org.uk/notaprimitivist.htm.

75. Bookchin, "Whither Anarchism?" p. 5.

76. Ken Knabb, "A Look at Some of the Reactions to Public Secrets" (2000), http://www.bopsecrets.org/CF/look.htm (accessed June 21, 2007).

77. Zerzan, "More Radical Than Thou?" p. 21.

78. Knabb, *Public Secrets*, p. 60.

79. Bob Black, "Withered Anarchism," unpaginated.

80. Ibid.

81. Ibid.

82. Griffin, "No Cure for Cancer," *Reclaim Rewild* 2 (2004): p. 3.

83. Manuel Castells, *The Power of Identity*, vol. 2, *The Information Age: Economy, Society and Culture* (London: Blackwell, 1997).

84. Kaczynski, *Industrial Society*, "Thesis 161."

85. Val Burris, Emery Smith, and Anne Strahm, "White Supremacist Networks on the Internet," *Sociological Focus* 33, no. 2 (May 2000): 232.

86. Castells, *Power of Identity*, 2:94.

87. John Connor, John Filiss, Leif Fredrickson, Lawrence Jarach, Ron Leighton, Jason McQuinn, John Moore, and Jonathan Slyk, "An Open Letter on Technology and Mediation" (Primitivism.com, 1999), http://www.primitivism.com/open-letter.htm.

CHAPTER 16

A "Tribe" Migrates Crime to Cyberspace: Nigerian Igbos in 419 E-Mail Scams

FAROOQ A. KPEROGI AND SANDRA C. DUHÉ

Nigerian e-mail scams, also known as Advance Fee Fraud or "419"[1] scams in reference to the Southern Nigeria Criminal Code[2] that criminalizes the impersonation of government officials for pecuniary gratification,[3] have been pervading cyberspace since the late 1990s. They have become so ubiquitous that trying to escape from them has now become almost as difficult as trying to hide from daylight: You can do it only with an effort so strenuous it reaches the point of absurdity. The scams inundate mailboxes of millions of e-mail account holders all over the world with such persistence and relentlessness that the U.S. Federal Trade Commission characterized them as having assumed "epidemic proportions."[4] The U.S. Secret Service, a major government body charged with the responsibility to combat this cybercrime, also described them as "a Mount Everest of fraud."[5] And the Washington, D.C.–based National Consumer League ranked them as the second-biggest consumer come-on on the Internet, outrivaled only by pitches for "herbal Viagra."[6]

According to the 2001 report of the Internet Fraud Complaint Center,[7] 419 e-mail scams accounted for 15.5 percent of all officially reported online fraud complaints in the United States.[8] What, then, is this so-called Nigerian e-mail scam? Perhaps the best operational definition that encapsulates its robustly variegated dimensions is the one provided by the National White Collar Crime Center:

> The Nigerian Letter Scam is defined as a correspondence outlining an opportunity to receive non-existent government funds from alleged dignitaries that is designed to collect advance fees from the victims. This sometimes requires payoff money to bribe government officials.

While other countries may be mentioned, the correspondence typically indicates "The Government of Nigeria" as the nation of origin. This scam . . . is also referred to as "419 Fraud" after the relevant section of the Criminal Code of Nigeria, as well as, Advance Fee Fraud.[9]

These unsolicited e-mails usually originate from Africa, mostly from Nigeria, but lately are springing forth from other parts of the world as well. Their trademark is their universal claim that colossal amounts of money are located in an African country either on account of the supposed death of some African dictator or of some foreign national who had a bank account in an African country but did not have the presence of mind to indicate a next of kin to claim his money in the event of death. The sender of the e-mail typically requests the recipient's help in transferring the money to the recipient's bank and, in turn, promises a huge reward (usually between 30 and 40 percent of the total money, which usually runs into millions of dollars) for this seemingly effortless assistance.

The scammers lend credibility to their fraud by claiming to be either high-ranking bureaucrats who have designs to cheat their governments but are hamstrung by a Nigerian constitutional provision that forbids public officers from having foreign accounts, or by pretending to be children or spouses of a well-known late African dictator. They claim that they can neither keep their late dictator father's loot, nor transfer it to a foreign account by themselves because a new, hostile regime is on the hunt for them. At this juncture, the prey is hooked.

But, at the last minute, the victim is told that unanticipated bottlenecks have mired the transaction, and money is needed to either pay some administrative fees or unforeseen taxes, or to bribe a disobliging government official to facilitate the release of the millions of dollars.[10] Already whetted by the anticipation of imminent wealth, victims dig into their own pockets to advance the process, figuring their near-term inconvenience is trivial compared to the millions to come. Devious perpetrators rely upon the alluring outcome of this risk/reward calculation, knowing full well that the promise of an easy windfall will frequently outweigh the otherwise preposterous notion of transferring thousands of dollars to a stranger in cyberspace. Hopeful euphoria is soon replaced by the harsh reality of being scammed, as preys opting for risk soon discover their monies are forever lost.

Estimates of money lost to the scam differ widely and, indeed, wildly. According to Sam Vaknin, statistics presented at the 2002 International

Conference on Advance Fee Frauds suggested that approximately 1 percent of the millions of people who receive 419 e-mails and faxes are effectively swindled and estimated that annual losses to the scam in the United States alone "total more than $100 million, and law enforcement officials believe global losses may total over $1.5 billion."[11]

However, Warren Richey, reporting for the *Christian Science Monitor* as early as 1996, quoted the U.S. Secret Service as having claimed that "letter scams from Nigeria rake in $250 million a year from gullible Americans."[12] The British National Criminal Intelligence Service disclosed that in 2002 alone, 150 Britons reported losses of 8.4 million pounds to the 419 e-mail scams.[13] Kimberly Noble reported that the Nigerian e-mail fraud had pulled in about $7 billion as of 1998 and that "of that amount, roughly $200 million to $300 million is thought to have come from Canadians." She added that the estimate is based on the assumption that "the $50 million so far reported to police represents only a fraction of the actual losses" because victims of the scam are often either too embarrassed or too afraid to report their misfortune to law enforcement agents for fear of inadvertently enmeshing themselves in the maze of a paradoxical criminal complicity in their own hardship.[14] In Britain, the average individual loss to the scam is $91,000.[15] MessageLabs also reported that, in 2003, the scam had grossed an estimated $2 billion, placing it as one of the top-grossing industries in Nigeria.[16] Although these figures and the claims that proceed from them are not corroborated by any systematic empirical verification or qualification, they represent an important measure of how the 419 scam e-mail phenomenon is perceived around the world.

The scammers have an amazingly robust assortment of ploys in their persuasive repertoire. Scams can take the form of "donations" to charities, academic institutions, religious groups, or other nonprofit organizations purportedly bequeathed from the "wills" of some dead Nigerian millionaire, but the prospective beneficiaries of these so-called donations are asked to pay an "inheritance tax" on them. The U.S. State Department made public the case of one church in Texas that was fleeced of up to $80,000 when it was told that a wealthy Nigerian benefactor had left millions of dollars to the church. But the bearer of the good tidings said a few financial details needed to be straightened up before the money could be released. The church ended up being sucked in.[17]

The sender of a scam e-mail can also purport to be an exalted bureaucrat in an African country who is fleeing his country as a result of political persecution. Consequently, he asks his victims to advance kickbacks in return for a generous cut of the material possessions he has supposedly stashed in some Western country.[18] Other insidious pleas take the form of requests to transfer money from overinvoiced contracts, "inside" deals on crude oil sales, currency conversion, or real estate.[19] No matter the form, each get-rich-quick temptation drains its victim's finances in the end.

The rhetorical armory at the disposal of the scammers in perpetrating this sophisticated cyberfraud is as broad as it is varied. However, the goal is by and large the same: to defraud unsuspecting and credulous, but sometimes well-intentioned or criminally inclined, people of enormous sums of money through deception, false pretenses, confidence trickery, and exploitation of the indwelling predisposition for rapaciousness in most people.

Although most of the scams merely bilk their victims of huge sums of money and leave them crestfallen, disillusioned, and financially denuded, some lure the victims overseas, where they are visited with violence, and occasionally death, when they run out of money. The fraudsters characteristically implore their prey to agree to pay for a trip to the site of the putative loot and demand utmost secrecy from them about the trip. They are told not to apply for a visa. The fraudsters then extend gratification to corrupt immigration officials who allow the victims into the country without valid travel documents. As the *Economist* put it, "the victim has then committed a crime, is on his own and is vulnerable."[20] Helpless, uprooted from their countries of origin, and hoaxed into becoming quasi-accomplices in a criminal offense in which they are at the receiving end, the dupes become susceptible to all kinds of intimidation and manipulation. Occasionally, too, victims have been willfully given counterfeit visas by the scammers, making their stay in the country illegal. This increases their vulnerability and exposes them to more acts of extortion.[21] Victims found in possession of advance fee documents in Nigeria are also in danger of running afoul of local laws.

According to *U.S. News & World Report*, "at least 15 foreign business people, including one American, have been murdered in advance-fee scams."[22] In 2002, Kenyan police helped save the lives of three kidnapped Americans who had been decoyed to travel to Nairobi, Kenya, by a notoriously ferocious 419 gang. In the same year, an American was held hostage in Johannesburg, South Africa, and another in Lagos, Nigeria.[23] A British citizen was also tormented and severely beaten by a 419 ring in Lagos in 2003 when he ran out of money to oblige the interminable demands of the scammers.[24] Similarly, in 2002, a Florida plumbing contractor who had been defrauded of about $67,000 was deluded into supposing that by going to London to meet with the scammers posing as businessmen, he could recoup the money he had invested in an elaborate, enduring, but, ultimately, evanescent plot of confidence trickery. He committed suicide when the cruel reality of his predicament hit him hard.[25]

Although it would seem that the e-mails largely target people in the United States and Europe, there is evidence that their target is more broadly transnational. In fact, the scammers also bilk their compatriots and other Africans. But they do more than that. They not only gravely hurt the image of Nigeria, its businesses,[26] and citizens, but their activities also increasingly expose Nigerian diplomats to lethal risks. For example, in 2003, a curious but tragic twist was introduced to this cybercriminality when a furious victim of the 419 scam in the Czech Republic vented his pent-up frustration by shooting to death an innocent Nigerian diplomat and severely wounding another embassy worker after losing $600,000 to scammers whom he believed were Nigerians.[27] Similarly, in 2005, a seventy-two-year-old Prague man, who had lost his entire life savings to the 419 scam, stormed into the Nigerian embassy in his city and shot two Nigerian diplomats. They did not have the remotest connection to the conmen.[28]

The victims of this crime transcend not only nationality but also social class and educational attainment. Several high-profile personalities, including academics, lawyers, doctors, businesspeople, even congressional representatives, have been ensnared in this intricate web of online fraud. The most celebrated case is the one that involved Edward Mezvinsky, a sixty-five-year-old former Democratic congressman from Iowa. Mezvinsky was beguiled into believing that he would make easy millions of dollars out of some putative ill-gotten wealth amassed by an African dictator by merely parting with a small advance fee to smooth the release of the money.

Following what began as payment of a nominal fee, he was irresistibly drawn into the complex vortex of a carefully organized confidence fraud that sucked up almost his entire life savings. He was reported to have lost approximately $13.3 million to the conmen. The former congressman borrowed most of the money from friends and banks under the false pretense of investing in a lucrative business venture. The bubble burst when David Sanders, a Virginia investor, sued him. Soon after, Mezvinsky declared bankruptcy, which revealed debts in excess of $7 million. The former congressman is reported to be confined to his home and suffering from manic depression.[29] A university professor in northern California likewise fell prey to the scam and lost $30,000.[30]

The snaring of prominent members of society into believing the legitimacy of an online request for a Nigerian funds transfer is, on the surface, perplexing. How could otherwise publicly lauded individuals fall for such folly? In his examination of other "investment" schemes, Dan Seligman hypothesized that temptations of easy money are "irresistible to babes in the financial woods, [because they believe] that there are invincible deals out there available only to the big, sophisticated insiders."[31] In cybercrimes, debonair dupes are not an anomaly; in fact, they are a target.

Victims of online scams have retrospectively claimed that deceptive offers seemed legitimate within the broader context of investment and market risks.[32] Many realize that most cyber-"opportunities" are scams, but still expect, or at least hope, that they have stumbled across a rare but authentic opportunity.

More fundamentally, a scammer's likelihood of success largely depends on the would-be victim's propensity to trust. Eric Uslaner differentiated strategic trust, which reflects experience with a particular person or circumstance, from moralistic trust, which is based on an optimistic worldview that most people can be trusted.[33] The latter provides potential dupes with the confidence to pursue risks online, and 419 scammers exploit this trust to their victims' irreversible detriment.

This online menace has become dreadful enough to attract the attention of U.S. lawmakers. On May 21, 1998, while declaring that seventeen people were murdered in Nigeria as a consequence of 419 scams, U.S. Congressman Edward Markey (D), representing the Seventh Congressional District of Massachusetts, introduced the Nigerian Advance Fee Fraud Prevention Bill to the U.S. House of Representatives to, among other things, "highlight the problem, to inform the public of the risks and to enable government action to be taken to prevent advance fee fraud."[34]

The bill provoked heated discussions in the House and focused attention on the mounting peril that Advance Fee Frauds posed to Americans, but it did not pass, perhaps in part because the United States government did not want to spark a diplomatic row with Nigeria by singling out and inscribing the name of the country in an unflattering piece of legislation. However, in December 2003, both houses of the United States Congress passed a bill, which was signed by President George Bush, to reduce and police unsolicited e-mails, but the 419 e-mails were not singled out for mention in the bill.[35]

Nigeria itself has passed several pieces of legislation to combat the fraud. Section 419 of the Nigerian Criminal Code Cap. 777, 1990,[36] from which the fraud derives its name, was promulgated to prosecute perpetrators of Advance Fee Fraud in southern Nigeria, which includes states in the eastern and western parts of the country, as well as Lagos, the commercial nerve center and former capital of Nigeria. Similarly, on April 1, 1995, a new national military decree incorporating northern and central states where the crime is almost absent, titled the Advance Fee Fraud and Other Fraud Related Offences Decree (No. 13 of 1995), took effect. Sub-section (1) of section 1 of the decree provides the courts and law enforcement agencies with extraterritorial jurisdictional powers to proscribe conduct carried out by individuals within or outside Nigeria who defraud persons located in any country of the world.

Accordingly, crimes syndicates, whether they are composed of Nigerians exclusively or Nigerians mixed with foreigners, are liable to be prosecuted in Nigerian courts for offenses committed within any part of Nigeria, or elsewhere.[37] The legislation also empowers law enforcement officers to try offenders *in absentia*, to convict them, and to penalize them when they return to Nigeria. Nigeria's current government also set up a special agency, the Economic and Financial Crimes Commission (EFCC), which has recorded "the arrest of hundreds of con-artists and the recovery of hundreds of millions of dollars in just two years."[38]

In March 2005, the president of Nigeria set up the Presidential Committee on Advance-Fee Fraud and Allied Criminal Activities in Cyberspace. While receiving the report of the committee, he was reported to have said, "The [incidence of] 419 has already become an embarrassment to the country. [It] costs us dearly. When you now practice 419 on the Internet, it becomes even more embarrassing."[39]

In addition, there has been a lot of recent collaboration between many U.S. government agencies and the Nigerian EFCC in the apprehension and recovery of money from 419 criminals. In one notable case, a joint effort between the U.S. Department of Justice and the Nigerian EFCC led to the recovery and return of $4.48 million to an eighty-six-year-old Hong Kong woman who fell victim to 419 scammers between 1995 and 2000.[40]

Despite their demonstration of multinational and bureaucratic prowess, these efforts have failed to eliminate the existence of the crime, as it still flourishes luxuriantly on the fringes of the cybercommunity.

The Igbo E-Mail Scam

Although it is usual to label 419 e-mail frauds as "Nigerian" e-mail scams, they are, in reality, largely an Igbo scam. As will be shown later in this section, the Igbos are just one of over 250 ethnic groups in Nigeria. However, they are predominant in the 419 e-mail scams. There is anecdotal evidence that many parliamentarians and even state governors from southeast Nigeria (home of the Igbos) rose to their present positions through money they fraudulently acquired from 419 scams.[41] The preponderance of the Igbos from southeast Nigeria in the 419 scams is hardly a contested fact among Nigerians, even in official circles.[42] Although no study has accounted for why the 419 scam phenomenon is virtually nonexistent in the northern and central states of Nigeria—and to a certain extent in western Nigeria, except Lagos—yet thrives among the Igbos, it is conceivable that the Igbo domination of the scam is the consequence of the scam's secretive nature. All underground economies are sustained by trust, secrecy, and high-level solidarity among their accomplices. Ethnic bonding, which comes from shared language, customs, and even ties of consanguinity, appears to be a major reason why the 419 scam remains largely among the Igbos. People from other ethnic groups who are attracted by the quick pecuniary gains of the scam and want to make inroads into it are usually repulsed, and sometimes murdered, by Igbo 419 kingpins. They are not trusted to be faithful to the oaths of secrecy that the nature of the scam demands. It must be said, however, that not all Igbos are 419 con artists. A majority of the people are entrepreneurial, industrious, and honest. But it is also the case that the 419 scams have an unavoidable ethnic coloration. And that coloration is Igbo.

But what predisposes Igbos to partake in 419 scams? Jean-François Bayart and his colleagues located the phenomenon within the context of what they called the emergent "criminalization of the African state."[43] Bayart, in fact, went as far as to suggest that the prevalence of the 419 fraud in Nigeria is evidence of the progressive atrophy of the African state from "kleptocracy to the felonious state."[44] For Andrew Apter, the problem can better be appreciated if it is gazed at through the social-anthropological lens. He traces the provenance and popularity of the 419 trend to preexisting, atavistic Igbo cultural practices that celebrated material possession at the expense of human dignity:

> Based on cultural idioms of money magic, whereby human blood and body parts are stolen and used to conjure illicit wealth, the 419 represents a nefarious trade, draining victims of their goods and cash through forged documents and staged performances . . . the 419 has migrated to the Internet, where it has proliferated and shifted through digital "cloning" from the circuits of oil to the information highway . . . [a] return to tropes of hidden bullion taken out of circulation and buried beneath the ground.[45]

Stephen Wright[46] made similar arguments when he said the incidence of 419 is the manifestation of a cultural success syndrome, which is lubricated by prebendalism, political patronage, and even elements of witchcraft that celebrate "big man" leadership.[47]

Brief Social, Economic, and Political Background of Nigeria

Nigeria is a West African country made up of thirty-six states, plus Abuja, the Federal Capital Territory, and over 250 ethnic groups, of which the Hausa, Yoruba, and Igbo are the major groups. It is the most populous country on the African continent, with approximately 150 million people, and it covers some 925,000 square kilometers. Lagos is the economic center of the country—and the hub of the 419 frauds— and was its capital city until 1991, when a new capital, Abuja, located almost in the dead center of the country, was created.

Nigeria's modern history is traceable to the time it became a British colony in 1861 under the administration of the Royal Niger Company Chartered and Limited. Prior to that, the territory was a concatenation of different ethnic-based empires and kingdoms. In 1900, the British government took over direct government of the territory and divided it into the Southern and Northern protectorates. In 1914, the Northern and Southern protectorates were amalgamated to form Nigeria.[48] On October 1, 1960, Nigeria became independent from Britain but retained elements of the British legal system and many other holdovers of British colonial rule. Because of its history of British colonialism, and the impracticality of adopting one of the over 250 languages as the lingua franca that would be acceptable to everybody, English was adopted as the official language of the country.[49]

As Sakah Mahmud pointed out, many observers of Nigeria at independence had invested enormous confidence and optimism in the country's potential for development.[50] A *Time* magazine special issue on Africa in January 1984, titled "The light that failed," justified the optimism in expectations that Nigeria would be a huge economic success in Africa when it said, "unlike many other African countries, [Nigeria] has a sizeable class of educated men and women who are well-trained to run its government, industry and armed forces."[51]

A commentator on Nigeria's early political/economic development also observed that "the wealth of Nigeria largely depends . . . on her agricultural production. Her land is relatively better than the rest of Africa and thus can feed a larger population."[52] Another analyst, twenty-nine years later, posited that "Nigeria has always been one of the most amply endowed territories carved out by the European colonizers."[53] Mahmud also called attention to the fact that in the early years of its independence, Nigeria actually attained "self-sufficiency in agricultural production, enough for both domestic consumption as well as for export."[54] In addition to achieving self-sufficiency in food production, Nigeria also witnessed what has been characterized as "bonanza development,"[55] which Richard Joseph defined as "earnings from petroleum exports considerably above the country's actual expenditure."[56]

Nigeria has vast deposits of oil, natural gas, coal, and iron ore, but its main source of foreign exchange earning is petroleum products. It is the eighth-largest exporter of oil in the world and the fifth-largest supplier to the United States. However, these gains and promises for even greater gains turned out to be transitory. After only six years of postindependence democratic rule, the country was engulfed in bitter internecine regional rivalries that snowballed into a Southern, Igbo-led, Christian military rebellion against the central government, which was dominated by Hausa Muslim northerners. After a Northern counter-coup, the Igbo ethnic group fought to secede from Nigeria and declared its own country, called Biafra. This secession bid precipitated a bitter and sanguinary civil war between 1967 and 1970 in which the whole country fought against the Igbos. Some accounts put the death toll at over thirty thousand.[57] Many commentators locate the preponderance of the Igbos in the Advance Fee Fraud crime to their postwar alienation from the orbit of governance and wealth distribution in Nigeria.[58]

The country has been ruled by a succession of brutal military dictatorships, with spasmodic periods of democratic rule. Sustained democratic governance was restored in May 1999 with the election of President Olusegun Obasanjo, who was a military ruler between 1975 and 1979 and was imprisoned by the previous military government for his caustic criticism of the lawlessness and venality of the government of the day. Now, as head of the People's Democratic Party, he has repeatedly vowed to put an end to much of the corruption that had plagued the previous military regimes, which held power for twenty-nine of the forty-five years since independence.[59]

The emergence of the 419 phenomenon has often been attributed to the plummeting of world oil prices in the mid-1980s and the devastating effect this had on the standard of living of Nigerians. The prosperity of the country began what appears to be an irretrievably downward slide. This, coupled with the activities of a progressively more venal military ruling cabal, led to a general decline in the quality of life of the average Nigerian. In order to survive in the increasingly difficult economic environment that this reality engendered, some Nigerians started to invent an assortment of deceitful designs calculated to bilk people in the more economically advanced parts of the world.

In particular, the Igbo proclivity for material wealth, combined with incessant exposure to brutal violence, political upheaval, blatant corruption, and glaring socioeconomic chasms, creates a sense of relative deprivation, which has motivated the group's involvement in "retaliatory" scams. The concept of relative deprivation has roots in Adam Smith's writings, in which he described the role of custom as equivalent to that of need in determining the "necessaries" of life.[60] That is, one looks to reference groups to ascertain one's relative well-being. Citing studies conducted on worker salary satisfaction and the happiness of people with wealthier neighbors, John Cassidy explained: "It appears that, while money matters to people, their relative ranking matters more."[61]

Nigeria, like many developing countries, is rife with crying disparities, and characterized by monumental, violent shifts in political economy. Perceptions of relative deprivation have been convincingly correlated with civil conflict in Nepal[62] and Côte d'Ivoire,[63] along with the emergence of secret societies and organized crime in China.[64] Valerie Møller asserted that "In the global era of communication, disparities in living standards have become more visible to fuel feelings of relative deprivation."[65] The Igbo 419 scams represent a nascent expression of discontent with relative deprivation in cyberspace.

In a sense, even a passing familiarity with Nigeria's political and social background—such as its notoriety as one of the most corrupt countries on Earth—nourishes the credulity of scam victims. It makes the scam propositions plausible.

In 1993, for instance, General Sani Abacha became head of state after democratic elections won by multimillionaire businessman Moshood Abiola were annulled by the military government of the day for no apparent reason. Abiola was later arrested for treason and imprisoned in 1994 for declaring himself president. He died of a heart attack in prison in early July 1998, following the death of General Abacha, also of a heart attack, in early June 1998.

During General Sani Abacha's regime, billions of dollars were blatantly stolen from the national treasury. The family of General Abacha has recently handed back several billions of dollars' worth of currencies taken from state funds, which have since been deposited in the Central Bank of Nigeria. Swiss banks, where the late general's loot has been deposited, are also gradually returning the money to the Nigerian government. A hint of the degree to which Nigeria is perceived as being corrupt is given in the 1998 Corruption Perception Index published by Transparency International. The index for Nigeria is 1.9 on a scale of 1 to 10, in which 1 represents the highest level of perceived corruption. By way of comparison, Canada has an index of 9.2 and Australia has an index of 8.7.[66] Nigeria has consistently ranked among the three most corrupt nations on Earth since the 1990s. In 2005, it was ranked the sixth-most-corrupt country on Earth, its best-ever performance in a long time.[67]

It is these political and social circumstances from Nigeria's past that created a scenario in which unsuspecting individuals could be persuaded to believe that funds located in Nigeria needed to be moved to Western countries in order to prevent them from either being impounded or devalued by the reigning regime. This scenario also provides the rhetorical staple for the scammers to nourish the gullibility of prospective dupes.

The Spanish Origins of Nigerian Scam E-Mails

Advance Fee Frauds (AFF) not only pre-date the Internet; they, in fact, antecede the birth of Nigeria. According to Harvey Glickman, Nigerian Advance Fee Frauds have roots that go deep into sixteenth-century Spain.[68] Originally known as the "Spanish Prisoner Letter," the scam has been historically perpetrated through ordinary postal mail. In its original form, affluent businessmen were contacted by an unknown person who usually falsely asserted himself to be a prison chaplain. The scammer would claim to be part of an effort to save the sheltered but endangered child of an estate-owning, incarcerated family member who was often reputedly said to be dying as a result of the harsh conditions of a Spanish prison.[69] The senders of the letters would solicit the financial assistance of the recipient of the letter either to free the child or the parent in return for a financial reward severalfold their initial investment, along with a promise of marriage to the distressed wealthy prisoner's beautiful daughter at the conclusion of the deal. It was often claimed that the putative rich prisoner could not disclose his identity without grim personal consequences to him and was therefore relying on the sender of the mail to raise money to arrange for his escape from prison.

Compassion and greed would usually strangely intermix to sustain the interest of the merchants in the deal. The first rescue attempt usually failed. What was initially an innocent, modest financial request for help in a "charitable" cause would morph into a more elaborate scheme that would require the businessman to travel to Spain. As soon as the dupe made the initial deposit, he would be told that unforeseen snags had arisen that required more money to fix, until the dupe was rendered bankrupt and the game ended. As an urban legends reference page Web site put it,

> In its earliest incarnation—which dates to the 1920s—it was known as "The Spanish Prisoner" con. In that long-ago version, businessmen were contacted by someone trying to smuggle the scion of a wealthy family out of a prison in Spain. But of course the wealthy family would shower with riches those who helped secure the release of the boy. Those who were suckered into this paid for one failed rescue attempt after another, with the fictitious prisoner continuing to languish in his non-existent dungeon, always just one more bribe, one more scheme, one more try, away from being released.[70]

Central characteristics of the Spanish Prisoner Letter are its excessive obsession with emphasizing the secrecy of the deal and the trust the confidence artist is reposing in the prey not to reveal the prisoner's identity, location, or conditions. The scammer often claimed to have carefully chosen the mark based on the laudatory estimation the mark had from his peers for truthfulness and probity; subsequently, the deal would be arranged so it appeared that the scammer's ultimate share of the reward would be bestowed at the putative discretion and benevolence of the prey.[71]

It is an ironic twist of history that the Spanish Prisoner Letter was so pervasive that in 1914, the year Nigeria was formally born, the British ambassador to Spain wrote to British colonial officers in Nigeria telling them to be wary of the swindle and to warn the people of Nigeria to keep their guard against it. The *Nigerian Customs and Trade Journal* of April 1914 reproduced the letter by the British ambassador to Spain, Arthur Hardinge, calling attention to "the Spanish Prisoner swindle . . . established in Madrid and other Spanish towns [and] assisted by accomplices in England." The letter added: "It appears that perpetrators of this fraud are still endeavouring to victimise residents of the British Colonies and it is considered advisable that the public in Nigeria should be warned to be upon their guard."[72]

It would turn out that several decades after this warning, a section of the Nigerian society would adopt, adapt, and perfect this fraud and even use it to torment the Spanish who "invented" it. It is conceivable, however, that the emergence of the Nigerian version of the time-honored scam is consequent upon the contact that citizens of the country had with British colonial rule, even probable, considering that the letter of the British ambassador to Spain made reference to "accomplices in England" with whom some Nigerians might have had reasons to interact. However, even if this speculation were proven true, it still leaves unresolved the mystery that, among all citizens of former British colonies in Africa and other parts of the world, Nigerians of Igbo extraction are dominant in this confidence trickery. This cultural dimension of the 419 phenomenon has never been explored in any scholarly or popular accounts of the origins of the scams, but, in a world that is becoming increasingly mediated in its communications and intercultural in its interactions, it certainly should be.

Notes

1. In Nigerian demotic usage, "419" (pronounced "four-one-nine") means more than scam e-mails or Advance Fee Fraud; it encapsulates a whole range of practices that are deemed guileful, dishonest, reprobate, and morally reprehensible.

2. It is a common misconception in popular and scholarly commentaries on the Advance Fee Fraud to state that 419 refers to a code in Nigeria's constitution. It actually refers to a code in the (Southern Nigerian) Criminal Code. Even though Nigeria has one federal constitution, it has two separate judicial systems. While the Criminal Code regulates the judicial system in Southern Nigeria,

where the 419 phenomenon almost exclusively exists, Northern Nigerian laws are guided by what is called the Penal Code. The Penal Code is a mishmash of neo-Islamic laws, British common law, and native Northern Nigerian customs. For a popular account of the history and evolution of the Penal Code and how it differs from the Criminal Code, see Farooq A. Kperogi, "The Shariah and the Penal Code: What's New?" *Weekly Trust*, November 5–11, 1999, p. 10.

3. Russell G. Smith, Michael N. Holmes, and Philip Kaufmann, "Nigerian Advance Fee Fraud," *Trends & Issues in Crime and Criminal Justice* (1999), http://www.isrcl.org/Papers/Nigeria.pdf (accessed September 18, 2005).

4. Thomas Catan and Michael Peel, "Bogus Websites, Stolen Corporate Identities: How Nigerian Fraudsters Steal Millions from Western Banks," *Financial Times*, March 3, 2003, p. 21.

5. David E. Kaplan, "A Land Where Con Is King," *U.S. News & World Report*, May 7, 2001, pp. 28–29.

6. Peter Carbonara, "The Scam that Will Not Die," *Money*, July 2002, Academic Search Premier.

7. The Internet Fraud Complaint Center (IFCC) is a collaborative effort between the Federal Bureau of Investigation (FBI) and the National White Collar Crime Center (NW3C) to combat fraud committed over the Internet. In December 2003, the Internet Fraud Complaint Center (IFCC) was renamed the Internet Crime Complaint Center (IC3).

8. See National White Collar Crime Center, *The Internet Fraud Complaint Center 2001 Internet Fraud Report: January 1, 2001–December 31, 2001*, http://www.ifccfbi.gov/strategy/IFCC_2001_AnnualReport.pdf (accessed September 17, 2005).

9. See ibid.

10. Warren Richey, "Pssst! Want to Earn an Easy $8 Million from Nigerian 'Officials'?" *Christian Science Monitor*, September 18, 1996.

11. Sam Vaknin, "Nigerian Scams—Begging Your Trust in Africa," *Global Politician*, May 25, 2005, http://www.globalpolitician.com/articledes.asp?ID=766&cid=8&sid=55 (accessed May 25, 2005).

12. Richey, "Pssst! Want to Earn an Easy $8 Million from Nigerian 'Officials'?"

13. Brian Brady, "Crackdown on 8.4M Pound African Sting," *Scotland on Sunday*, March 2, 2003, http://web.lexisnexis.com/universe/document?m=7460 2ee1f997ee38d5d5d7575b8369c5.

14. Kimberly Noble, "The Nigerian Scam," *Maclean's*, March 16, 1998, p. 1c.

15. Nicholas Thompson, "You've Got Fraud!" *Foreign Policy*, May 2003, pp. 2–3.

16. MessageLabs is the world's leading provider of e-mail security and management. It can be accessed at http://www.messagelabs.com/Threat_Watch.

17. Ted Coombs, "Nigerian Bank Fraud Scam Lives On," *Byte.com*, July 12, 1999.

18. Vaknin, "Nigerian Scams."

19. Kaplan, "A Land Where Con Is King."

20. "The Great Nigerian Scam," *Economist*, January 7, 1995, p. 1.

21. Benton E. Gup, *Targeting Fraud: Uncovering and Deterring Fraud in Financial Institutions* (Chicago: Probus Publishing Company, 1995).

22. Kaplan, "A Land Where Con Is King."

23. See Associated Press State and Local Wire, "Musician Survives Encounter with African Scam Artists" by Ken Dey, *Idaho Statesman*, August 7, 2000, accessed September 18, 2005, from http://web.lexis.com. Also see Cramp R. Roberts, "Scam Artists from Africa, Caribbean Increasingly Successful in Con Schemes," *The News Tribune [Tacoma, Washington]*, September 10, 2002, http://web.lexis-nexis.com/universe/document?_m=74602ee38d5d5d7575b8369c5.

24. Brady, "Crackdown on 8.4M Pound African Sting."

25. Carbonara, "The Scam that Will Not Die."

26. A good example of the ways in which the 419 scam has tarnished Nigeria's image and hurts its businesses can be gleaned from the recent rejection, by all online merchants, of credit/debit cards emanating from Nigeria. Nigerian banks, in conjunction with such reputable credit card companies as MasterCard and Visa, introduced credit/debit cards to Nigeria in late 2005, but all Western online merchants not only rejected the cards, but have unanimously refused to honor even credit cards issued in the West with a Nigerian billing address, or ship goods to a Nigerian mailing address. For details on this, see Sonny Aragba Akpore, "Foreign Firms Reject E-payment from Nigeria," *Guardian*, January 24, 2006. Also, read the strong editorial commentary written on the issue by the *Guardian*, Nigeria's leading daily newspaper, "Laying the Groundwork for E-payment System," February 8, 2006, http://www.guardiannewsngr.com/editorial_opinion/article01.

27. The victim, who was later identified as Jiri Pasovsky, 74, a retired army doctor, was sentenced to eight years in prison for the murder. But on January 9, 2006, he was freed by the court on grounds of ill health. For details, see BBC, "Court Frees Czech Diplomat Killer," http://news.bbc.co.uk/1/hi/world/europe/4597186.stm (accessed January 9, 2006).

28. Bob Sullivan, "Nigerian Scam Continues to Thrive," MSNBC Interactive, http://msnbc.msn.com/id/3078489/ (accessed September 30, 2005).

29. Carbonara, "The Scam that Will Not Die."

30. John C. Dvorak, "The Great Nigerian Scam," *PC Magazine*, May 2003, p. 61.

31. Dan Seligman, "Swindles of the Year," *Forbes* 163, no. 12 (June 14, 1999): para. 6 (retrieved July 19, 2006, from EBSCOhost database).

32. Anne Kates Smith, "What Were They Thinking?" *Kiplinger's*, April 2002, pp. 94, 96.

33. Eric M. Uslaner, "Trust Online, Trust Offline," *Communications of the ACM* 47, no. 4 (April 2004): 28–29.

34. Smith, Holmes, and Kaufmann, "Nigerian Advance Fee Fraud," p. 7.

35. See Wendy Tanaka, "House Approves Bill to Cut out Spam," *Philadelphia Inquirer*, December 9, 2003, p. C1. Also see Saul Hansell, "Junk E-mail and Fraud Are Focus of Action," *New York Times*, August 25, 2004, p. C1.

36. Uche J. Osimiri, "Appraisal of Nigerian Advance Fee Fraud Legislation 1995," *Journal of Financial Crime* 4, no. 3 (1997): 271.

37. Ibid., p. 272.

38. "Go South, Con Man," *Economist*, August 2004, p. 67.

39. "Cyber Crime: Obasanjo Receives Draft Bill," *ThisDay*, March 10, 2005, p. 1. The president was making reference to how earlier versions of 419 before the Internet not only exposed the image of Nigeria to a lot of scorn but caused several Nigerians in Nigeria to lose a lot of money.

40. See Economic and Financial Crimes Commission, "EFCC Recovers and Returns $4.48m to 86-year-old Hong Kong Woman," http://www.efccnigeria. org/index.php?option=com_content&task=view&id=667&Itemid=2. Similarly, on November 23, 2005, the Nigerian Economic and Financial Crimes Commission returned U.S. $17 million to a Brazilian bank—the first installment of $242 million that Nigerian 419 scammers persuaded the bank to part with willingly. This 419 scheme—which led to the bank's crash—marks one of the biggest cases of 419 fraud that government officials have cracked. For details, see IRINNews.org, "Nigeria: Financial Crimes Agency Returns Millions to Brazilian Bank," http://www.irinnews.org/report.asp?ReportID=50266&Select Region=West_Africa.

41. See Farooq A. Kperogi, "Being Robbed with Your Consent: A Rhetorical Analysis of the Cybercriminal Persuasive Techniques of Nigerian 419 E-mail Scams" (Master's thesis, Department of Communication, University of Louisiana at Lafayette, 2006).

42. It is a well-known fact among Nigerians that Advance Fee Fraud scams are almost the exclusive preserve of the Igbos. Festac Town in Lagos, where the most vicious 419ers (Nigerian expression for advance fee fraudsters) live, is almost an exclusively Igbo neighborhood. It is said that the 419 kingpins so jealously guard the dominance of the Igbos in the fraud that they sometimes murder people from other ethnic groups, mainly the Yoruba, who attempt to make entry into the scam "business." Another indication of the perception, even in official quarters in Nigeria, that 419 is the exclusive province of the Igbos came to light in 2005 when the Nigerian Economic and Financial Crimes Commission sponsored ads on national television calling attention to the dangers of 419. It used subliminal messages that pathologized the Igbos as inherently criminal. The ad had a character called Chike, a popular Igbo name, who affected an Igbo English accent. However, the umbrella cultural organization of the Igbos in Nigeria, Ohanze Ndigbo, took umbrage at this and demanded the immediate withdrawal of the ads. The group issued a statement saying, "The advert is not only capable of discrediting Ndigbo [i.e., Igbos] wherever they are found on the face of the Earth but also exposing [them] and their entire generations yet unborn to the risk, scorn, and shame of public opprobrium, contempt, and ridicule with its attendant consequences of loss of face, respect, trust, faith and standing among the other ethnic nationalities of Nigeria and indeed the entire world." For details of this controversy, see Ndidi Onuorah, "Ohaneze Protests EFCC Sponsored '419' Advert," *Champion*, August 25, 2005, p. 21.

43. Jean-François Bayart, Stephen Ellis, and Beatrice Hibou, *The Criminalization of the State in Africa* (Oxford and Bloomington: James Currey and Indiana University Press, 1999).

44. Jean-François Bayart, "Conclusion," in *The Criminalization of the State*

in Africa, ed. Jean-François Bayart, Stephen Ellis, and Beatrice Hibou (Oxford and Bloomington: James Currey and Indiana University Press, 1999), p. 131.

45. Andrew Apter, "'Dear trusted friend': Dislocations of Value in Nigerian Scams" (discussion paper, Roundtable, Annual Meeting, African Studies Association, Boston, November 1, 2003). From these authors' knowledge of Nigeria, there is no evidence that the incidence of 419 is rooted in the cultural idioms of any Nigerian society. The fact that the 419 confidence trickery did not originate from Nigeria, but from Spain, as will be shown later in this study, invalidates this observation.

46. Stephen Wright, *Nigeria: Struggle for Stability and Status* (Boulder, Colo.: Westview Press, 1998).

47. For an insightful discussion of the preponderance of the Igbo ethnic group of southeast Nigeria in the 419 fraud, see Bayart, Ellis, and Hibou, *The Criminalization of the African State*, p. 10. They slightly differ from Apter by locating the dominance of Igbos in the 419 fraud in the fact of their economic and political exclusion after the Nigerian Civil War, which pitted the Igbos against all other Nigerians.

48. Up to this point in Nigeria's political history, it is traditional to delineate the country into North and South. These demarcations are not merely cartographical; they are also political, cultural, and historical. Northern Nigeria, which is predominantly Muslim, has nineteen out of Nigeria's thirty-six states and occupies more than three-quarters of the entire landmass of Nigeria. Southern Nigeria, on the other hand, is predominantly Christian and consists of seventeen states.

49. It should be noted, however, that the Hausa language, native to Northern Nigeria, is the most widely spoken language in Africa in terms of numerical strength. It is spoken by over 70 million people in Nigeria, Niger, Ghana, and some parts of Sudan. But because the language has been identified with a particular ethnic group, there is reluctance to adopt it as the lingua franca.

50. Sakah S. Mahmud, *State, Class and Underdevelopment in Nigeria and Early Meiji Japan* (London: Macmillan Press Ltd., 1999).

51. Cited in Ibid., p. 175.

52. Brian G. Stapleton, *The Wealth of Nigeria* (London: Oxford University Press, 1958), p. 1.

53. Richard Joseph, *Democracy and Prebendal Politics in Nigeria* (Cambridge: Cambridge University Press, 1987), p. 221.

54. Mahmud, *State, Class and Underdevelopment in Nigeria and Early Meiji Japan*, p. 3.

55. David G. Becker, "Bonanza Development and the New Bourgeoisie," *Comparative Political Studies* 15 (1982): 88.

56. Joseph, *Democracy and Prebendal Politics in Nigeria*, p. 236. The period witnessed what in Nigeria has come to be known as the "Udoji era," in reference to the recommendations of a certain Justice Udoji who suggested that the government increase the Nigerian national minimum wage exponentially in light of the windfall from crude oil sales. This dramatically increased the percentage of the middle class and generally led to hitherto unthought-of im-

provement in the general standard of living in the country. The head of state of Nigeria at that time, General Yakubu Gowon, was often quoted as saying that Nigeria's problem was not with money, but how to spend money.

57. John de St. Jorre, *The Nigerian Civil War* (London: Hodder and Stoughton, 1972).

58. For an in-depth overview of the ethnic alienation of the Igbos in postwar Nigeria, see Eghosa E. Osaghae, *Crippled Giant: Nigeria since Independence* (London: Hurst, 1998).

59. Steve Robinson, "Hands Up for Democracy," *Time*, March 1999, pp. 36–38. President Obasanjo has shown more commitment than any previous ruler in Nigeria in confronting corruption. His fight against corruption has seen many high-profile Nigerians, including a former Inspector-general of Police, a state governor, and many government ministers, prosecuted and put behind bars. But there are valid allegations that his apprehension of corrupt officers is selective and politically motivated.

60. As cited in John Cassidy, "Relatively Deprived," *New Yorker* 82, no. 7 (April 3, 2006): 42–47 (retrieved July 19, 2006, from EBSCOhost database).

61. Ibid.

62. Sonali Deraniyagala, "The Political Economy of Civil Conflict in Nepal," *Oxford Development Studies* 33, no. 1 (March 2005): 47–62.

63. Arnim Langer, "Horizontal Inequalities and Violent Group Mobilization in Côte d'Ivoire," *Oxford Development Studies* 33, no. 1 (March 2005): 25–45.

64. An Chen, "Secret Societies and Organized Crime in Contemporary China," *Modern Asian Studies* 39, no. 1 (February 2005): 77–107.

65. Valerie Møller, "Happiness Trends under Democracy: Where Will the New South African Set-Level Come to Rest?" *Journal of Happiness Studies* 2, no. 1 (March 2001): 33–53.

66. Transparency International, "Corruption Perception Index 1998," *TI Newsletter*, December 1998, p. 2.

67. Transparency International, "Corruption Perception Index 2005," *TI Newsletter*, http://www.transparency.org/cpi/2005/2005.10.18.cpi.en.html.

68. Harvey Glickman, "The Nigerian '419' Advance Fee Scams: Prank or Peril?" *Canadian Journal of African Studies* 39, no. 3 (2005): 460–489.

69. For a popular account of the cognacy between the Nigerian 419 scam and the Spanish Prisoner swindle, see "New Initiatives to Slam Million-dollar Scams," http://parlsec.treasurer.gov.au/parlsec/content/pressreleases/2002/013 .asp. The news story notes that the 419 scam is a variation of the Spanish Prisoner swindle, which dates back to 1588. "The only difference," the article quotes Australian Senator Ian Campbell, Parliamentary Secretary to the Treasurer in charge of fighting scams, as saying, "is that the original scam used parchment and the promise of a hidden treasure chest."

70. See "Nigerian Scam," http://www.snopes.com/crime/fraud/nigeria .asp. The reason some sources date the Spanish Prisoner swindle to the 1920s is that the phenomenon captured global attention at that period because of the incipient economic depression and upheaval in Spain—much like Nigeria in the

1980s and now. For a full account of this, also see The Head Heeb, "419 and Its Ancestors," http://headheeb.blogmosis.com/archives/014878.html.

71. For an excellent scholarly account of the nature and form of the Spanish Prisoner swindle—which is uncannily redolent of the Nigerian 419 scam—see Joseph L. Holmes, "Crime and the Press," *Journal of the American Institute of Criminal Law and Criminology* 20, no. 2, (1929): 246–293. Holmes's concern was with the manner of newspaper reports of con swindles in 1926. His research convinced him that the frequency, persistence, detail, and vividness with which newspapers reported the scams armed the "swindlers [with] valuable hints as to human cupidity and gullibility" and furnished "the blueprint . . . for the guidance of persons with criminal tendencies but who have not the capacity to successfully plan a crime" (246). Also see Arthur A. Leff, *Swindling and Selling: The Spanish Prisoner and Other Bargains* (New York: Free Press, 1976).

72. Nigerian Customs and Trade Journal, April 1914, p. 189.

About the Contributors

STEVE ABRAMS is a Ph.D. Candidate in the Interactive and Collaborative Technologies program in the Donald Bren School of Information and Computer Sciences at the University of California, Irvine, where he received his M.S. in 2004. He also received an M.A. in Communication, Culture, and Technology from Georgetown University in 2004. His dissertation research investigates sensemaking networks for managing innovation in distributed teams; details can be found at http://www.ics.uci.edu/~sabrams.

TYRONE L. ADAMS, PH.D., is the Richard D'Aquin Endowed Professor of Journalism and Communications at the University of Louisiana at Lafayette (Ph.D. and M.S., Florida State University; B.A., University of Florida). As coeditor of *Electronic Tribes* with Professor Stephen A. Smith, he found the writing and ideas presented in the essays to be of immense personal and professional value. He specializes in new media applications in interpersonal and organizational communication, and is a former President of the American Communication Association (2005–2006). He can be e-mailed at theswampboy@gmail.com and browsed at http://www.swampboy.com.

THOMAS W. BRIGNALL III, PH.D., is with the Department of Sociology at Lewis University. His research interests include racism, social movements, the social impact of technology, and globalization. He is currently involved with several studies measuring the erosion of public meeting spaces and the impact of virtual societies. He spent more than nine years in the computer industry while attending college and still closely monitors new technological innovations. He can be e-mailed at tom@criticalsociology.com.

DAVID R. DEWBERRY is a Ph.D. Candidate in Human Communication Studies at the University of Denver. His research uses interpretive and critical perspectives to examine communication and rhetoric within and surrounding government and politics in traditional and mediated settings. He would like to thank Susan A. Sci, University of Denver, for her careful reading and thoughts on earlier drafts.

SANDRA C. DUHÉ, PH.D., is Assistant Professor and Coordinator of the Public Relations program at the University of Louisiana at Lafayette and Associate Director of Communication at UL's Center for Business and Information Technologies (Ph.D. and M.S., University of Texas at Dallas; M.S., University of Southwestern Louisiana; B.S., Louisiana State University). Prior to joining academia in 2004, she worked as a public affairs manager for three multinational corporations. Based on that experience, her interests lie in political economy, new media, and new science perspectives in corporate public relations. She can be reached at scduhe@louisiana.edu.

SMARAGD GRÜN is an active member of several online and meat-space slash-fiction communities. More than ten years ago, using this pseudonym, she began participating in the slash community, where she continues to seek innovative solutions to protect individuals while advocating community building, envelope pushing, and freedom of speech. She can be contacted at smaragdgrun@yahoo.com.

FAROOQ A. KPEROGI is a Ph.D. student in Communication at Georgia State University, Atlanta. He completed his M.S. in Communication at the University of Louisiana, Lafayette, and his B.A. in Mass Communication at the Bayero University, Kano, in Nigeria. He worked as a staff writer for a Nigerian weekly newsmagazine, as a reporter and later news editor for many Nigerian newspapers, as a researcher in a unit of the Nigerian Presidency called the Presidential Research and Communications Unit, and as a news writing instructor at the Ahmadu Bello University, Zaria, in Nigeria. His research interests, which are perpetually evolving, are new media; the intersection among media, religion, and national identity construction; and Diasporic identities in cyberspace. His chapter on Nigerian 419 e-mails, coauthored with

Dr. Duhé, is a small portion of his M.S. thesis, which explores the linguistic, rhetorical, and sociohistorical singularities that underpin the discursive practices of the scam e-mails. It lays bare the form and essence of the e-mails, illuminates their grammar of deception, and constructs a prototype of their discourse patterns. He can be reached at farooqkperogi@gmail.com.

LEONIE NAUGHTON, PH.D., is a Fellow in Cinema Studies at the University of Melbourne, Australia. Author of *That Was the Wild East: Unification, Film Culture, and the "New" Germany* (Ann Arbor: University of Michigan Press), her work has been published widely in Australia and the United States, and is in translation throughout Europe. Her e-mail is leonienaughton@ozemail.com.au.

BOLANLE OLANIRAN, PH.D., is Professor in the Department of Communication Studies at Texas Tech University in Lubbock, Texas (Ph.D., University of Oklahoma). His research interests include computer-mediated communication in groups and organizations. He can be reached via e-mail at B.Olaniran@ttu.edu, and he maintains a Web presence at http://www2.tltc.ttu.edu/Olaniran.

MATHIEU O'NEIL, PH.D., is a Senior Research Associate at the Australian National University's Research School of Social Sciences. This volume's use of the tribal metaphor gave him an opportunity to connect sociological and anthropological concerns. His current project focuses on the relationship between online autonomy and authority procedures. He can be contacted here, mathieu.oneil@anu.edu.au, and looked at there, http://acsr.anu.edu.au/staff/mathieu.html.

JIM PARKER, PH.D., has been the Webmaster at Vanderbilt University since 1994 (Ph.D., Florida State University). He has been teaching communication courses for over thirty years at a variety of institutions. He presently teaches a course in virtual communities at Vanderbilt University. He is a consultant for Rheingold Associates, an international virtual network of contractors offering expert guidance in creating and maintaining successful sustainable virtual communities. He can be reached at jim.parker@vanderbilt.edu.

RONALD E. RICE, PH.D., is the Arthur N. Rupe Chair in the Social Effects of Mass Communication in the Department of Communication, and Codirector of the Carsey-Wolf Center for Film, Television, and New Media at the University of California, Santa Barbara (Ph.D. in Communication Research, Stanford University; B.A. in English Literature, Columbia University). He has coauthored or coedited *Media Ownership: Research and Regulation* (2007); *The Internet and Health Care: Theory, Research and Practice* (2006); *Social Consequences of Internet Use: Access, Involvement and Interaction* (2002); *The Internet and Health Communication* (2001); *Accessing and Browsing Information and Communication* (2001); *Public Communication Campaigns* (1st ed., 1981; 2nd ed., 1989; 3rd ed., 2001); *Research Methods and the New Media* (1988); *Managing Organizational Innovation* (1987); and *The New Media: Communication, Research and Technology* (1984). See http://www.comm.ucsb.edu/rice_flash.htm and http://www.cftnm.ucsb.edu for additional details.

ANN ROSENTHAL, PH.D., LT. COL., USAF (RETIRED), is Director of Open Source Intelligence, Inc., List Owner, Cloaks and Daggers (academic study of intelligence organizations), founding board member of the InterAmericas Council, and President of the American Communication Association (2006–2007). An Aristotelian rhetorician, she specializes in information warfare and sent her first e-mail in 1967. As a Native American, she especially enjoyed writing about electronic tribes, while also being able to pay tribute to Dr. Gerald M. Phillips, an eminent electronic communication scholar. Google her or e-mail dr.ann.rosenthal@gmail.com.

JODY M. ROY, PH.D., is Professor of Communication and Assistant Dean of Faculty at Ripon College in Ripon, Wisconsin. Her chapter, "Brotherhood of Blood," reflects both the scholarly research and field experience that are hallmarks of Roy's career. Roy is the author of *Love to Hate: America's Obsession with Hatred and Violence* (Columbia University Press, 2002), a member of the board of directors for the National Association of Students against Violence Everywhere, and an affiliate of the Midwest Gang Investigators Association. She regularly trains members of the law enforcement community and K–12 educators, as well as her own undergraduate students. Roy has been honored with more than a dozen awards for civically engaged teaching; in 2005, the Carnegie Foundation named her "Professor of the Year" for the state of Wisconsin.

TERRI L. RUSS, PH.D., is a guest lecturer of Communication Studies at Purdue University North Central (Ph.D., Purdue University; J.D., DePaul University; B.A., Purdue University). Her research focuses on the intertextuality of cultural, media, and interpersonal discourses and the power dynamics created by them. She is particularly interested in the embodied practices of media discourses and the lived experiences of women's body dissatisfaction. When she's not immersed in power and discourse analysis, she's a fiber artist striving to create postmodern representations of the goddess. She especially enjoyed writing about the Craftster tribe, as it provided an opportunity to blend her scholarly and creative sides. She can be contacted at tlruss17@hotmail.com.

JONATHAN SKINNER, PH.D., is a Lecturer in Social Anthropology at The Queen's University of Belfast. He has carried out long-term fieldwork on the island of Montserrat, investigating colonial and post-colonial relations as expressed through calypso, poetry, development work, and political debate (*Before the Volcano: Reverberations of Identity on Montserrat* [Arawak Publications, 2004]). He also has interests in tourism and dance, edits the journal *Anthropology in Action*, and serves as European Association of Social Anthropologists (EASA) Publications Officer. His e-mail address is j.skinner@qub.ac.uk.

STEPHEN A. SMITH, PH.D., is Professor of Communication at the University of Arkansas, Fayetteville (Ph.D., Northwestern). His research interests include political communication and freedom of speech, and he continues to be fascinated by the transformative power of computer-mediated communication to emancipate the intellectually oppressed and geographically isolated.

CHRISTINA STANDERFER, PH.D., is an Assistant Professor at the University of Arkansas Clinton School of Public Service (Ph.D., University of Colorado). She coordinates the school's Field Service Educational Programs. Her research centers on the investigation of the rhetorical construction of civic engagement, public issues, and public opinion. Her investigation of rhetorical constructions of civic engagement extends into cyberspace and has resulted in the publication of a coauthored chapter in *Arguing Communication and Culture* (2001). She currently serves on the editorial board of *Women's Studies in Communication*. She may be reached at standerf@sbcglobal.net.

DEBORAH CLARK VANCE, PH.D. (Howard University, 2002) is an assistant professor in and chair of the Department of Communication at McDaniel College, where she teaches courses in media studies, cultural studies, and rhetoric. She has presented competitive papers and participated on panels each year since 1998 at one or more of the prestigious ICA, ECA, and NCA conferences. She is frequently quoted nationally in newspapers on media and cultural issues, has published articles on free speech and identity topics, and has authored articles and chapters that appear in several books. She has taught for over ten years at Towson University, The College of Notre Dame of Maryland, and has been at McDaniel College since 2003.

MICHAEL C. ZALOT, PH.D., is Associate Professor and Chair of Business at DeVry University in North Brunswick, New Jersey (Ph.D., New York University; M.A., Montclair State University; B.A., the College of New Jersey). His research focuses on the analysis of cultural objects and properties, particularly music, and he teaches technical courses in Web development, graphics, and object-oriented programming. He was formerly a Web and multimedia author for AT&T Labs, has played electric guitar for more than two decades, and can be e-mailed at mzalot@devry.edu; his Web site is http://www.nj.devry.edu/~mzalot.

Index

Italic page numbers refer to figures and tables.